The *Jet Race*
and the Second
World War

The *Jet Race*
and the Second
World War

Sterling Michael Pavelec

NAVAL INSTITUTE PRESS
Annapolis, Maryland

Naval Institute Press
291 Wood Road
Annapolis, MD 21402

Library of Congress Cataloging-in-Publication Data

Pavelec, Sterling Michael.
  The jet race and the Second World War / Sterling Michael Pavelec.
    p. cm.
  Originally published: Westport, Conn. : Praeger Security International, 2007.
  Includes bibliographical references and index.
  ISBN 978-1-59114-666-7 (alk. paper)
  1. Jet engines—Design and construction—History—20th century. 2. Jet planes, Military—Design and construction—History—20th century. 3. World War, 1939–1945—Aerial operations. I. Title.
  TL709.P38 2010
  629.134'353309044—dc22
                                    2009049170

Printed in the United States of America on acid-free paper

16 15 14 13 12 11 10   9 8 7 6 5 4 3 2
First printing

For Jennifer, my distraction

Contents

Acknowledgments

There are a number of people that deserve recognition for their generous assistance and guidance on this project. First and foremost, I would like to thank Dr. John F. "Joe" Guilmartin for his insight in the completion of my dissertation, the basis for this book. He not only pushed for me to attend Ohio State, but he also guided me through some rough times with critical detractors. Without his help and encouragement, this project would have been much more difficult. Also at Ohio State, Dr. Allan Millett was instrumental in this book, my candidacy exams, exciting coursework, and his assistance in several important Fellowships and conferences. His input on this and other projects has been helpful. Finally at Ohio State, Dr. Alan Beyerchen was one of my most influential teachers. His classes were always difficult but made me think. I became a better historian and critical thinker because of his classes and our frequent conversations. I hope that this will, in some small way, give back to these three historians what they gave me.

Furthermore, the professors at University of Calgary have continued to be a source of inspiration and insight. From the initial steps of this journey in Dr. John Ferris's *World War II* class to the guidance from Dr. Tim Travers and Dr. Holger Herwig who oversaw my Master's thesis in 1999, I have benefited from constant interaction with the excellent Calgary programs.

This project was funded through numerous grants and awards from the Department of History at Ohio State, as well as the Mershon Center for Strategic Studies, Ohio State University. Special thanks go to Dr. Matt Keith for his constant updates about Mershon funding.

The archivists who helped and provided assistance were numerous, and I will no doubt forget some. But special mention goes to the excellent staff at the Imperial War Museum (London and Duxford), the Public Record Office/National Archive (Kew), as well as Sebastian Cox of the Royal Air Force Historical Society, who provided insight into the British portions of this project. Special thanks to my relatives in London, Sue and Des Ryle, who let me stay with them. In Germany, Dr. Helmuth Trischler at the Deutsches Museum continues to provide invaluable information. Dr. Horst Boog was also helpful notwithstanding his recent retirement from the Bundes Archiv-Militär Archiv. In the United States, I have to thank above all Dr. Jeffrey Underwood and Brett Stolle at the U.S. Air Force Museum (Dayton, Ohio) for getting me into Wright-Patterson AFB in the midst of continuing crises. Dr. Underwood opened the USAFM archives to a lowly civilian when the entire base was sealed tight after September 11. We will always share the memory of the attacks on the World Trade Centers as we watched the horror unfold in his office as I was digging through the archive materials. Thanks also to "Squire" Brown at the USAFM for the personal assistance. The library staff at the Dunbar Special Collections at Wright State were very helpful in locating both the Whittle Papers and General Electric Aircraft Engine Archives housed there. I was also able to spend a short but helpful visit at the Bell Aircraft Museum (Mentone, Indiana; birthplace of Larry Bell) and want to thank Tim Whetstone, the curator. Further thanks go to Dr. Michael Neufeld at the National Air and Space Museum (Washington, DC), for comments and sources, the staff at Stormbirds.com for information on the Messerschmitt Me 262 rebuilding project, and the friends and colleagues who collected photos and tidbits for this project.

In a more personal note, thanks to my grandma, who sparked my curiosity at an early age. Thanks to Sterling Davies, my grandfather, who was my namesake and also provided financial assistance throughout my academic career. To my parents Dave and Mo, who provided encouragement, a place to visit, and funds for my ever-expanding library. For my sister Kirsten, follow your heart. To all my friends who have been patient (and most think I am completely insane for staying in school so long): Todd, Rod, CK, Todd, Aaron, Dutch, Rob, and "webmaster" Rich, my never-ending appreciation and apologies for being unavailable. Last but most important, to my sunshine, Jen. You have been there through thick and thin, good and bad, and this is dedicated to you. You are my strength, I love you.

What follows is my analysis alone; any errors of omission are mine.

Introduction: The State of Aeronautical Engineering and Aircraft Technology in the World, 1919–1939

The years between the end of the Great War and World War II saw swift and unprecedented change in aviation technology. Change was particularly rapid in the 1930s when aviation was shaped by a number of factors.

The plane had proven itself as a viable weapon in the Great War, and was developed following the war based more on its potential than on the realities. During the interwar period, the evolution of the airplane for military and civilian uses continued and expanded. While nascent national programs instituted commercial flights, funded by passengers and mail, sport flying also became popular. Initially a rich man's hobby, flying had wide appeal and interest. New companies were born and died in an attempt to expand man's domination of the air. Pilots flew and crashed as new technologies were tested. Records were set and broken as airplane evolution progressed. The science of aviation was put into practice and taught in a number of different ways—ways that differed according to national proclivities and governmental support, or lack thereof—as military and civilian programs alike discovered the potentialities of powered flight.

During the course of the Great War, the airplane became a viable weapons platform as well as a more expedient mode of transportation. Experiments during the war proved decisively that the airplane was useful in a number of new roles and operations. The plane was used for observation and liaison, as an air-to-air fighter, for antishipping, and for aerial bombing. The plane was used from land bases, over land, over the sea, and from newly constructed aircraft tenders and carriers. During the war, the plane was used to project the war against the civilian populations of all of the belligerents—save the Americans—in the form of "strategic" bombing.[1] Although it was not effective or efficient in the grand scheme of things, civilian populations were shocked by the immorality of aerial bombing campaigns.

The airplane, and the destruction it prophesized, was one of the threats addressed specifically in the treaties that finally ended the war. In the Treaty of Versailles, Germany was forbidden from having or building a military air force based on the fears and memories from World War I.[2] The 1920s began with Germany forcibly disarmed, and the other European powers in various states of demilitarization. One of the important issues with aircraft was, and has remained, the impact of advanced technology. First, aircraft in production quickly became obsolete as new technology evolves. Second, aircraft rely heavily on active theoretical investigation as well as research and development (R&D) to remain competitive. In the years immediately following World War I, each of the world powers disbanded air forces and cancelled contracts for new military aircraft. It fell to R&D establishments, civilian aircraft manufacturers, and government procurement agencies to keep aircraft technologies competitive in the world of aeronautical development. In the following pages, I will deal with each of the major world powers—those with the capacity to produce high-technology aircraft—in regard to their responses in the interwar period.

In the wake of Versailles, the Germans chose to conduct covert aeronautical research. By the time the Pact of Paris (1926) relaxed the restrictions on German aviation development,[3] there were already rearmament plans in the works. The Fokker Aircraft Company had relocated to Holland and was secretly selling airplanes to Germany. Further, the Germans were procuring planes from covert German companies in other countries. The Heinkel Aircraft Company was selling aircraft back to the German government through Sweden.[4] Thus, even though the Germans were not producing aircraft, they were still at the cutting edge of scientific theory and engineering research and development.

In the interim between the war and rearmament the German aviation establishment pursued academic research and theoretical analyses of dynamics and materials. When the Germans began building military aircraft again, they were able to build on up-to-date research, and designed some of the most advanced aircraft in the world. Further, the Germans had some of the best technical schools and academic programs and trained a body of remarkably proficient aeronautical engineers during the interwar period.

By the 1930s, the Germans developed a structured and efficient academic program for their engineers and machinists. The basis for German aeronautical engineering and aircraft development was sown and cultivated in their academic system. Machinists were indoctrinated into their profession in *Machinenbauschulen* (MBS—Machine Builders Schools)[5] that were responsible for the hands-on approach to engineering, while engineers attended the

Technische Hochschulen (Upper-division Technical Schools) where students learned theoretical physics, chemistry, and materials engineering. These two approaches combined to produce some of the finest aeronautical engineering in the field of aviation.

During the interwar period, one of the most productive schools in the fields of aerodynamics and thermodynamics was the University of Göttingen, home of the *Aerodynamische Versuchsanstalt Göttingen* (AVA—the Aerodynamics Research Institute at Göttingen).[6] Ludwig Prandtl, one of the world's finest theoretical physicists lectured there to a captivated young doctoral student, Hans Joachim Pabst von Ohain.[7] Prandtl concurrently held positions at the Kaiser Wilhelm Institute (KWI) as the director for Fluid Dynamics Research (*Strömungsforschung*) as well as the recently appointed copresident of the Lillienthal society for Aeronautical Research (*Lillienthal-Gesellschaft für Luftfahrtforschung*) as of 1936.[8]

The theoretical work at the KWI and government-sponsored research institutions allowed the Germans to develop a basis of theoretical knowledge that was arguably the best in the world. The Germans were at the forefront in academic fluid mechanics, airframe development, and high-speed theory. Prandtl was one among many who led the way in the development of German scientific research. Further, he was an important influence on Hans von Ohain, one of Prandtl's students. As we will see, Ohain later went on to develop first the theory and later the reality of turbojet propulsion in Germany.

The importance of the German system is that while Germany was denied the right to build military aircraft, their research and development did not stop. German research in physics, aerodynamics, and metallurgy determined future aeronautical development. German scientific advancement facilitated aeronautical development so that when the Germans began to rebuild their air force they had a qualitative advance on the rest of the world. German military aircraft by 1938 were the best in the air, and developments in German aeronautical theory outpaced everyone.[9] Although the Americans led them in the field in transport and long-range aircraft development, U.S. aeronautical R&D was fundamentally different than the Germans' during the 1930s, a point that will be clarified below.

Furthermore, the new German government, led by the Nazis after 1933, not only pushed aggressive rearmament, but also increased funding into scientific research. The newly formed *Reichsluftfahrtministerium* (RLM), the German Ministry for Air, was headed by *Reichskommisar* for Aviation Hermann Göring (effectively Hitler's number two man), reflecting the Nazis affinity and value placed on technology in general and aviation technology specifically. The RLM was founded in the early days of the Third Reich, on May 1, 1933, and became responsible for all aspects of German aviation. Through the technical office (*Technisches Amt*), the RLM controlled research, development, production, contracts, and testing of aerial related material proposed to or solicited by the RLM.[10]

The Germans were intent on building a strong Luftwaffe (air force) and began plans to rationalize the aircraft manufacturing industry early.[11] The RLM, sponsored by the Nazi government, threw money at rearmament programs intending to make Germany without equal in the air. The principal beneficiaries were the German aircraft manufacturing firms Heinkel, Messerschmitt, Junkers, and Dornier, and the engine companies BMW, Daimler-Benz, and the engine division of Junkers.

The Third Reich also created dedicated research organizations, including the *Deutsches Versuchsanstalt für Luft* (DVL—the government-sponsored German aeronautical research organization). But for all the resources committed to R&D by the Nazis, German research organizations were not coordinated and lacked clear focus.[12] There was funding for aviation research, but the money often chased its own tail in duplicated effort. In the 1930s this was acceptable, even beneficial in stimulating alternative lines of development: there was plenty to go around. But after the war started, this dangerous practice continued unabated. As in other areas of the German war economy, this multiplicity of overlapping and competing programs stretched scarce resources to the breaking point—and beyond.[13]

The real innovations came from private industry; two specific aircraft manufacturers were willing to work outside of official permission on programs of personal interest. It is enough to say that the Germans were interested in improving aircraft and building an impressive air force. The government-sponsored organizations did have input, but it was the theoretical fundamentals that guided aircraft evolution in the interwar years.

One aspect of aeronautical engineering that was especially appealing to German theoreticians—perhaps spurred on by the Versailles proscriptions on conventional engine development—was the idea of turbojet-powered flight. Aircraft manufacturers and designers for the most part were content to pursue incremental improvements of conventional piston-engine-powered aircraft. In all of the world industrial powers, development and innovation of conventional aircraft types and models, with the introduction of new yet conventional types, was the norm. Throughout the 1930s there were vast improvements of existing aircraft technology. One indicator was the rise in absolute top speed for aircraft during the interwar period.

Steady improvements to existing technologies yielded significant improvements in performance, but a select few turned their interests and talents elsewhere. A handful of more perceptive engineers recognized that the combination of piston engine and propeller was rapidly approaching a point of diminishing returns. Despite increases in efficiency afforded by variable-pitch propellers, significant improvements in drag reduction and a host of lesser supporting technologies, increasingly huge improvements in engine power were yielding smaller and smaller increases in speed.[14]

A handful of men, almost exclusively in Europe, became interested in the theoretical use of turbojet engines as prime movers for aircraft. These innovators each had different motivations and predictions, but their end goals were similar, to create turbojet engines for use in aircraft. Their efforts led to a revolution in aircraft propulsion that occurred directly before and during World War II. But, as the record will show, although the individuals were important, the development of turbojet aircraft systems were expensive endeavors; too expensive for individuals. The development of turbojet aircraft was dependent on both funding and ancillary technologies for success.

The origins of the process in Germany are instructive; it came down to individual companies and their interest in turbojet aircraft. Ernst Heinkel, the owner of his own aircraft company, was contacted by a colleague who taught at Göttingen, Professor Robert Pohl. Pohl recommended in a letter that Heinkel consider the young doctoral student Hans von Ohain and his revolutionary powerplant ideas. Heinkel was immediately interested and put Ohain to work. He was able to fund Ohain's interests through contract money from the RLM. The German government did not even initially know of Heinkel and Ohain's project. Heinkel's rearmament contracts and money set aside for civilian applications[15] enabled him to support his own in-house R&D. Heinkel used his money well; he gathered some of the finest young aeronautical engineers and designers together to work at his aircraft manufacturing firm. Two of the outstanding young men who became instrumental in the German jet aircraft program were Sigfried and Walter Gunther. The "Gunther Twins" were excellent—bordering on radical—airframe designers, young and full of ideas, who had also been shepherded by Heinkel to further his R&D. The Gunther twins began their tenure at Heinkel by developing the world's first turbojet airframe and the first rocket-powered airframe.[16]

The RLM did eventually see the fruit of Ohain's labor—coupled with the Gunther twins' airframe—and offered contracts based on the theories and potentialities of turbojet aircraft. In Germany there was interest in development of turbojet technology at the highest levels of government and industry; there was also ample funding to commit to R&D. The Germans, as exemplified by Ohain, and later Anselm Franz, were scientists who applied theory to develop technology.

Across Europe, the mood was in favor of aircraft development. In Italy, theory abounded, but both industry and financial assistance lagged. The joint Caproni-Campini project developed a radical new aircraft, the CC.2 (official Italian Air Force designation N.1). The Italian plane, often mislabeled as a "jet," was in fact a ducted fan aircraft. A conventional piston engine powered a three-stage variable-pitch fan embedded in the fuselage. Additional plumbing was added for fuel to be burned in the exhaust phase, theoretically raising thrust. The first flight on August 27, 1940—a year after the first German jet flight—showed that the plane was a failure. Heavy and underpowered, the aircraft had a top speed of only 325 kmph (195 mph), slower than the contemporary Caproni Vizzola F.4 piston-engine fighter.[17] The prototype CC.2 program was disbanded and the only existing examples of the Italian "jet" were relegated to museums. A complete example, and the first to fly, went to the Aeronautical Museum of Vigna di Valle, near Rome, where it can be found today. The second prototype airframe—sans engine—went to the *Museo Nazionale della Scienza e della Tecnica* (The National Museum of Science and Technology) in Milan. The Italians were interested in high-speed flight, but did not have the industrial resources or the theoretical knowledge to support a successful turbojet program. Furthermore, their piston-engine program was underfunded and fraught with difficulties. After building some of the most powerful and innovative aero engines in the 1920s and 1930s, the Italian engine manufacturers reverted to conventional, relatively low-powered designs. Significantly, the Italians depended on German engines for high-output applications during World War II. Finally, Italian industry had difficulties keeping up with wartime demand; the Italians had overcommitted to hostilities during the Spanish Civil War (1936–1939)[18] and were inextricably involved in the Axis cause already by the summer of 1940. The Italians simply did not have resources to commit to turbojet R&D programs.

The situation in France varied in detail. Funding for aircraft R&D was available, but direction was lacking. Although French policy was generally antiwar, French air doctrine dictated a strong air force to take the fight to the enemy. Thus, the French were dedicated to building a strong air force to prevent another World War I. The *Ministère de l'Air* committed finances to Dewoitine, Morane-Saulnier, Bloch, and the Avions Henri Potez Company. But in 1936, the new Popular Front government nationalized all defense industries, confusing aircraft production capabilities. Thus, the French faced inefficiency in industry as well as a lack of reliable engines. France in the interwar years was in no condition to further aeronautical R&D for radical projects. For all the combined advancements in French scientific theory, and interest in development, French military procurement was hamstrung by political infighting in Paris. Subsequent aircraft development suffered.

The Soviets were perhaps in the best position to lead in world aeronautical engineering and development. Industry had been nationalized and modernized rapidly after 1928. Because of the complete control of the State, added to almost complete economic autarky, the Soviets deftly avoided the worldwide economic crisis of the 1930s. The Soviets were on the cutting edge of aircraft technology and also had the industrial base to support their military building programs. The Polikarpov I-16 became the first modern fighter design to see production,[19] and proved capable in the Spanish Civil War against modern German designs.[20] But, the Soviets were hindered by two major setbacks: the purges of the Soviet officer corps effectively left the military without direction and leadership after 1936, and the overbearing State control of industry did not foster competition; instead it suppressed it.

The Soviets were in an excellent position to maintain their lead in aviation technology, but did not.

Further analysis shows that Soviet air doctrine was antithetical to high-technology turbine ideas. Soviet design efforts went toward high-speed, short-range fighters to defend against the Luftwaffe and sturdy, capable ground-attack aircraft that complemented Soviet tactical doctrine. The only indigenous Soviet turbojet program began in 1936 under Arkhip Lyul'ka, an engineer at the Kharkov Aviation Institute in Leningrad. He began development of an eight-stage axial-flow turbojet in 1938 that was still under construction in 1941 when the Germans besieged the city. Continued development eventually produced the TR-1 turbojet engine, but it was not flight tested until 1947.[21] Prior to the war the Soviet aircraft industry did make a mark on aeronautical engineering, but the Soviets did not perceive a need in the 1930s for the radical changes that were underway in Western Europe.

In Britain, the emphasis was on bomber construction. Royal Air Force (RAF) doctrine was based on the theoretical possibilities of the heavy bomber and the British were proponents of heavy, multiengine bombers. The British were determined to make sure that their RAF lived up to the potential of the aircraft. British planning and procurement followed the teachings of Hugh Trenchard, their airpower prophet. The British were delighted that dependence on airpower offered a number of advantages. First and foremost, the RAF promised to avoid the trenches of the last war: airpower equaled mobility. Further, the RAF could be built up with substantially less funding than either the Royal Navy or the Army, and, finally, was ideally suited to colonial duties. Mobility provided operational ability to interior regions of the British Empire not easily accessible to land or sea power. In the contemporary Somaliland crisis, the Air Ministry was vindicated through the use of airpower.

Still, the British opted for heavy multiengine bombers. In exercises every year in the late 1920s and early 1930s, the emphasis was on the self-supporting bomber formations and their abilities to "crush opponents from the air."[22] This bomber emphasis continued until 1936, when for a number of reasons, the British began the serious development of Fighter Command under Air Chief Marshall Hugh Dowding. By 1939, at the outbreak of the European war, the British possessed the only organic fighter defense system because of one simple fact: a single-engine fighter aircraft is easier and cheaper to build. Fighter Defense grew out of Dowding's determination and prescient application of meager funding.[23] Other important factors that contributed to the formation of Fighter Command were the development of radar in Britain in 1935, and the conscious decision to centralize Fighter Command under Dowding. Thus for economic, political, strategic, and technological reasons, the British were able to develop the best antiaircraft interceptor force in the world. But defense does not win wars.

The RAF's Air Ministry did support engine development, but only piston engines. Fortunately for Western democracy, the British did design the one of the best liquid-cooled aircraft engines of the interwar period,[24] the Rolls-Royce *Merlin* series of engines. The *Merlin*'s precursors set a number of speed records, and the *Merlin* itself was arguably the most important aero engine of World War II. The *Merlin* powered the Supermarine *Spitfire* and Hawker *Hurricane*s that won the Battle of Britain and the majority of heavy bombers that leveled German cities in the British half of the Combined Bomber Offensive, 1943–1945. Moreover, the *Merlin* was backed up by a family of excellent air-cooled radial engines built by Bristol. But, ironically, the very excellence of British conventional aero engines diverted attention from more radical solutions to aircraft propulsion.

The British did not systematically consider advanced or revolutionary aircraft propulsion systems prior to the war. In fact, the entire British turbojet developmental program can be attributed to a single RAF Flight Officer who was fortunate to have a number of very timely breaks. Frank Whittle single-handedly introduced innovation into British aircraft technology.

In the United States, the Army dominated the development of military aviation technology—above and beyond the Navy's influence—and was in close contact with civilian R&D programs. The National Advisory Committee for Aeronautics (NACA) was founded in 1915 to coordinate aircraft research in the United States, and, although the NACA made impressive strides in the interwar period, and made major contributions to Allied victory in World War II, its impact on this story is quite negligible. Except for a 1924 study on "Jet Propulsion for Airplanes,"[25] NACA was not involved in the early stages of turbojet development in the United States. The study concluded that "jets" of multiple definitions were inefficient for aircraft, and the study set the tone for American aircraft propulsion research well into the war. Only after America was flying its first turbojet aircraft did NACA complete in-depth studies of the phenomenon.[26]

The development of American aviation technology in the interwar period came from three institutional bases, and it is important to note that none were mutually exclusive. There was significant input into aircraft development from the civilian aviation industry as well as continued R&D and contracts from both the Army and the Navy. In the United States, airframe manufacturers were civilian firms that were funded both by commercial interests and government contracts. The three direct influences often led to different requirements and restrictions on aircraft; there were different considerations in the development of commercial versus Army versus Navy aircraft. Significantly, and most importantly, the American aviation industry was concerned with the economic viability of civilian aircraft and aviation technology, which was driven by the perceived need for long-range, low-maintenance aircraft for commercial transportation. But the military also influenced various technologies that had an enormous impact on both military and civilian applications, specifically the variable-pitch propeller and high-octane aviation fuels.[27]

The U.S. Army initially played the most significant role in the development of American turbojet technology. The Aeronautical Division of the U.S. Army Signals Corps was changed to the Army Air Corps in 1926, then later was renamed the U.S. Army Air Forces. The Army Air Forces—as it was titled in 1941—was blessed to have an avid aviator with a strong interest in technology as its commander, and General Henry Harley "Hap" Arnold shaped the Air Forces leading up to and during World War II. Arnold's influence from the top was vital in the development of the first American turbojet aircraft. The Americans relied on foreign developments for their turbojet program; the British literally supplied America's first jet engines. But, once American industry coordinated with the military, the Americans quickly recovered from initial failures and took center stage in high-technology weapons platform production. But it is important to point out two things. First, the American aviation industry in the interwar period concentrated on perfecting piston-engine aircraft for commercial potential. By investigating high-reliability and long-range variables, the Americans designed some of the best transport aircraft—technology that later translated directly into heavy multiengine bomber aircraft.[28] Second, with regard to turbojet technology and other revolutionary propulsion systems development, it is important to keep in mind that the Allies developed the technology and later applied science to perfect it. The Allies were dedicated to the reality of turbojet aircraft before the theoretical basis was established.

The Japanese were quick to appreciate the potential of military aviation. But the Japanese, who possessed both theoretical aptitude and industrial capacity, did not develop native turbojet programs. One reason was that the concept of turbojets was antithetical to Japanese doctrine. The Japanese concentrated on range above all, then maneuverability and speed in their aircraft. Japanese aircraft, especially Imperial Japanese Naval planes, were constructed for long-range operations. The turbojet engine is inherently thirsty, and all of the early turbojet aircraft were plagued by extremely short-range restrictions. The fact that the Japanese did not develop turbojet aircraft is not a criticism; I agree with the majority of aviation historians who argue that the Japanese went to war with some of the most advanced piston-engine aircraft of all the industrial powers for what they were designed to do. Indeed, in terms of range, payload, and reliability, the Japanese developed the finest naval aircraft leading up to the war. This, however, was done at a cost in that Japanese aircraft were vulnerable to enemy fire and had a tendency to explode when shot.[29]

One interesting turbojet development that has been lost to the historical record is the effort of a Hungarian, György Jendrassik. During the interwar years he was responsible for the development of the world's first turboprop engine. He developed a 15-stage axial-flow compressor that fed reverse-flow combustion chambers that exited over an 11-stage turbine. The attached propeller produced thrust and the engine was rated at 1,000 shaft horsepower. It ran in bench tests for the first time in August 1940, but the program was almost immediately disbanded. The Hungarian Air Force went to war with German conventional piston-engine planes and not revolutionary turboprop-powered aircraft.[30] The necessities of war preempted Hungarian fame.

At this point, a look backward at the development of high-speed aircraft technology in the interwar period is in order. International competitions and air races influenced not only airplane design and modifications during the interwar period, but also facilitated interaction between countries and companies. The Gordon Benett Aviation Cup was one of the first of these international competitions. Proposed by an American, Gordon Benett, a series of trophies were offered for speed competitions on land and in the air.[31] In the first competition, held during the Rheims Aviation Meeting in 1909, Glen Curtiss, the American aircraft designer, won in a plane of his own manufacture. His average speed was 47 mph. The event attracted competition from both Britain and France. The cup returned to America the next year as per the rules; the winner's home country hosted the race, but the British won and the cup moved across the Atlantic for 1911. In 1912 the French won (125 mph), and won again in 1913 without foreign competition. The race was not held again until after the war, when the French won it for the third and final time in 1920.[32] The trophy that replaced the Benett Cup was the Deutsch Cup, but was in no way German; it was named after the Deutsch de la Meurthe family of France. This short-lived race was only held twice, in 1921 and 1922. There was less interest in this race in the era of a more important aerial competition.

The most famous air race series was the Schneider Trophy. Proposed in 1912 by M. Jacques Schneider, a Frenchman, it was a speed competition for seaplanes.[33] The first Schneider Trophy was held at the Monaco Seaplane Meeting in April 1913, but was poorly attended for such an important competition. The race was governed by the F.A.I. (*Fédération Aéronautique Internationale*), which had been founded in 1905 as an international governing body over aviation.[34] The F.A.I was formed to oversee international rules dealing with licensing and customs; it became important because airplanes could circumvent traditional ports and harbors. The F.A.I. was also interested in air safety, and thus became the natural choice to officiate aerial contests and international meetings.

The Schneider Trophy set the standard for all speed records in the interwar period. The race was resurrected after World War I and continued until 1931 when the British won it for the third year in a row, giving them permanent possession of the Schneider Trophy.[35] Over the course of the contest, the competitors included French, American, Italian, Swiss, and British teams. Interestingly, the only German entry into the Schneider

Trophy race was in 1914; unfortunately it crashed before the race. The Germans never reentered.

In the quest for absolute speed, the Germans faired better, making and breaking speed records at frequent intervals before World War I and into the interwar years. The first credited "official" air speed record was presented to Alberto Santos of France, when he flew a plane of his own design and construction to 25.65 mph in 1906. The record was broken regularly after the Great War, based on the intense development of aviation science. France, Italy, Britain, and the United States all held speed records at one time during the interwar period. But, interestingly enough, it was the chief test pilot for the Messerschmitt Company, Fritz Wendel, who set the longest-standing record for piston-engine aircraft. In April 1939, Wendel flew a prototype Messerschmitt Me 209[36] to a speed of 755.1 kmph (469.22 mph).[37] His flight broke the record of another German, Hans Dieterle, who had set the record in March 1939 with the top speed of 746.6 kmh (463.7 mph) in a Heinkel He 100 prototype.[38] Wendel's piston-engine speed record lasted for 30 years. It was not until August 1969 that an American flew a piston-engine aircraft faster.[39]

This ongoing competition, which ended in 1939, points out a number of factors in the development of aviation during the interwar period. First, the German speed record, as the world approached war again, suggests that German aviation was staging a strong comeback after the severe restriction of Versailles. The German aircraft companies Heinkel and Messerschmitt began developing aircraft that were cutting-edge technology and the fastest in the world. This is a testament to both the airframe and engine designers in Germany. This German "comeback" led directly into the second development, namely, the intense rivalry that was developing between Messerschmitt and Heinkel on a professional level. The two competed over contracts and manufacturing during the course of the war, and eventually both developed turbojet aircraft for the Luftwaffe. The air speed records also indicate the intense rivalry in the international sphere of aviation development. The record was set and broken frequently, often within weeks. Further, the record transferred from country to country chaotically; at various times the record was held by France, Britain, Italy, or the United States, with the Germans making a strong showing in 1939. Finally, the 1939 air speed record also calls attention to *Flugkapitän* Fritz Wendel, the chief test pilot for Messerschmitt. Wendel became an important person in the development of the German jet aircraft program in general, and the Messerschmitt Me 262 in particular. He was not only the chief test pilot for the Messerschmitt Aircraft Company, he was also an accredited aeronautical engineer who suggested and implemented important improvements into several Messerschmitt aircraft.

At the same time, there was international competition in transport and commercial aircraft development. The American designed and built Lockheed *Vega* and later *Orion* set the early standard for best combination of speed, range, and payload of the interwar period. The American dedication to the development of long-range and high useful load aircraft translated into fantastic multiengine, long-range aircraft. The Americans, while not as concerned with absolute speed records, were dedicated to designing and building commercially viable planes for transport. Europeans were entranced by the American Lockheed aircraft; the Swiss bought several *Orions* as mail planes.[40]

The Americans did set the standard in the early 1930s for excellent aircraft design. The *Orion* incorporated a number of technological advances that led the field. The incorporation of the NACA cowl increased speed and efficiency of radial engines, low-wing monoplanes and retractable undercarriage combined to offer unforeseen advantages in aircraft design. Further, these improvements were not lost on the Europeans, especially after the Swiss started flying the American designs. By 1934, three major German companies (Heinkel, Junkers, and Messerschmitt), one British design (from Gloster), one French plane (from Dewotine), and the Soviet Polikarpov I-16 and I-17 incorporated some if not all of these improvements. The emphasis on airframe design became streamlining for speed.

Other American planes were also making their mark on the international aeronautical scene. Douglas "DC" series aircraft were showing promise as long-range transports. A Royal Dutch Airlines/KLM flown Douglas DC-2 was registered in the 1934 MacPherson Robertson England–Melbourne Air Race. The race was for a cash prize, its unintended consequence was exposure for international air mail routes; one of the conditions of the race was that the planes had to carry mail. A De Havilland DH 88 twin-engine speed plane won first place and carried a handful of letters to their recipients in Australia. The second arrival was the DC-2, which carried 400 pounds of mail and three fare-paying passengers from England to the South Pacific. Its top speed did not match the DH 88s, but the DC-2s did not stop for fuel as often as the British racer. Interestingly, the DC-2 was only 10 hours behind the DH 88, and only 10 hours ahead of the third finisher, an American Boeing 247-D flown by an American crew.[41] Range and payload, for the Americans, were the decisive variables. But the Americans were content to perfect existing technology; there was little interest in the revolutionary turbojet.

Aircraft were traded around Europe for a variety of reasons as well. Lufthansa Junkers Ju-52 tri-motor transports were flown under the banners of Sweden, Spain, and Italy, as well as Germany. Rolls Royce engines were swapped for airframes, most of which were subsequently built under license in foreign countries. American aero engines were sold to the Soviets. French aircraft and engines went to Eastern Europe and the Soviets. Interestingly, only the Americans declined purchase of European aviation technology. Each of the industrial European powers was able to build on the other's ideas as well as mistakes. The Germans, who were dedicated to building a brand-new Luftwaffe—openly after March 1935—invested most financial and intellectual capital into aircraft R&D.

One of the most interesting documents from the interwar period pertaining to the development of turbojet technology came out of the week-long Volta Conference for the study of the Physical, Mathematical, and Natural Sciences, held in Italy, in October 1935.[42] The theme of the annual Volta conference that year was *Le Alte Velocita in Aviazione*: High-Speed Flight.[43] The 1935 Volta Conference included panels on the theories of high-speed flight and physics. The conference was truly international: the participants came from across Europe and the United States and each of the presenters wrote in his native language.[44] The conference record was printed in English, French, German, and Italian. The importance of the conference was that it served as a clearing house for cutting-edge theoretical physics, and the question of high-speed flight was broached. The participants for the most part consented that the aircraft piston-engine was approaching the apex of its efficiency, and that new avenues needed to be explored. German and French participants discussed the possibilities of revolutionary new designs in turbines, turboprops, and reaction jets; other conference participants argued that there were no viable uses for high-speed, high-altitude aircraft. On the whole, the conference showcased the theoretical knowledge of the continental Europeans and the lack of interest of the British and American participants.[45] It is also important to note that the Germans and French, in different contexts, were interested in and investigating turbojet technology in the mid-1930s.

Among the participants was Harry Wimperis, representing the British Royal Academy. Wimperis discussed the development of the Rolls-Royce "R" engine that powered the winning Schneider Trophy aircraft in 1931, but even he did not conceive of radical new propulsion systems, though he recognized that further research needed to be done on high-speed (supersonic) flight, predicting that "a totally new aerodynamic regime [will be] entered—one of which little indeed is at present known." He speculated that, "the future will show whether that unknown region will be explored first by the patient researchers of the laboratory and wind tunnel, or by some daring attempt by bold pilots and venturesome constructors."[46] Wimperis was pessimistic about the proposed research into high-speed flight. He was of the opinion that high-speed and high-altitude flights could be achieved but believed that "...our remaining task will merely be the discovery of passengers who wish to fly at such altitudes." He was not optimistic about selling the idea of novel aircraft transportation technology to the paying public.[47] Nor in fact were others. Few were willing to speculate on the commercial interest in high-speed aviation. The irony was that commercial concerns would not be the driving factor.

The interaction initiated during the Volta Conference undoubtedly carried on afterwards, but two points arise from the record: first, the Germans were at the top of the learning curve with regard to presentations and papers offered; and second, there is little indication that the information filtered down from the prestigious, but academic, attendees to their respective aircraft industries.

To the last generalization there was a partial but important exception. From the record of the participants, there is a clear connection between the participation of the three Göttingen representatives and in-depth theoretical discussion during the conference.[48] Prandtl, von Kármán (who was German-trained, but employed in the United States), and Pohl were deeply involved in both the presentations and discussions that centered on the theme of the conference: High-Speed Flight. From the Volta conference to the Göttingen classroom is an obvious bridge that would have exposed Ohain—through his advisors—to state-of-the-art international theory. The evidence is circumstantial, but persuasive. We can state with confidence that Ohain, who was finishing his doctorate at the time, was at least implicitly exposed.

While Ohain benefited from strong academic traditions, Frank Whittle in Britain had to actively seek out education and mechanical proficiency to complete his innovations. In Germany, Ohain was fortunate to get early support from industry and later government, whereas Whittle in Britain had to fight tooth and nail for funding and workspace. The Germans developed turbojets first primarily because of high-level interest. In Britain the process took longer.

In considering the early history of turbojet propulsion, we must remember that in the interwar period, theoretical and actual turbojet development was brand new. It was as if industry were rebuilding the *Dreadnought* battleship. There were obvious precedents in airframe technology. Even the jet airframes would have to be improvements on their ancestors, but the engines were the revolution. In Germany, then Britain, and still later the United States, turbojet technology was novel in every sense. The idea that a jet thrust from a three-cycle turbojet engine could be used as a prime mover for aircraft was the ideal that the designers pursued. The national approaches were different. The Germans, beginning with Ohain and continuing through Franz, were interested in new forms of propulsion for aircraft. Ohain commented that piston engines were too rough, noisy, and dirty. He was looking for "elegance" in aircraft propulsion. His reaction after his first flight in a Junkers Ju 52—a definitely inelegant airplane—was to seek to develop a new, quieter, propulsion system so that passengers could enjoy the inherent beauty of flight.[49] Franz continued the German quest and added the variable of speed to his concept of the beauty of flight.

In Britain, the perceived purpose of turbojets was a bit more straightforward. Whittle, a test pilot and engineer, was interested in high-speed and high-altitude flight. He was concerned with theoretical issues: the efficiencies and output of the machine and the performance possibilities of his innovation. But at the outset, he was more concerned about building his prototype engine, making it work (no easy feat), making it better, and making it fly. He did not comment on the ultimate change turbojet technology would offer the pilot or passenger. His sole concern—appropriate for a serving RAF officer—was speed. Thankfully, Whittle had more tenacity than the British Air Ministry and British industry combined; in the face of heavy adversity and scarce funding Whittle built the first turbojet outside of Germany.

The approach in development was sharply different in Germany. The record shows that Ohain, Franz, and the German turbojet design teams developed the theoretical background before the actual development of the turbojet engines. All of the German designers were accredited physicists, engineers, and academics who spent years on theoretical analysis before the first physical development began. This was clearly a major factor behind the eventual German disregard for centrifugal-flow turbojets and their pursuit of axial-flow designs. The axial-flow turbojet was more difficult to design, more expensive to construct, and also took longer to develop. Axial-flow compressors, however, were theoretically more efficient and powerful and for the Germans it was an easy decision to make. The Germans banked on their potential for developing high-technology weapon systems throughout the war.

In Britain Whittle adopted a more empirical approach. He developed his engine according to existing principles making full use of his mechanical ability. His design was innovative, but not without precedent. His advanced engineering education began in earnest after his first proposals and attempts to build a working engine. Further, although substantially refined in development, the Whittle product was in many senses designed to work rather than to satisfy a theoretical optimum. In sum, the Whittle engine was "good enough" for prototype development. Moreover, it was sufficiently successful and interesting for consideration by the government and industry. Whittle was given opportunity to develop his ideas, but the British were not banking on his innovation; British piston-engine aircraft were fine as they were, thank you very much. Whittle's designs proved to be a good foundation for an Allied turbojet program, but were not developed with the same insistence as in Germany. Allied turbojet development would go through revision and modification, but the issue was that an innovative power plant was manufactured without thorough scientific analysis. Whittle did apply theoretical analysis to his engine to improve it, but the Allies were content to use conventional aircraft throughout the war; the Allies did not show the same need for turbojet aircraft that the Germans did.

By the end of the 1930s the conventional piston-engine aircraft industry was in full swing. As Germany prepared for a new war, and as the former Allies prepared to defend themselves, production lines ran at a furious pace. Industry and aircraft would go through substantial modification over the course of the war. By the end of the war, piston-engine aircraft were exceeding 450 mph,[50] flying at altitudes of 30,000 feet,[51] and carrying impressive payloads.[52] But in spite of these improvements one series of aircraft would make an impression on the war that lasts to this day. German, and later the Allied, jets marked the break from piston-engine aircraft to the next generation of aircraft design.

1

The Birth of the German
Jet Program

The account of the German jet program begins with a young doctoral student freshly minted from the University of Göttingen in 1935. The young Hans Joachim Pabst von Ohain devised a hypothetical turbojet engine for use in aircraft after having been interested in the idea by one of his lecturers, Dr. Anselm Franz. Through the financial and material assistance of Ernst Heinkel, aircraft magnate, who had reasons of his own for assisting Ohain, the 25-year-old *Doktor Ingenieur* was able to produce the world's first operational turbojet engine and materially aid in the development of the first flying jet airplane. Based on these early experiments, the Germans took the lead in turbojet engine and jet aircraft technology in spite of wartime restrictions, and were able to commit the first jet fighters and bombers to combat operations. In the end, the appearance of jet technology in the skies over Europe did not alter the course of the war in the German's favor, but the history of the German jet program is an illustration of excellent science and research dedicated to the potential of turbojet technology. During the war the Germans introduced the world to jet engine and aircraft technology that set the pace for all future high-performance aircraft development.

In the early 1930s Ernst Heinkel was interested in producing the finest and fastest aircraft. He had dedicated his aircraft manufacturing firm, which carried his name, to the development of fast, clean aircraft designs.[1] Heinkel's designs were structurally as well as aesthetically pleasing, but for various reasons in competition for government contracts Heinkel was always second to his main rival, Willi Messerschmitt.[2] Thus, although his designs were excellent and on the cutting edge of innovation, Heinkel was over-looked for military contracts for his fighter aircraft.[3] In 1935 Heinkel's He 112 was placed second to Messerschmitt's Bf 109 in the competition for what would become the Luftwaffe's biggest and most important fighter contract. Heinkel was able to sell only a few dozen aircraft to Spain and Romania.

Heinkel did set a number of trends in aircraft design, including retractable undercarriage, incorporation of a nosewheel in a tricycle undercarriage, and his trademark elliptical wing design. He was also responsible for the development of some of the fastest aircraft during the interwar period.[4] Although Heinkel was not making much from fighter contracts, he was making a decent living from commercial aircraft and clandestine bomber development and production.[5] Therefore, Heinkel was in the financial position to delve deeply into research and development; he was in a position with his company to build new and interesting aircraft. He had the mindset to accept new and radical ideas in the development of flight; the stage was set for the birth of the German jet program.

Hans Joachim Pabst von Ohain was the son of a career German army officer who was left without a career at the end of World War I. His father returned to Berlin and began a successful career as a light bulb distributor, working for the electrical company Pintsch. The young Ohain was successful in school and chose to go to the prestigious University of Göttingen, a well-known center of aerodynamic research, to pursue his studies in physics. His education was cultivated by great minds such as Frederick Courant, Robert Pohl, Ludwig Prandtl, and Theodore von Kármán, the last two of whom taught at the nearby Göttingen Kaiser Wilhelm Institute for Fluid Mechanics. While at Göttingen, Ohain studied physics as his main focus with aeromechanics and math as his secondary fields.[6] But, as Ohain recounts, his classes and work were all within the realm of theory.[7] He learned a great deal in lectures about theoretical mathematics, fluid mechanics, and physics, but it was not until much later that he became interested in the theoretical application of physics and math to the turbojet engine.

Initially, Ohain was involved in the development of an optical microphone, basically, sound for film. His dissertation, "The Application of Zero Order Optical Interference for Translation of Sound Wave Directly into Electrical Impulses," was accepted in 1935, and he received his Ph.D.[8] Ohain's patents for the optical microphone were bought by Siemens Company for DM 3,500,[9] which gave him both time and money to pursue another interest, the turbojet engine. His years at Göttingen had given him an outstanding basis in theoretical physics and math, and he was ready to pursue another course.

The birth of the turbojet engine in Germany came down to an eventful meeting between Ohain and his advisor, Professor Robert Pohl. The professor was not impressed with Ohain's grasp of the theoretical physics and suggested that he work on "creative applications." The advisor continued,

"When you have something which really revolutionizes technology by using physics this is fine, but don't do mediocre stuff."[10] Ohain was encouraged to apply his talents to development rather than limit himself to theory. Thus with his background in fundamental physics, and supplemental education in aerodynamics and math, Ohain set out to build his own "pet project" based on theoretical science.

Ohain related that his initial interest in turbojet power plants stemmed from his love of gliding. "Gliding is a beautiful outdoor sport you know; I also got a bit interested in the aerodynamics of flight. This led me to look into what could make the normal airplane a little bit faster and smoother. I thought the reciprocating engine was a horrible monster and that the propeller lacked elegance. I thought that it should be possible to drive an airplane fast and smoothly through the air like a very fantastically fast glider."[11] Ohain thought in terms of aesthetics as he approached the theories of flight. He applied his educational training to developing an engine based on the laws of thermodynamics.

Although Ohain built a prototype engine while still in school, it was not self-sustaining, and only ran on propane. Ohain had befriended his auto mechanic, Max Hahn, and engaged his services and workspace in a local Göttingen auto repair shop. After completing a theoretical cycle analysis of the three-stage turbojet engine (compressor–combustor–turbine), the men set out to build the contraption. In a period of 3 months, Hahn built the model according to Ohain's calculations, with important implications. Although the technological predecessor, steam turbine components were disregarded as too large and heavy; the new engine was fabricated from scratch. Further, because Hahn preferred working with sheet metal, as well as traditional fasteners such as nuts and bolts, the lightweight engine was constructed out of sheet steel without welds. Ohain related that he did not "engineer" the engine in that he specifically built it with regard to weight and size considerations. He argued that "an engineer would have said: first prove the principle and forget about weight restrictions. But I tried to make the model light and compact because I had the illusion the thing could propel a plane."[12] Interestingly, Ohain did not think of the turbojet engine as an advancement in turbine development in the same vein as steam turbines; he thought his invention was something completely "unclassifiable" and dissimilar.[13] The engine constructed had a two-stage compressor, with one axial compressor stage followed by a single-sided centrifugal compressor stage, an annular combustion chamber, and a radial turbine. The model engine was constructed at a cost of 500 DM;[14] money borrowed from Ohain's father for the project. Although the project was a failure as a turbojet power plant, Ohain's theoretical analysis and rudimentary prototype proved the validity of turbojet technology. In the end, it was not powerful enough to fly, but the machine was self-sustaining: it kept running when fuel was delivered to the combustion stage.

It was more important that he had been encouraged to sit down and actually work out the theoretical analysis to determine the viability of his ideas. His advisor, Professor Pohl, was adequately impressed with the figures that he stated, "... this is sound ... Tell me what company you would like to work with on your engine and I'll write a letter of recommendation for you to its director."[15] Ohain chose Ernst Heinkel and the Heinkel Company because "... he [Heinkel] has the reputation of being a little bit crazy. I am considered crazy too so maybe we'll make a good team."[16] It was settled, and Pohl sat down to compose a letter on Ohain's behalf to Ernst Heinkel.

Heinkel was always interested in new ideas, and when he received the letter from Pohl, he was sufficiently interested in the young theorist's ideas to write back inviting Ohain to his house. The meeting was set for March 18, 1936.[17]

Ohain visited Heinkel in Rostock and discussed his ideas for the engine. Heinkel's engineers listened and commented on Ohain's presentation. They mentioned that the idea was an old one, but had not yet been realized; they consented that maybe the time was ripe for reassessment. Their noncommittal suggestion to Heinkel, after analyzing Ohain's theories, was "Well, there may be something to it; it is not as good as he thinks, but it is worth some consideration."[18] Ohain was given a contract, and in April 1936, with Max Hahn in tow, he began work for Heinkel.

By March 1937, Ohain, Hahn, and the design team (to which Heinkel had added *Dipl. Ing.* Wilhelm Gundermann, a specialist in aeroengineering) had developed the Heinkel HeS 1 turbojet engine. The experimental engine was the product of rigorous combustion chamber testing, to meet the high-heat requirements of earlier experiments.[19] The original engine burned gaseous hydrogen for fuel—it would not have worked otherwise—but lived up to theoretical expectations and confirmed Heinkel's opinions on turbojet technology.[20] The team impressed Heinkel with the engine and its output in relation to projected efficiency, and was funded for the next stage in the developmental process, a liquid-fuel turbojet engine.[21] The continuing difficulty in Ohain's engine was the combustion stage: it was clear that the combustion stage would involve enormous pressures and unprecedented high sustained temperatures. Finding materials that could withstand these conditions would be an ongoing problem.

Over the next 18 months, development continued on the separate stages of the Heinkel-sponsored Ohain engine, with particular attention to the combustion chamber. It was not until this time that Ohain learned that a similar effort was underway in Britain. Ohain learned of this when he tried to take out patents on his engine; he was rejected based on a number of precedents. The French engineer Guillaume should have had the most comprehensive patent rights on the axial-flow turbojet that he registered in 1921; but by the 1930s his engine remained merely a paper proposal.[22]

Ohain's patent rejection was based on the 1930 Whittle patents, and also Swedish patents registered to Milo Aktie-Colegat.[23] When Ohain saw the patents, he was convinced that they were merely "paper" patents, as yet unbuilt. Specifically, he knew that the Swedish patents were not being built; more to the point, he was convinced that the Whittle design was inherently flawed. Ohain saw Whittle's engine as unstable and impractical, and thought that ". . . the Whittle idea was not being seriously worked on. I had not the slightest idea that Whittle was, at that very time, developing his ideas with great vigor. We were both working along similar lines but with different approaches."[24] The Germans continued with the perception that they were the only viable project under construction, and that they were pursuing the correct theoretically based development of turbojet engines for aircraft. They were correct in one of their assumptions.

Ohain spent a considerable amount of time on the problem of combustion. The HeS 1 had run well with clean-burning, easy-to-ignite hydrogen, but Ohain ran into troubles trying to convert the engine to liquid fuel. And, Heinkel complicated matters by insisting on a flying engine. Under pressure, Ohain revisited the principles of combustion and traveled to seek council with leaders in the field. Finally, with the combination of Hahn's practical knowledge, and theoretical knowledge gained from experts and trade shows, the team assembled working liquid-fuel combustors for their turbojet.

Another problem to overcome included high-volume fuel pumps for the turbojet. The engine consumed fuel at an unforeseen rate. Because of the experimental nature of the first aircraft power plant, and time constraints imposed from above, Ohain suggested pressurized fuel tanks to force the fuel into the engine at a constant rate. Clearly, this was not a long-term solution. He commented to Heinkel, "It is as if we are building an astronomical telescope with lenses made of beer bottles with the hope that we will later obtain facilities to make proper lenses."[25]

After surmounting a series of frustrating difficulties, the Heinkel/Ohain turbojet engine, designated HeS 3b, was ready for flight by early spring 1939. The engine was redesigned, then built, and construction begun on the first turbojet airframe.

The design chosen as the first turbojet airplane was designated the Heinkel He 178. It was designed by the Günther brothers, Seigfried and Walter, a pair of young aeronautical experts also working for Heinkel. The small, shoulder-wing plane was an experimental prototype built to test an experimental power plant: nothing more, nothing less. Like another contemporary experimental Heinkel aircraft, the He 176 rocket plane,[26] the He 178 was built to the physical specifications of the chief Heinkel test pilot Erich Warsitz. Two prototypes were built, the He 178 V1 ("V" for *Versuchs*—experimental) was fitted with a fixed undercarriage because the "bugs" were not yet worked out of the retractable landing gear; the second prototype—V2—was built with working retractable landing gear.

In June 1939, these two aircraft, Heinkel's rocket plane and turbojet plane were shown to Hitler in hopes of winning coveted government contracts as well as official recognition for technological development.[27] At the demonstration, the rocket flew (with nearly catastrophic consequences) and the jet was shown, Ohain providing expert responses to the Führer's and the others' questions. The German Air Ministry, the *Reichsluftfahrtministerium* (RLM), was finally let in on the closely guarded Heinkel turbojet secret. Although there were other German turbojet projects under theoretical development, Heinkel's led with a marginally working engine, an actual airframe, and a proposed first-flight date. Ohain and his team concentrated all efforts on making sure that the promised "end of July" flight would indeed become a reality.

The engine was modified to acceptable levels of output. The impeller was stress tested and the fuel system was modified for the first flight. Because of the time constraints imposed by Heinkel, Ohain was forced to forgo liquid fuel and fabricated a compressed hydrogen fuel system for his engine. The first flight was powered with compressed hydrogen forced into the combustion chamber to prove the viability of the engine; this was plainly a temporary expedient. Ohain was determined to construct a liquid fuel engine but he was equally determined to make his existing engine work by the deadline. The hydrogen-fueled turbojet engine was married to the He 178 airframe and prepared for the first flight. On August 27, 1939, Heinkel test pilot Erich Warsitz lifted off the airfield at Marienehe completing the first ever jet flight. The Heinkel team had ushered in a new era of aeronautical engineering.

The first flight of the He 178 was historic, but not without problems. The He 178 V1 was designed for a retractable conventional undercarriage,[28] but in the interest of saving time, the V1 had fixed landing gear. The Günther brothers predicted their plane would fly at speeds of 800 kmph (approximately 500 mph) based on their figures and Ohain's calculations, but, the reality was disappointing. The fastest flight recorded that year was Fritz Wendel's record-setting flight of 755.14 kmph (469.25 mph) in a highly modified piston-engine-powered Bf 109 (actually a prototype Me 209).[29] It was an impressive achievement that was not overcome until 1969 by an American pilot.[30] The Günther brothers, Ohain, and Heinkel hoped the future would belong to jets.

The HeS 3b turbojet that powered the Günther's He 178 V1 produced 500 kg (1,100 lbs) thrust. The plane was designed around the engine, with the air intake in the nose and a tubular frame that housed the centrifugal-flow engine. Warsitz took off for the first time in a turbojet-powered aircraft and achieved a top speed—with the wheels down—of 300 kmph (187 mph). Warsitz was also the first to suffer a jet bird strike, which cut his flight short, but without substantial damage to the airplane or engine.[31]

Ohain recounts that Heinkel rushed to the phone to telephone Berlin. Although Heinkel was visibly excited by the first jet flight, the response was rather curt when General Ernst Udet, Head of the Technical Department said, "Everyone is asleep in Berlin," and hung up.[32] Notwithstanding, the Heinkel design team was in a festive mood and excited about their successes.

In the afterglow of the first flight, Heinkel tried to get official RLM visitors to come and see his newest creation, but the government had other concerns. Germany invaded Poland on September 1, 1939, and it was not until November that RLM representatives visited Marienehe. The delegation included Milch, Udet, and Helmut Schelp, the latter an engineer in the technical department of the RLM. The demonstration almost ended in disaster when a fuel pump seized during taxi. Heinkel took the officials for breakfast with the explanation that a tire had blown, and the plane was quickly repaired in frantic haste; Heinkel thought it was his last chance to impress the RLM.[33] The plane was fixed, the officials returned, and test pilot Warsitz prepared for takeoff. The flight went off without a hitch, but Milch, Udet, and Schelp were unimpressed with the new technology. Ohain's recollection was that they did not understand the revolution they were witnessing.[34] The RLM officials returned to Berlin without so much as a word. Heinkel and Ohain were stunned that they had not made a deeper impression. There are a number of reasons for "official" disinterest. First and foremost, the officials were preoccupied with the new European war, and had strategy and planning to consider. Secondly, the He 178, although revolutionary from a technical standpoint, was not a military aircraft. Concurrent designs were faster and bristled with guns. The He 178 was the recognized first step toward improved aircraft technology, but was still in its infancy. Finally, the RLM was roundly disappointed at Heinkel's production schedules. His aircraft company had fallen behind and the RLM officials were probably disappointed that he was "goofing around" with nonproductive aircraft developmental programs. That being said, the RLM did devote money to the programs in development on the potential that they would come to fruition.

Subsequent flights with He 178 V1 were few and far between. The fixed landing gear was not modified, which limited the plane's capabilities. Furthermore, the unconventional compressed hydrogen fuel delivery system was neither ideal nor convenient; the He 178 was relegated to show status.

The second prototype was a considerable improvement on the first. The V2 had retractable landing gear and increased wing area; improvements for speed and maneuverability respectively. Most importantly, the V2 was powered by the next Ohain development, the HeS 6, with a proposed 590 kg (1,300 lbs) thrust. The new engine model burned liquid fuel, as was Ohain's initial intention, and was more powerful but at the same time heavier.

Only two He 178 prototypes were built; after a short experimental life the He 178 V2 was sent to Berlin as a museum display. It was lost during the war in a bombing raid. Heinkel instead turned his energies to competing projects that offered the potential of greater gain and prosperity. But at the same time Heinkel also continued research and development of turbojet projects. He ordered his best designers and engineers to come up with a fighter concept. The result was the twin jet-engine Heinkel He 280 coupled with improved Heinkel engines to power it.

Interestingly, although the first jet flight was a significant milestone, it did not represent the only line of German turbojet development. The decision had already been made to pursue other avenues of engineering. Engineers at Göttingen and elsewhere around the country had independently developed the scientific basis for the development of a German jet program. At the 1935 Volta conference on high-speed flight, well attended by German engineers and theorists,[35] conferees had determined that the reciprocating piston engine was reaching its useful limits. This "presumptive anomaly" led theoretical scientists to develop ideas, frequently absurd, on the future of high-speed flight.[36] The reciprocating engine had a lot of development left in it—it did, after all, win World War II—but scientific theorists correctly perceived limitations. Prandtl and Kármán, leaders in the aeronautical field were among the Volta attendees. The historian of technology, Edward Constant, argues with statistics that the Germans were producing twice as much pure scientific analysis on high-speed aerodynamics than their closest competitor, the United States.[37] Suffice it to say that the Germans were well advanced and considering the possibilities of alternate power sources for high-speed aircraft.

In some respects, the RLM had arguably benefited from the Treaty of Versailles and the limitations it imposed on aviation development. Because the Luftwaffe had to start literally from scratch, by the 1930s there was little sentimental baggage from the first air war to hinder development or design. German engineers were able to experiment and gained substantial government sponsorship for cutting-edge designs and technology. As early as April 1, 1939, the RLM had issued a directive outlining theoretical development of turbojet aircraft for the Luftwaffe. It specified technical guidelines for turbojet aircraft proposals based on a twin-engine single-seat interceptor/fighter design of all metal construction. The plane should carry adequate firepower for air-to-air combat, and be capable of operations in night and in weather. It was to have a high rate of climb, and "highest possible" maximum speed. Range and endurance figures were noted as well as takeoff and landing guidelines, indicating the specifications writers were cognizant of the compromises to be considered in regard to nascent turbojet technology.[38]

The RLM had asked for and received proposals based on the guidelines before the first flights of the Heinkel He 178. In short, the German scientific and technical communities appreciated the potential of the turbojet aircraft; the Heinkel/Ohain project simply confirmed their prognostications. The German engineers and aerodynamicists also saw limitations in the early centrifugal-flow designs. Instead of concentrating on further developments on the centrifugal-flow design, the RLM, with considerable input from Dr. Anselm Franz, decided to pursue the potentially more powerful axial-flow type turbojet engine. Heinkel would continue work on further centrifugal-flow designs, such as the HeS 8a, but did not receive official funding or RLM support. In the meantime, the RLM had offered contracts to both *Junkers Motorenbau* (*Jumo*) and *Bayerische Motoren Werke* (BMW) to propose turbojet engines as early as 1939, just as the Heinkel He 178 project was reaching fruition. Guided by the theories of Dr. Franz, *Jumo* decided on an axial-flow type engine.[39]

The axial-flow turbojet had a number of advantages over the centrifugal-flow design. The axial-flow engine had a smaller cross section and intake radius thus the axial-flow engines could be mounted in external nacelles. The Germans were able to design their airframes and, in effect, add the engines as accessories: necessary, but added on. By contrast, the British, who stayed with the proven centrifugal-flow turbojet throughout the war, had to build their plane around the engine, severely restricting design flexibility. In practical terms, the centrifugal compressor's larger diameter dictated either a single-engine design with the engine in the fuselage (He 178 and later Gloster *Pioneer*) or multiengine designs with the engines embedded in the wings. Furthermore, the Germans believed that the centrifugal-flow turbojet was quickly reaching the limits of its design potential.[40] Although the centrifugal-flow turbojet would vastly improve (and continues to improve to this day), the gamble paid off for the Germans. The axial-flow turbojets developed by the Germans during the war were far superior to Allied centrifugal-flow models in construction and efficiency.[41]

There were drawbacks to the axial-flow type, but each of these was overcome by German insistence. The design was more difficult to develop, but the German engineers were able to "freeze" development and mass-produce the engine, making the construction as simple as possible. By the end of the war unskilled workers were forcibly turning out hundreds of axial-flow turbojet engines each week.[42] Further, the axial-flow type was more expensive to construct, both financially and in terms of material requirements. The Germans circumvented this problem by making the jet engine program a government high-priority project.[43] Funding was provided and materials were allocated.

The projected German airframes enforced the decision in favor of axial-flow turbojets. The plans submitted by both Heinkel and Professor Willi Messerschmitt's respective aircraft companies called for underwing engines, the exact application for which the axial-flow types were designed. The revolutionary new aircraft were proposed to carry the axial-flow turbojets under wing, and consideration was also made for a number of different axial-flow engine proposals from competing engine manufacturers such as BMW and Junkers. The Heinkel program, the He 280, was proposed in 1939 and envisioned a twin-engine jet fighter airplane. The competing program, the Messerschmitt project 1065—the basis for the future Me 262— was proposed as early as 1939, following the RLM request of 1938. Both were designed *from the beginning* as frontline combat jet aircraft, building on the advances already accomplished in the field, and expanding on brand-new aeronautical engineering technology in the form of axial-flow turbojets.

But, the German jet program was almost preordained to failure. As early as February 9, 1940, *Reichsmarshall* Hermann Göring, the commander in chief of the Luftwaffe, working under a direct order from the Führer, decreed that all military production projects that would not be operational within 6 months to a year were to be scrapped.[44] All experimental programs were to cease immediately in favor of producing the greatest quantity of aircraft, regardless of quality. In the minds of the German High Command, the war was not supposed to last long, therefore there was no immediate need for experimental projects, only a dire need for, in this case, as many planes already in production as soon as possible. The order was repeated and strengthened the following year in an infamous *Führerprotokoll* (Führer directive). On September 11, 1941, Hitler reiterated that all experimental projects that would not reach fruition within 6 months were to be terminated.[45] But the directive was reworded with regard to the Luftwaffe in January 1942 that read: "The State Secretary and Inspector General, Luftwaffe, however, is required to evaluate all development projects in terms of their feasibility as regards to the current status of raw materials and production capacity."[46] Göring had conveniently created a loophole that would have a decisive impact on the fate of the German jet program.

Paradoxically, the jet aircraft program was given the highest priority status supporting the experimental programs. The RLM under Field Marshal Erhard Milch, the State Secretary of Aviation, issued "*Projekt Vulkan*" in December 1942 prioritizing several experimental aviation projects. In his words it was for "the absolute demand for qualitative superiority of German air force equipment over that of the enemy countries has led me to order the creation of an urgent development and production program under the code name 'Vulcan.'"[47] The program gave priority of equipment and materials to German projects that would produce jet fighters and bombers, their engines, and guided weapons. The projects that were given the code "Priority DE" included the Me 163 (the Messerschmitt rocket fighter), Me 262, He 280, the Ar 234 (Arado's jet bomber), and the Me 328 (Messerschmitt's pulse-jet fighter). This directive illustrates the importance of the jet programs to Milch and the RLM, and shows that the RLM sensed a need for a qualitative advantage that these planes would provide. Although Hitler and Göring were ready to shut down programs that would not be available immediately, the decision by Milch shows foresight and planning for the future of the Luftwaffe.

Both Heinkel and Messerschmitt initially ignored the restrictive Hitler order, and both continued to develop their respective experimental jets. After both aircraft were built, and initial tests had been completed, the Milch order of December 1942 allowed them to continue the development of their jet programs with official RLM sanction.

In the midst of this "official" turmoil, Heinkel submitted proposals based on even more advanced technology. In the heady days of interwar aviation development, Heinkel was insistent on producing an all-Heinkel turbojet aircraft incorporating Heinkel-built airframes and engines. His proposals included plans for a twin-engine aircraft powered by two axial-flow turbojets. Ohain's early centrifugal-flow turbojet engines were constructed using an impeller that forced air outwards from the center through diffuser vanes and through a manifold, changing the air flow direction 90 degrees before it was ignited by the fuel to form thrust. The inherent problem with the centrifugal-flow engine was that there was only one compressor unit; the combination of the impeller, diffuser vanes, and manifold. The axial-flow turbojet was theoretically more efficient because it employed as many compressor stages as were necessary.[48] In addition, the axial-flow engine could be dismantled and each section tested as compared to the centrifugal-flow engine which could not be dismantled and was tested on a trial-and-error basis. The centrifugal-flow engine was, however, easier to construct, and was the first form of jet engine to be flown by both the Axis and the Allies. But, the axial-flow engine offered better efficiency and was more easily tested and modified. Thus Heinkel, following his initial successes with a centrifugal-flow turbojet engine, focused on the development and testing of axial-flow turbojet engines.

It was not until 1941 that adequate engines were constructed for the German second-generation jet planes. Heinkel had recruited Max Müller to build axial-flow turbojets at the Heinkel factory workshops. Side by side with Ohain, Müller created the HeS 30 axial-flow engine while Ohain was improving his centrifugal-flow type, the HeS 8.[49] The choice between centrifugal- and axial-flow turbojets was a concern for Heinkel. Ohain had only been able to produce 500 kg static thrust—of a proposed 700 kg—from the HeS 8. Meanwhile Müller was producing his planned 700 kg thrust from the HeS 30, and as it was modified over the course of the year eventually delivered 900 kg thrust. Heinkel's decision, supported by the RLM, was in favor of the axial-flow turbojet engine over the centrifugal-flow engine designed by Ohain.[50] The axial-flow engine design team, led by Müller, was moved to Stuttgart, and work continued on the HeS 30 (also known by its official RLM designation 109-006) as well as the next generation axial-flow turbojet engine, the 109-011, designed to produce 1,300 kg thrust. However, work on the HeS 30 was abandoned by order of the RLM's Technical Department in order to concentrate on the (proposed) more powerful 109-011, and the He 280 program was once again delayed due to a lack of engines.[51] It was a major setback for the He 280 program when Helmut Schelp of the RLM Technical Department dropped the HeS 30 (109-006) in favor of the 109-011, an entirely new design. Had the development continued on the HeS 30, it could have proven to be an adequate power plant for the fledgling He 280. Instead, the RLM decided on a new design, and farmed out proposals from other companies for jet engines: the forerunners in the competition included Junkers and BMW. Heinkel and Messerschmitt would eventually have to depend on these companies for engines.

Testing continued, and both the Heinkel and Messerschmitt designs continued to improve and show potential. The He 280 airframe was prepared, and the anticipated HeS 8a engines were finally ready by March 1941. The HeS 8a jet engines were the culmination of Ohain's theoretical abilities to that point. The HeS 8a was a centrifugal-flow turbojet engine, incorporating the designs and modifications that Ohain proposed from the beginning of the project in 1936. His HeS 8a was a liquid-fuel (diesel) burning jet engine specifically built for Heinkel jet aircraft at the Heinkel engine manufacturing plant. The first engines were delivered, the plane was readied, and the chief test pilot Fritz Schäfer was able to make the first flight in the twin-engine He 280 on March 30, 1941.[52] The plane tested well and on April 5, 1941, a demonstration was held for Luftwaffe and RLM officials including General Ernst Udet, the Luftwaffe's Director of Air Armament. The response was good, but there was general consensus that work needed to be done to improve the aircraft's engines.[53] As testing continued, work was in fact done by Ohain and the designers at Heinkel to improve both the airframe and the engines. Ohain supervised the development of the next generation of Heinkel engines, the axial-flow HeS 11 (RLM 109-011); the airframe was redesigned with the original tail strengthened for stability at high speeds.

Concurrently, work proceeded at the Messerschmitt factory on project 1065, the future Me 262. There were complications that almost finished the Messerschmitt project early in its testing stages. Early development was hindered first and foremost by a lack of engines. Willi Messerschmitt had designed an airframe that was literally years ahead of its proposed power plants. It was designed from the beginning to be an air superiority fighter. Flight testing began on the prototype Me 262 airframe powered by a Junkers Jumo 210 piston engine to test the stability of the plane, however, the piston engine was not powerful enough to adequately test the airframe. The results were therefore inconclusive. The heavily armed and armored airframe needed high-speed testing to prove the viability of both the airframe design as well as the necessity for turbojet engines. The high wing loading[54] meant that the plane needed to go fast to adequately test the flight characteristics of the airframe. Piston-engine testing determined only that the airframe was acceptable at low speeds such as takeoff, landing, and stall speeds. Wind-tunnel testing of the Me 262 was more beneficial, showing Messerschmitt that his design was sound and that his projected performance figures were attainable. But the Me 262 airframe was only tested as a model in the wind-tunnel, there were no wind-tunnels in Germany large enough to accommodate a full-scale mock-up. Although Messerschmitt did gain invaluable information, a lack of wind-tunnel testing on a full-scale airframe did not expose some of the manufacturing faults that would crop up in later flight testing.

One of the most persistent myths about the Me 262 program is the question of the aircraft in the bomber (or at least fighter/bomber) role. It is important to note that the original plans for the production version of the Me 262, as submitted by Willi Messerschmitt, included provisions for bomb racks. Moreover, Messerschmitt's final design plans submitted on March 4, 1943, included specific instructions that the Me 262 be able to carry bombs: "as per an order from the Führer, every fighter must henceforth be capable of performing in the fighter-bomber role. An installation capable of carrying 500 kg of bombs is foreseen for the Me 262."[55] This is important for it makes clear that the Me 262 was intended to be able to carry bombs *from the beginning* of the project.

At the time, in compliance with the wishes of the RLM, all production fighter aircraft were to be constructed to perform the dual role of fighter-bomber.[56] As offensive weapons, they were to carry small bomb payloads to aid in tactical strikes, in addition to their purely defensive fighter roles.[57] The Luftwaffe concentration on combined operations with land forces, along with a lack of strategic direction from Göring, allowed the air arm of the German military to be used effectively as a tactical attack element.[58]

The German fighter had been initiated into the close air support role during the final stages of World War I, and that role was experimented with and continued throughout the German involvement in the Spanish Civil War. After the stunning successes of the campaigns against Poland and France, the principal German fighter, the Messerschmitt Bf 109, was produced as a *Jabo* (fighter/bomber).[59] This was not unusual: the British at the same time produced a fighter/bomber version of the famous Spitfire, the FB Mk.V.[60] In fact, even American fighter planes were outfitted for dual-purpose air warfare and close-air support roles. However, it is important to note that the Messerschmitt Company had already dealt with the RLM order that fighters had to be able to perform the dual role of fighter/bomber. The documentation suggests that Willi Messerschmitt consciously knew in 1943 that the production Me 262 would have to be able to carry bombs as per Hitler's orders. Suffice it to say that Messerschmitt was cognizant of the requirements for his future fighter project in 1943, and it was no shock to him that the Me 262 was supposed to carry bombs when it went into production.

In the meantime, as both the Heinkel and Messerschmitt airframes were being tested, intense effort was being put into turbojet development. A detailed discussion of the engines themselves is therefore warranted. Conventional piston engines were reaching the apex of their efficiency.[61] As power in the form of thrust was increased, corresponding weight increased exponentially. In other words, if horsepower was doubled, the weight of an engine quadrupled (2 to the second power).[62] The piston engine was used and improved throughout the interwar years, but the Germans actively pursued alternative power plants for airplane designs. The Germans began with theoretical work on the compressibility of fluids and theories on high-speed flight. Leading physicists were working on the theoretical questions that opened discussion of alternative power plants for aircraft. And it is also important to remember that the Nazis, in power since 1933, were also very interested in advanced technology and its technical application to warfare. The beginning of the turbojet revolution[63] was initiated by Hans von Ohain and Frank Whittle with their respective centrifugal-flow turbojet engines. The centrifugal-flow turbojet engine is composed of three stages: the compressor, the combustion stage, and the exhaust turbine. Both of the early designers built the simple engines in order to test their theories of propulsion. The centrifugal-flow engines proved the viability of turbojet power, and had obvious benefits. Their simple construction meant that they were easy to build. The combination of the impeller and turbine on a common shaft meant that there were no reciprocating parts, therefore less vibration and fewer moving parts. The lack of propellers negated the compressibility problems that were being observed in piston-engine aircraft. But, there were drawbacks too. The high rotational speeds—15,000–17,000 rpm as compared to 3,500–4,000 for piston engines—translated into problems in lubrication and temperature. And, materials development had to evolve with the development of turbojet engines. Combustion chamber temperatures approached 1800°F and new materials had to be developed to deal with the novel temperatures and rotational speeds being faced by the early designers. Furthermore, the centrifugal-flow turbojet engine was limited with regard to upgrading. It was difficult to test centrifugal impellers, and development was frequently trial-and-error. Further, since compression stages were difficult—if not impossible—to add to a centrifugal-flow engine, upgrading was much more inconvenient. For better performance the engine had to be entirely redesigned and manufactured. Thus, following the early successes of the centrifugal-flow turbojet engines, interested Germans at all levels conceded that the centrifugal-flow type did not show the same promise as the more complicated but higher potential axial-flow turbojet engine.

The decision in favor of the axial-flow turbojet engine over the centrifugal-flow engine was a question of technological necessity. Although the axial-flow engine was more expensive and more difficult to build, it was preferred by the RLM and the engineers.[64] The axial-flow engine had a smaller intake diameter because the air flowed straight through the engine rather than being compressed centrifugally. Thus, there was less drag in flight. It was also a more efficient engine. More compressor stages could be added for higher compression ratios to produce more thrust. Finally, both the He 280 and Me 262 were designed to carry two axial-flow engines under the wings, whereas the He 178 (as well as the British Gloster E.28/39 and the American Bell XP-59A) were aircraft designed around centrifugal-flow turbojets, with the airflow directed through the fuselage of the plane. The drawback, for the Germans, was that the axial-flow turbojet engine was more difficult to construct, even without RLM interference. The airframes were ready literally years before their corresponding engines; the concurrent German engine technology was delicate and unreliable. Although the German engines proved to be more powerful, they required constant maintenance and care. And there was a lack of reliable engines for the German jet program throughout the war.

The discussion of the development of the German axial-flow turbojet engine begins with the BMW. BMW was the first to complete jet engines for the Me 262 program. But, in the initial flight with the BMW turbojet engines on March 25, 1942, both failed, and the plane was nearly lost. Fortunately for the Me 262 project, the piston engine used for low-speed airframe testing was retained for the first flight with the BMW 003 jet engines. The jet engines failed directly after takeoff, but the pilot was able to land the plane safely thanks to the piston engine.[65] In a postmortem examination, it was determined that the compressor blades on both engines had failed and seized; BMW went back to the drawing board.[66] Although the plane had been saved, the failure of the BMW engines was a major setback for the Me 262 program. The RLM reduced its initial order of 20 Me 262 prototypes to a mere five; the reinstatement of the initial order was dependent on successful tests with the Junkers Jumo 004 engines.[67] The Jumo 004s were not ready until July 1942 when they were finally fit to Me 262 V3. Junkers had successfully completed two axial-flow turbojet engines, designated Jumo 004, but the road had been long and hard.

Work had begun on the Junkers Jumo 004 (Model T1) axial-flow turbojet engine as early as 1939. Dr. Anselm Franz, after completing his doctorate in Switzerland, was offered a position in the engine development department at Junkers. The RLM contracted Junkers motor division—known as *Jumo*, the combination of the names *Junkers Motorenbau*—to produce a prototype turbojet engine.[68] The prototype, which was constructed to run on diesel fuel, was first tested in October 1940 without an exhaust nozzle. After configuring the various pieces and assembling them, the designers' bench tested the engine at the end of January 1941 to a top thrust of 430 kg (930 lbs). Work continued to increase the output of the engine, the minimum set by the RLM contract was 600 kg thrust.[69] The engine finally reached minimum requirements in August of the same year after the original alloy compressor blades were replaced with steel. Flight tests were initiated using a Me 110 flying test bed to run-up the engine in flight. These flying tests began in March 1942. Following a series of successful tests, the RLM ordered an additional 80 Jumo 004s in late summer 1942.[70] Therefore, it is important to note that engine tests were still underway when the Me 262 made its maiden jet flight on July 18, 1942. The engines and airframe would require further modification before either was ready for operations.

The revolutionary engine design from Franz was an axial-flow turbojet created for a single purpose. Franz initially designed the engine as the answer to the engine-starved German jet program. The prototype Jumo 004 had an eight-stage axial-flow compressor, eight annular combustion chambers, and a single exhaust turbine. The shaft speed of the Jumo 004 was estimated at 16,000 rpm, and the designed thrust rating was 900 kg (1,980 lbs). Franz's Jumo team realized theoretical output of the Jumo 004 relatively early in the program, the prototypes achieved design parameters.[71] But problems soon emerged in the postprototype turbojet engine development.

However, the initial engines, built to power the Me 262 V-series prototypes, were built as experimental engines. There were no restrictions on the materials used to construct the first Jumo 004 engines, and they used large quantities of scarce raw materials such as nickel, cobalt, and molybdenum. The quantities used in the prototype engines were unacceptable in production; the Germans were running short on precious raw materials even early in the war. Furthermore, Dr. Franz realized this dilemma. He understood that once the Jumo 004 was ready for production it would have to be redesigned incorporating less of the valuable and scarce raw materials that were simply not available.[72]

However, Jumo, led by Franz, was able to redesign the entire Jumo 004 with regard to materials shortages. The new production engines used far less strategic raw material per engine, and the German designers were able to make extensive use of substitute materials in engine construction. The drawback was that the engine's operational lifespan was shortened. The benefits were that the engines could actually be constructed with limited raw materials, they became increasingly easier to construct, and the Germans could employ semi- and unskilled labor in the manufacturing process. For the Germans in wartime, the benefits easily outweighed the costs. The Germans, in the midst of shortages, produced the most technically advanced aeronautical designs and power plants.

Following successful flight testing, which we will return to later, the Jumo went through a number of refinements. The engines were redesigned using less and less of the scarce raw materials and more substitute methods were employed. In June 1943 the Jumo 004 was "frozen" for production.[73] The main problem faced by Junkers was the lack of strategically important raw materials. Whereas the prototype engines had been constructed without regard for the amount of scarce raw materials used, there were severe restrictions placed on the production models. Less reliable materials and construction techniques were employed in the production engines and there were corresponding failures in the power plants. For example, in the original prototype engines the combustion chamber was made of a high-alloy steel, but the production model was built with a mild steel sprayed with an aluminum coating.[74] The use of *Ersatz* materials constrained the Junkers Jumo 004 to a short 10-hour operational lifespan before complete overhauls were necessary. Although the engine was improved and made more reliable, the lack of important raw materials led to a relatively short operational lifespan for the engine during its entire career as a Luftwaffe power plant. Subsequently, there was a constant shortage of engines from Junkers for the Me 262 jet program; it was not until April 1944 that there were enough engines available to outfit an entire squadron of Me 262s.

Junkers continually improved the engines. The Jumo 004A was replaced by the 004B-1 by June 1944. The 004C, using air-cooled turbine blades evolved from the 004B-1. The 004B-4 series engine also used this technology and was in production by December 1944.[75] The 004B-4 series was a technical marvel; it used no nickel and only 2.2 kg chrome in each engine.[76] The engine's high-altitude performance was improved a great deal, but the low-speed characteristics remained unchanged. To the German pilot's chagrin, the engines performed poorly on takeoff and landing throughout the war; eventually it was so bad that the Me 262, the most advanced fighter design in the world, required conventional piston-engine fighter escort during takeoff and landing procedures. The Luftwaffe was forced to use fighters to protect fighters!

The German jet program was given a morale boost in early 1942 when Albert Speer was appointed the Minister of Armaments and Production and implemented a program to husband precious raw materials.[77] After initial conflict with Göring, Speer was able to increase fighter production to higher levels than ever before realized within the Reich. Speer was responsible for streamlining the German war economy so that production could be increased. In order to do this he established an efficient system for ordering military hardware and setting up production schedules. He was also responsible for husbanding the dwindling supply of raw materials in Germany in order to reduce wastage. Finally, he was able to rationalize the war economy, and removed military officials from supervisory positions in the munitions plants. This final move directly increased the efficiency within German factories.[78]

More importantly for the German jet program, Speer was responsible for the creation of the *Jägerstab* (Fighter Staff) on March 1, 1944. By centralizing all fighter aircraft production, efficiency was increased through cooperation.[79] Fighter planes (and their engines) received top priority for materials and the Me 262 was eventually provided with all the necessary materials for production.[80] However, supplies were dwindling, and even the Jumo 004 engines had to utilize substitute materials in their final construction.

The airframes also went through changes and modifications from their inception to their production. The planes were requested by the RLM as early as 1938,[81] and both Heinkel and Messerschmitt submitted designs. The Heinkel He 280 was an aesthetically pleasing airplane, which combined Heinkel's attention to detail, need for speed, and beautiful designs. The low-wing, twin jet-engine design incorporated a straight wing with an elliptical trailing edge and a twin horizontal stabilizer tail design. The inadequacy in the He 280 was that its operational range was very limited and its armament was poor as compared to Messerschmitt's proposed design. The RLM chose the Me 262 over the He 280 on the basis of range and firepower.[82] But the overarching problem was still a lack of engines for the revolutionary airplane design. In the end it was a poor decision by the RLM, the He 280, which was to use first Heinkel engines (HeS-8), and later BMW engines (003), would have been another jet aircraft that the Luftwaffe could have put into operations. The decision to cancel the program meant that the Luftwaffe only had one viable jet fighter in any significant numbers instead of two. Heinkel was ordered to continue development of his heavy bomber, the He 177 *Greif*, which was plagued with technical problems throughout the war. The most promising heavy bomber design cancelled the Luftwaffe's second viable jet fighter design. Heinkel completed only prototypes, which were employed throughout the war as flying test-beds.

Conversely, Messerschmitt's design was accepted. Messerschmitt was the obvious choice to provide the Luftwaffe's newest jet fighter; he was the mastermind behind the Bf 109,[83] the backbone of the Luftwaffe fighter force. This design had projected German might in Spain during the Spanish Civil War, and all over Europe as Hitler practiced his geopolitics in the Saarland, Austria, and the Sudetenland. Bf/Me 109s had destroyed Polish air power in the very short yet very decisive Polish campaign; and 109s had been responsible for the destruction of the French *Armee de l'Air* in the 1940 campaigns. By the Battle of Britain, the Me 109 E-3 and E-4 models were coming online, and proved their worth against the best British design in the Supermarine Spitfire Mk I. Limited by range and numbers, the Germans lost the battle, but returned to the skies to counter British bombing over Germany. Messerschmitt's designs proved their worth as he developed new, more powerful models.

But, the fact that Messerschmitt was the main producer of fighter models was also a hindrance to the nascent jet program. In addition to Messerschmitt's Me 109 program, another Messerschmitt plane competed for vital materials, engineers, and manufacturing space. The proposed Me 209, a second-generation development of the Me 109, was under consideration by the RLM concurrently. In a meeting in May 1943 the Me 209 was struck from the developmental roster of production aircraft in favor of the Me 262.[84] The dilemma was this: the Me 209 was already in preproduction—the jigs and tools were already in place—and the engines were being produced—the DB603 A-1—and more importantly were available. At this time the Me 262 were still in early testing, only five airframes were available, and the engines were still undergoing substantial development and revision. The RLM recognized the potential of the Me 262 and banked on it. Whereas the Messerschmitt Company was ready to produce the Me 209, the Me 262 promised a significant leap in technology and the Me 209 was dropped.

The next month, June 1943, Messerschmitt himself was called before the RLM to report on the status of proposed production of the Me 262.[85] While it was still in testing, he predicted that his company could not commence delivery of operational Me 262s before January 1944. Messerschmitt was optimistic about the Me 262 program, but he was realistic about his company's manufacturing capabilities. He predicted that his company could start production in January 1944 and be able to deliver by the end of each month 8 in February, 21 in March, 40 in April, and 60 in May. Thereafter, he promised 60 aircraft each month through November 1944. At this point he noted that these were only airframes! He specifically pointed to the fact that he was in control of producing the aircraft, the Junkers engines were another matter altogether. The delivery of operational jet aircraft was dependent on the manufacture of the jet engines in as much as it was dependent on the airframes. But he outlined the maximum airframes that his manufacturing could produce. Messerschmitt told the members of the RLM meeting that the most he could promise per month was 400 airframes, and this figure would not be attained before September 1945.[86] Interestingly, at the same time Messerschmitt was producing over 500 Me 109s alone each month.[87] Messerschmitt proposed jet fighter production over and above all current Messerschmitt production!

Furthermore, in the June meeting Messerschmitt argued against his own Me 209 project. He wanted the contract—and subsequent funding and materials—for the jet program.[88] Messerschmitt argued that the Me 209 jigs and tools were not in fact ready, and that the proposed Daimler Benz engines were not working up to requirements. He stated that at that point, his company could produce equal numbers of either Me 262s or Me 209s, but not both.

As well, by this time the Focke Wulf FW 190 was replacing the Me 109 in the air as the mainstay of the Luftwaffe fighter force.[89] The FW 190 A-4, and by the end of 1943, the D-9 replaced the Me 109 G and K series fighters, and allowed Messerschmitt to refocus production lines.

The RLM insisted on continued production numbers, even of the obsolete Me 109, in order to keep the Luftwaffe supplied with planes.[90] The RLM requested of Messerschmitt that he produce 1,000 Me 262s a month by September 1945, a figure that he agreed to. His acceptance was hailed by both Milch and Adolf Galland, the Luftwaffe's general of fighters who had personally flown the Me 262 and championed its production. However, Messerschmitt noted again that his jet planes relied on Junkers and BMW for engines.[91] Production figures for the Me 262 were set at 1,000 per month, an unrealistic dream in war-torn Germany where the situation was becoming more tenuous each day.

Incredibly, in addition to the projected 1,000 per month Me 262 production, the Me 209 project was resurrected. At the August meeting the RLM requested not only 1,000 Me 262s per month, but added (a total of) 3,000 Me 209s and FW 190s to the production list.[92] RLM officials ordered that there was to be no loss of projected production of the Me 262, even though the Messerschmitt company had to almost completely retool for two new production models.[93] It was not until November 1943 that the Me 209 project was finally, and officially, scrapped. In the interim, between August and November, the Me 209 program consumed vast quantities of resources that could have been put to better use toward the Me 262. But it was not the materials misdirected to the Me 209 program that hindered the Me 262—without the essential power plants the Me 262 was no more than a high-tech glider.

The Me 262 airframe itself was a modern marvel. Messerschmitt had been designing and constructing cutting-edge aircraft for years; he was responsible for a number of novel aircraft technologies. The Me 262 would push him and his company to the limits of aircraft technology. In the beginning Project 1065 was envisioned as a straight wing, twin-engine, single-seat fighter design. The initial designs incorporated the clipped-wing made famous by the Me 109 with the engines slung under the wing. The tubular fuselage was a standard Messerschmitt design, but would undergo many developmental changes during its lifetime. The body of the aircraft was redesigned before prototype construction into the easily recognizable triangular shape. The triangular cross section facilitated lift, reduced drag, thus enhanced speed. The straight wing was reconsidered, and in order to balance the plane and accommodate the heavy engines Messerschmitt swept the wings from the engine to the tip while maintaining the straight wing from the root to the engine nacelle. This novel approach, taken for other considerations, had an enormous impact on the development of aircraft technology. Messerschmitt did not realize that by sweeping the wings he would promote speed, he did it for stability. But it did increase speed, which led to other experiments and ideas.

With the combination of the completion of the airframe at Messerschmitt in the midst of political wrangling, and the fabrication of the Jumo engines in the midst of materials shortages, the entire aircraft was assembled for its maiden flight. With the Junkers Jumo engines finally ready, following the ill-fated attempt with BMW engines, Me 262 V3 was fit and ready for testing. On July 18, 1942, Fritz Wendel took to the air under pure jet power from the airfield at Leipheim in an Me 262 V3 (PC+UC). At that point, Messerschmitt and his designers found flaws that only became apparent with the advent of high-speed jet-powered flight.

In the first flight, Wendel found that the tailwheel configuration of the landing gear was inappropriate for the novel power plants. In a conventional piston-engine plane, the airflow from the engine moves over the control surfaces in low-speed taxiing and flight. In the Me 262s configuration, the airflow from the jet engines did not move over the elevator controls, and the tailwheel would not come off the ground. The experienced test pilot took a novel approach and stabbed the brakes at 112 mph. This caused the nose to drop, the tail to rise, and the plane to "grab" the air. Wendel took off and flew a 12-minute circuit in the jet.[94] The Me 262 still needed work, however, and suggestions were immediately made for its improvement.

Wendel, an experienced test pilot, a confidant of Messerschmitt, and an accredited engineer in his own right, was able to suggest improvements, which were later incorporated into production. Upon landing the jet prototype, he immediately suggested improvements to the craft. He related the dangerous braking procedure, and recommended a tricycle landing gear incorporating a nosewheel.[95] The designers recognized the importance of his suggestion, but this in turn required a weight shift toward the nose of the aircraft, and a redesign of the entire undercarriage. The shift in the center of gravity was made with the planned addition of armaments in the nose, and the landing gear was subcontracted out to the Opel factory. It was not until the construction of Me 262 V5, equipped with a fixed nosewheel, and V3 retrofit with tricycle gear, that the Me 262 had the new landing-gear configuration. Up to that point the dangerous braking procedure had to be used to make the jet plane take off.

Furthermore, Wendel suggested that the entire wing be swept back, from root to tip. He explained to the designers that the plane, while fast, was unstable in turns and unmaneuverable. He suggested a redesign of the wing for increased lift and maneuverability, design modifications that were incorporated into future prototypes. The wing modifications led to a 30 percent increase in wing lift.[96]

The first RLM test pilot to fly the new jet was Heinrich Beauvis. On August 11, nearly a month after the first flights by Wendel, Beauvis took the controls of Me 262 V3. Although coached by Wendel, Beauvis could not duplicate the dangerous braking procedure and quickly ran out of runway. He crashed the plane without ever taking to the air, causing significant damage to the Me 262 in particular and the German jet program as a whole. The Me 262 V3 required substantial repair, and Messerschmitt was without a flying prototype until October, when the Me 262 V2 was again fitted with engines and flown. Despite the accident, the RLM ordered five additional prototypes and ten preproduction models. The ten 0-series aircraft (Me 262 A-0), to be designated V11 through V20, were to include the safer tricycle landing gear system. When Beauvis did finally fly the jet in October, the RLM again expanded its order to thirty 0-series aircraft, with the stipulation that they would be completed by the end of 1943. However, Messerschmitt rejected the order on account of his lack of production capabilities; he promised only 10 airframes by the deadline.[97]

The highest praise for the Messerschmitt jet came from one of the Luftwaffe's own, *General der Jagdflieger* (General of Fighters) Adolf Galland. He made his first jet flight on May 22, 1943. Three days later he presented a written and oral report for the viability and necessity for the jet aircraft.[98] He was overwhelmingly impressed with the jet plane, even in the testing stages, and demanded that the Me 262 replace all other Messerschmitt production (including the Me 109) immediately. He argued that the FW 190 could be produced as the main piston-engine fighter for the Luftwaffe, and that Messerschmitt should concentrate all production on the Me 262. Galland requested the impossible figure of 1,000 Me 262s per month for the Luftwaffe fighter arm. In Galland's opinion, the Me 262 was more advanced than the proposed Me 209; the Me 209 was immediately obsolete when compared to the new jet fighter. In his diary he outlined his intentions, "Drop Me 209, put Me 262 in its place."[99] His opinion influenced the conference and an RLM order for the first 100 Me 262s was posted to Messerschmitt.[100] Galland had flown and evaluated the newest German technological wonder, and his sentiments can be summed up in his description of the plane, "It was as though angels were pushing."[101]

2

Frank Whittle and the "Squirt"

The story of the Allied jet program began in Britain. The basis for both the British and American jet programs was the engine designed, built, and manufactured by Frank Whittle, an Englishman. The Allied jet program was built around his jet engine, the Power Jets W.1. The account of the British turbojet program thus begins and ends with a dedicated and determined Whittle, who virtually single-handedly designed and built a working turbojet prototype in the midst of opposition and ignorance. The fact that Whittle was able to construct his revolutionary power plant is a testament to his perseverance in trying times as Britain attempted to avoid future war.

Born in 1907, Whittle was raised under the influence of his father, a tinkerer and self-employed "engineer," actually closer to a mechanic in the generalized sense. The owner of a small manufacturing business, the Leamington Valve and Piston Ring Company, Moses Whittle often worked in his shop alone satisfying a small number of contracts. Young Frank was therefore exposed at an early age to the machine tools, materials, and an inventive spirit that would guide him to his ultimate fame. By the time he was 10, he was doing piecework for his father's business in return for pocket money.[1] A self-instructed engineer like his father, he spent many hours in the local library reading popular science accounts in magazines and journals. His particular interest was in flight, and he considered himself well read enough that he knew enough to fly a plane without "going through the formality of being taught."[2] The best way for young Whittle to further his career as an engineer and satisfy his passion for airplanes was to join the exciting world of the Royal Air Force (RAF).

The RAF had a number of apprenticeship programs for the instruction of mechanically minded young men. Called engineers upon completion of their training, these early machinists and mechanics were hired as RAF personnel, indoctrinated into the government military structure, and taught how to care for the latest technological marvels. Whittle saw his opportunity to work with his knowledge and his hands around airplanes and decided to put his expertise to use in the RAF. At age 15, shortly after Christmas 1922, he attempted to enlist as an RAF "boy apprentice engineer." He was rejected on medical grounds, even after scoring high on the written exams, and returned home dejected. For 6 months he modified his training regimen and diet, and retook the physical battery in June only to be rejected again. This might well have been the end of the story of the Allied jet program, but Whittle decided to give it "one more go." He resubmitted paperwork in September 1923 under the guise of an initial application (even though he had already applied twice!) and was finally accepted as a first-time candidate for the RAF mechanics apprentice school at Cranwell.[3]

Assigned as an aircraft apprentice to No. 4 Apprentices Wing RAF Cranwell, Whittle was quite excited about his curriculum and professional training. He did not, however, adjust well to the military discipline in the RAF. His spare time (often at the expense of his physical development during "sport time") was dedicated to a newly formed group known as the Model Aircraft Society. He and his colleagues used their knowledge gained in their apprenticeship training, combined it with spare and unused parts and pieces in and around the school, and dedicated time to the construction of flying model airplanes. One such model was a 10.5-foot wingspan plane powered by a two-stroke engine of Whittle's design and manufacture. The plane was built in Whittle's third and final year as an apprentice, and his wing commander suggested that Whittle demonstrate his model for graduation day. Unfortunately for the young engineer, the spark plugs fouled, and the plane did not fly. Whittle himself suggests that the embarrassing nonperformance of the plane's engine may have been the source of his "strong prejudice against piston engines."[4]

In the event, things worked out well for Whittle, barely. His intricate work and dedication to aircraft earned him the fifth slot for admission to the RAF College for further instruction, leading to an officer's commission, but only after one of the cadets above him failed his physical! Whittle was promoted to the Cadet Wing at Cranwell where he furthered his technical knowledge in an academic setting. More importantly, Whittle learned to fly.

Whittle began the two-year period of instruction at Cranwell in 1926. He was finally a Flight Cadet, and learned hands-on flying to supplement his academic knowledge. After 8 hours of dual instruction Whittle flew his first solo flight in his second term. Needless to say, early training methods were vastly different than the modern day. The Flight Cadets were thrown "into the fire," and accident rates were high. Pilots themselves were still seen as daredevils and thrill-seekers in their nascent technology. Whittle was no exception and his flying was frequently hazardous. He had his share of accidents, but was saved by an amazing ability to escape danger during his stunts and did not suffer injury. But more than once Whittle was grounded for stunt flying or confined to base for motorcycle hijinks. He devoted his occasional incarceration to his studies, and progressed toward revolution.

He spent three of his first four terms studying chemistry, for which he had an affinity. His chemistry instructor, Professor O.S. Sinnatt, encouraged Whittle's ideas and devotion. Then, in his fourth and final term, Whittle developed the idea that would change the course of aviation. His term project was titled "Future Developments in Aircraft Design." In it he outlined his interest in high-altitude, high-speed flight.

Behind his shift to the study of flight from chemistry was his love for flying. He was obsessed with speed at a time when the fastest planes, indeed the very ones on which he was training, were flying at speeds of no more than 150 mph. Whittle envisioned an aircraft that would fly in the stratosphere at speeds of 500 mph.[5] He considered ducted-fan engines, gas turbine–driven propellers, and even rocket engines, but according to his own admission, he did not initially consider "pure" turbojet engines.[6]

Even though he was full of bright ideas, the RAF had other plans for the young pilot officer. Whittle was posted to Number 111 Fighter Squadron (Hornchurch) as a fighter pilot where he added to his flight log and also to his acrobatic skills. According to his own testimony, it seems that during his cadetship and pilot years Whittle was quite the "show off" in the air, and was frequently reprimanded for his dangerous flying techniques.[7] Although his actions are a testament to his bravery and experimentation, it is fortunate that he was never seriously injured or even killed because of his hijinks. The free time allotted at the regular RAF posting allowed Whittle the invaluable opportunity to develop his turbojet ideas further. The squadron's "official" workhours were only eight to four during the week, with every other weekend completely free.[8] His time was not constrained as it had been in Cadet School, and Whittle was free to experiment. Work continued on the development of his prototype while he was at No. 111.

Whittle continued his RAF duties when he was posted to pilot trainers school at Wittering in 1929. Initially a student, he eventually became a pilot instructor. Once again, his ample free time allowed him to theorize on high-speed, high-altitude flight. During this time he finally disregarded the idea of a ducted-fan engine. This arrangement involved a piston engine that drove a series of fans within a hollow fuselage, providing thrust. The Italians continued their work on this configuration and flew a ducted-fan aircraft—the Caproni Campini CC.2—in August 1940.[9] However, the plane was underpowered and unusable. The novel configuration offered no advantage over conventional Italian designs and development was terminated.[10] Whittle, in a flash of brilliance, decided to substitute a turbine for a piston engine in the system, proposing, in theory, a "pure" turbojet engine.[11] Whittle discussed the idea with one of his instructors at the Central Flying School, a man named W.E.P. Johnson, who eventually became intimately involved in the development of the turbojet engine.

The new-found friendship led first to a meeting with the school commandant, Group Captain Baldwin, who forwarded a strong recommendation for an audience with the Air Ministry. Whittle was instructed to report and propose his power plant ideas in person. Unfortunately, Whittle's turbojet idea was rejected because of mistakes in Whittle's calculations and overoptimism.[12] After rehashing the figures, Whittle was confident that he had been correct, and resubmitted his ideas to the Air Ministry only to have his proposal rejected again. The stated reason the second time was that the material requirements for the high stresses and temperatures involved in his project were unavailable, indeed beyond contemporary comprehension. In 1929 the Air Ministry shelved the project indefinitely even though Whittle continued his research. In 1930, Whittle, with the assistance of the erstwhile patent officer Johnson, filed a Provisional Specification for his turbojet engine.[13] Interestingly, after the Air Ministry was notified, according to regulations, the patent was not protected as "secret," and the information was published in a number of sources over the next 2 years.[14] The information was available; it remains a question as to whether it aroused attention in anyone at all. The Germans by 1936 were well on their way to jet-powered flight, but the Americans, as we will see, could have benefited substantially from this breach of security.

Whittle continued his work independently on jet engine technology. He was transferred after completing instructor training at Wittering to Number 2 Flying Training School at Digby, and promoted to the rank of Flying Officer. His instruction duties were exciting, and once again Whittle found himself with plenty of time on his hands. It was while he was at Digby that Whittle went beyond the Air Ministry to seek out support for his radical power plant idea.

His initial contact was the Reid & Sigrist Company in Brooklands. George Reid, cofounder of the company, had developed the aerial turn indicator[15] and was actively involved with aircraft technology. Although Reid was interested, he indicated to Whittle that his small company could not fund such a potentially expensive project. For Whittle, the news was a mix of good and bad: he was disappointed that he still had no funding, but was encouraged that at least one other person was excited about his patent.[16] His old friend W.E.P. Johnson was responsible for Whittle's next contact with the British Thomson-Houston (BTH) Company. BTH showed interest, but because of the financial crash of the previous year had little extra money for research. The BTH representatives at the meeting were the chief engineer, F. Samuelson, and his deputy R.H. Collingham. They showed only mild interest in Whittle's work and calculated that start-up costs for the technology would approach £60,000, a sum they were unwilling to invest. In declining support they cited financial reasons observing the detail that they were an industrial turbine company, not an aircraft engine manufacturer. Whittle was disheartened, but not offended. He related that "if anything, it now surprises me that they should have given such a patient hearing to a young man of twenty-three with no academic qualifications."[17]

At the end of the year Whittle, now newly married, asked for a transfer and was posted to the Marine Aircraft Experimental Establishment at Felixstowe as a floatplane test pilot.

While there, Whittle continued his quest for funding and turned to Armstrong-Siddeley for support. Although Armstrong-Siddeley found Whittle's ideas sound, the chief engineer turned down his proposal due to lack of necessary materials. Whittle's turbojet engine proposal called for extremely high compression and temperatures. The design objectives pushed known boundaries of both metallurgy and engineering.[18] Some of Whittle's pilot friends were dubious of his interests; one went so far as to nickname the idea "Whittle's Flaming Touch-hole."[19] But, Flying Officer R.D. Williams assigned to Felixstowe was a great supporter and would have an enormous impact on further development of Whittle's turbojet. One of the immediate problems Whittle faced was that he was proposing unheard-of performance improvements with his engine. He argued that his idea would be made up of a compressor with a 4:1 pressure ratio with 75 percent efficiency. At the same time, the most advanced British aircraft engine was the Rolls-Royce Type R experimental engine that only produced a 2:1 compression ratio with 62 percent efficiency.[20] But, Whittle's figures were only estimates; inasmuch as there was no comparison available his ideas remained purely theoretical.

Whittle continued his test-flying duties, and became proficient in several types and under a wide variety of conditions. He made a good record of himself as an experimental pilot and excelled at flying boats and floatplanes.

At this juncture, RAF rules and regulations came to Whittle's rescue. After 4 years' service, permanent officers were expected to attend specialist courses in either engineering, signals, armament, or navigation. As Whittle recounted, "Naturally, I elected to specialize in engineering, and with the backing of the recommendation in my confidential report I was posted to the Home Aircraft Depot, Henlow, to attend the Officers' Engineering Course in August, 1932."[21] In a show of remarkable aptitude, Whittle excelled in the entrance exams, scoring a composite 98 percent. He further amazed his instructors and mentors by completing the 24-month course on a compressed 18-month schedule.

The RAF had discontinued a program of sending exceptional officers to Cambridge University to attend a further 2 years studying Mechanical Sciences, but Whittle offered an exceptional case. His personal application was supported by his commander at Henlow, and the Air Ministry consented to Whittle's wishes in a letter stating "that in view of this Officer's excellent work on the Specialist 'E' Course they have decided as an exceptional case to allow this Officer to proceed to Cambridge University for the two years 'E' Course."[22] Whittle was going to Cambridge.

In the 6 months between the end of his stint at Henlow and his entrance to Cambridge, January to July 1934, Whittle was promoted to Flight Lieutenant and posted to the Engine Repair Section as the Officer in charge of the Aero-Engine Test Benches with enough time and opportunity to continue nonsanctioned work on his novel propulsion system. His official RAF time was spent keeping the Henlow planes in the air; during his off hours he worked on turbojet engine blueprints. His jet engine idea was going nowhere, and during this interval Whittle lost almost all faith in his idea. He entered Cambridge intent on furthering his engineering education. Whittle had just been through 18 months of intensive RAF engineering training so the nominal 3-year program was shortened to 2 in his case. One indication of his dwindling enthusiasm for the jet engine came in January 1935 when his 1930 patent fees ran out. He was informed first by the patent office of the due date, then by the Air Ministry that they were still uninterested, and Whittle's patent for the jet engine in England ran out for lack of the £5 renewal fee.

Thus, at the beginning of 1935, it is interesting to note two points. First, Whittle was still in the employment of the RAF. The Air Ministry had recognized the potential in the young officer and decided to send him for additional academic training at the most prestigious engineering school in the country. They were in effect hoping that his intuition and expertise could have an impact on future air technology. But, at the same time there was no official support for the turbojet engine. Whittle could have an impact on technology, but the Air Ministry did not think jets were the answer. Second, Whittle had decided that his engine idea was "before its time."[23] The turbojet engine was theoretically possible; this could be proven mathematically. But the necessary materials for construction, as well as the financial means for development, were not available. Whittle decided that the material requirements had not been developed for the estimated temperature and pressure requirements for the turbojet engine. Consider that the most advanced aircraft in 1935 still employed wood and fabric construction, and were flying at top speeds of 260–315 mph.[24] Whittle's proposal *was* before its time, but not impossible under the right circumstances. Unfortunately, Whittle also lacked funds. From his early soliciting he realized that he was going to need large amounts of capital for his project. The deepest pockets were at the Air Ministry, and they would not even pay the £5 to renew his patent. The Ministry was not convinced of the viability of the project. Further, Whittle had been turned down by private-sector investors and companies because he was unable to make his proposal applicable to civilian applications. The right conditions for the development of the turbojet in Britain were absent, and its innovator became despondent. Whittle gave up hope of developing a working prototype turbojet engine.[25]

Then, at his lowest point, Whittle received news that resurrected the jet engine program. In May 1935, he received a note from R. Dudley Williams, a former cadet colleague at Felixstowe. The letter read,

> This is just a hurried note to tell you that I have just met a man who is a bit of a big noise in an engineering concern and to whom I mentioned your invention of an aeroplane, *sans* propeller as it were, and who is very interested. You told me some time ago that Armstrong's [Armstrong Siddeley] had or were taking it up and if they have broken down or if you don't like them, he would, I think, like to handle it. I wonder if you would write me and let me know.[26]

This was the first indication to Whittle that there was any interest at all in his project. Whittle met a short time later with Williams and his partner J.C.B. Tinling to talk about the possibility of jet engine technology. In exchange for a quarter interest in their scheme, Williams and Tinling would finance patents and drum up sponsorship while Whittle worked out the engineering; it was, after all, his idea. Whittle believed that there were components of the technology that could be promoted as lucrative, even if the entire system was not, and Whittle was willing to barter future shares in jet engine technology for initial investment. Whittle was to be the "brains" and Williams and Tinling were to act as agents and financiers. The men agreed on the figure of £50,000 as the start-up costs for the first turbojet engine. Whittle's new agents were sent out to secure funding.

In the interest of secrecy the team had decided not to investigate funding sources in the aircraft industry itself; there was a danger that because of the lapsed patent some other company could initiate its own experimentation. Instead, they sought funding elsewhere. Their first substantial interest came as both exciting and worrisome. Mr. M.L. Bramson, intimately involved in aeronautical circles, became aware of Whittle's engine idea. Whittle thought he would make a good contact, but was afraid that he would pursue the matter himself. Thus, Whittle and his team approached Bramson to garner direct support. Bramson was a welcome supporter and immediately put in motion events that culminated in full financial support for Whittle's engine.

With Bramson's assistance, Whittle, Williams, and Tinling approached the investment firm of O.T. Falk and Partners. Bramson wrote the official proposal, the intermediary document between Whittle's engineering specifications on the one side and the importance of the technology to consumers on the other, and the draft was accepted.[27] The BTH was once again contacted—they had denied support in 1930—and contracted on a piece-by-piece basis to construct components. The Air Ministry took immediate notice and became the fourth "member" of the contract. Thus, in March 1936, Power Jets Limited was formed, with Whittle as the chief engineer and technical consultant, Williams and Tinling as primary "A" shareholders, and L.L. Whyte and Maurice Bonham Carter, both from Falk and Partners, represented the "B" shareholders. The Air Ministry set the requirement that Whittle, under the employ of the RAF, could not work at the company as his primary RAF posting, but could be involved up to 6 hours per week.[28] This was a restriction the young officer disregarded on a regular basis. The investment firm allocated the requested resources, and hands-on work finally began on Whittle's jet engine.

Whittle had designed his engine to push the boundaries of known aerodynamic theory. His proposed experimental engine—it was obviously designed with flight in mind, but the first prototype was intended as a test bench model—was to be a radical improvement on existing turbines. The closest relative to the turbojet was the conventional engine turbosupercharger; designed to provide compressed air/fuel mixture at high altitude. Contemporary single-stage–centrifugal compressor turbosuperchargers could provide 2.5:1 compression ratios with 65 percent efficiency. Whittle calculated that his double-sided centrifugal-flow turbojet engine, with a rotational speed of 17,500 rpm, could produce a 4:1 compression ratio at 80 percent efficiency; thus producing an estimated 1,400 pounds of thrust. Whittle surmised that his engine, once perfected, could power an aircraft to 500 mph at 70,000 feet![29]

Whittle faced two immediate challenges. First, he had to overcome the problems associated with compression. For the impeller to compress the air to the required ratio and efficiency, the turbine, the engine's final stage, would have to generate 3,000 shaft horsepower. This figure was well above contemporary piston engines, and was not realized on any but the largest steam turbines. Whittle's engineering prowess would prove equal to the task; he was able to overcome this incredible hurdle. Secondly, the development of the second stage of the engine, the combustion chamber, caused Whittle endless anxiety. He estimated that the small chamber of no more than 6 cubic feet would burn 200 gallons of fuel each hour.[30] His calculations indicated that this would lead to temperatures and pressures that were heretofore unheard of; Whittle was in a dilemma of how to approach this novel problem. Typically, he sought out novel solutions. He consulted a number of combustion specialists at the British Industries Fair in February 1936, visiting boilermakers and heat engineers. He reports that, "I met with blank astonishment and was told that I was asking for a combustion intensity of at least twenty times greater than had ever before been achieved."[31] Whittle came across an independent Scottish firm, Laidlaw, Drew, and Company, who were more enthusiastic about the challenge and Mr. A.B.S. Laidlaw accepted the contract for building Whittle's combustion chambers. Unfortunately, the combustion chambers continued to plague the Whittle engine project, and caused serious delays and anxiety.

Whittle continued his personal involvement in the development of the engine, ignoring the Air Ministry 6-hour per week restriction, and neglecting his Cambridge studies. He went about the country, between Laidlaw, BTH, the Hoffamn Company (bearings), Alfred Herberts (shaft assembly), and home, and fell behind in his "official" duties. With his exams approaching, Whittle settled in to study. He crammed for 5 weeks, and in a testament to his ingenuity and intellect, Whittle graduated with a "First" on his Tripos (exams). With the completion of his schooling Whittle was concerned that he would be reassigned, possibly overseas. Fortunately for the British jet engine program, the Air Ministry was persuaded by one of Whittle's advisors, Roy Lubbock, to allow Whittle to stay for a year of postgraduate work at Cambridge—time Whittle spent exclusively on the development of his jet engine.

Freed from school and Air Force work, Whittle poured his time into his project. His designs were sound; the compressor impeller was being fashioned at High Duty Alloys, and the turbine construction began at Firth Vickers. Toward the middle of the summer, the mechanical pieces of the turbojet were in the final phases of construction. But problems remained with the combustion chambers at Laidlaw. The first combustion experiments did not begin until October, when adequate materials and configurations were developed to deal with the extreme temperatures and pressures. Whittle ferried frequently to Laidlaw to supervise and consult on the progress. Testing the individual components was not financially possible, so Whittle decided to build the engine and test it as a complete unit, a high-risk high-gain strategy. It had the benefit of low cost and relative quick results, but testing the complete engine meant that problems could not be isolated or easily identified within the three-stage process of compression, combustion, and exhaust.[32] By the end of 1936, the individual components were still under development; Whittle would have to wait for the new year to begin assembly of the engine.

Testing began literally in the BTH backyard. The engine, later known as the "Whittle Unit," or W.U. contained the three stages designed by Whittle. The compressor impeller was a double-sided centrifugal compressor 16 inches in diameter. There were no diffuser vanes on the impeller casing; Whittle relied on the "vortex space" to provide compression with the compressed air entering the nozzle-less scroll turbine inlet. For his initial trials Whittle decided on a single compression chamber, where the compressed air mixed with fuel and was ignited. The expanded, fuel-fired air flowed through the last stage, the exhaust turbine, which, in theory, would provide the 3,000 shaft horsepower to drive the impeller and continue the turbojet cycle.[33]

Whittle was fortunate that his technology was so cutting edge; even the BTH employees, in and around the Power Jets workshop, had no idea what he was up to. Some thought he was working on an improved flamethrower![34] In an interesting anecdote of the dangers and novelty of the project (and a case for "I wish I was there") Whittle recounts,

> The apparatus was usually anything but leak-proof, and large pools of fuel would collect underneath. Sooner or later flaming drops would set them alight and we, conducting the tests, would be stepping between the pools of flame like demons in an inferno.[35]

The engine was assembled, tested with compressed air, and was finally cleared for the first run-ups.

Even if not fully supported by the Air Ministry, Whittle's work did not go unnoticed. The efforts of his small experimental company were watched with interest by the Aeronautical Research Committee, the Air Ministry, and the engine section of the Royal Aircraft Establishment (RAE). Whittle's required written reports kept them appraised of his centrifugal-flow engine trials, and the Ministry, prodded by the RAE, invited Metropolitan Vickers to build an experimental axial-flow turbojet engine. Metrovick (the short name for Metropolitan Vickers Electrical Company of Trafford Park, Manchester) had led the field in axial-flow steam turbines and was an intelligent choice for an experimental turbojet engine. The axial-flow design was more troublesome than Whittle's centrifugal-flow design, and took considerably longer to develop. But prototype Metrovick F.2 and F.3 engines were finally developed and tested as the first Allied axial-flow turbojet engines during the war. The importance of the Metrovick engines, to which we will return later, was that the Ministry began to notice the potential for the proposed aircraft prime-mover and began to make forays into experimental research and development of turbojet engines. And, although Metrovick did not compete directly with Power Jets, the dilemma posed by the choice between centrifugal-flow and axial-flow would become a hot topic in British aircraft engine development.[36]

In early 1937, Whittle and his team prepared for their first running trials with the W.U. On April 12, the W.U. was started for the first time. The bench test was successful in that the engine ran under its own volition, but Whittle recounts the experiment was uncontrollable. The engine, after initial run-ups with the starting motor, was fed with fuel. With Whittle at the controls, the engine quickly raced up to 8,000 rpm, "as Whittle's assistants raced out of the building!" Whittle finally stopped the engine by shutting off the fuel supply. Whittle recounts that "this incident did not do my nervous system any good at all. I have rarely been so frightened."[37] Experiments the next day were similar, but added the danger of flame. Flames were "leaping and dancing above in mid-air above the engine," and "sheets of flame belched from the jet pipe" as the engine ran out of control again.[38] Whittle was once again able to shut it down without serious damage to the engine or himself—once again his design team had fled harm's way—but Whittle resorted to alcohol therapy (in the form of red wine) to calm his nerves. The problem, which was resolved immediately, was that fuel was "puddling" in the lowest part of the combustion chamber, providing—literally—fuel for the fire. Once this was recognized appropriate redesigns were enacted, a drain for the combustion chamber, and downstream injection for the fuel. The fourth test run was almost without incident, "almost" meaning that the combustion chamber still overheated and set fire to one of the ignition cables.

Whittle found that the limiting component to the efficiency of his now successful engine was the combustion chamber. He was able to run the W.U. up to 8,500 rpm, but no further increase in revolutions, and therefore power, was unattainable. He found that adding extra fuel did not work; it simply burned past the final turbine stage. The combination combustion chamber/fuel delivery system would have to be completely revamped to reach his goals for his engine. Attempts with vaporized kerosene came to naught; the engine ran out of control again because of too much fuel. And a return to the downstream injection was equally as bad; the engine seized at 12,000 rpm, and work had to begin anew on the W.U. Whittle decided that it was time for radical redesign, and was concurrently asked to vacate his workshop at BTH; his trials were disruptive to the "real" work on the other side of the wall. Power Jets was moved to another BTH facility at Lutterworth, an abandoned foundry.

To add to Whittle's worries, finances once again became an issue. Falk and Partners were unable to come up with the promised assistance and money was running low. At this point, Power Jets found an important friend in an effort to gain Air Ministry funds. Sir Henry Tizard, the genius behind the development of British radar and the chairman of the Aeronautical Research Committee, posted a letter to the Air Ministry on behalf of Whittle and Power Jets. It stated,

> You ask for my opinion about Whittle's scheme.
>
> I think there is nothing inherently unsound in his ideas. He may possibly be somewhat optimistic in some of his predictions, but even allowing for that, I think it highly probable that if he has the necessary financial support and encouragement, he will succeed in producing a new type of power plant for aircraft. I am particularly interested in this work because I think that if we are to provide the high powers which will be necessary for aircraft of the future, we must develop some type of turbine. Further, the fact that such an engine would use heavy oil is of great importance from the point of defence and commerce.
>
> I have a very high opinion of Flight Lieutenant Whittle. He has the ability and the energy and the enthusiasm for work of this nature. He has

also an intimate knowledge of practical conditions—this combination of qualities is rare and deserves the utmost encouragement. I sincerely hope he will get the necessary finance because I think you will have to make up your mind that a large expenditure will be necessary before final success is reached. My general opinion of the importance of this work leads me to express the hope that the money will be raised privately so that the knowledge that it is going on will not be widespread.

     P.S.—Of course, I do not mean to imply that success is certain. All new schemes of this kind must be regarded as 'gambles' in the initial stages. I do think, however, that this is a better gamble than many I know of on which money has been spent.[39]

This was high praise coming from Tizard, and no doubt influenced the decision of the Air Ministry. The Air Ministry offered financial support to Power Jets to the tune of £10,000. The money was allocated thus: the first £1,000 was for a report on the work and engine tests already completed, the next £2,000 for research money for a test run of the engine up to 14,000 rpm (the W.U. had only been up to 12,000 rpm, and that was out of control!), the following £2,000 would be for full-speed trials (Whittle had proposed that his engine would run at 17,500 rpm full speed). The final £5,000 was allocated for the purchase of the engine after these successful test run-ups.[40] But, the Air Ministry decided, in September, that they did not want the W.U. engine after testing; thus, the contract was reduced to £5,000 total. Falk and Partners could not come up with the promised money and were slowly marginalized from the company and the boardroom, while the Air Ministry became an increasingly more important partner in every sense. Added to this was a small amount of support from BTH itself, in addition to the workspace. The most important Air Ministry offering came in July 1937. Whittle had completed his 1-year postgraduate work at Cambridge, and instead of posting Whittle, the Air Member for Personnel assigned him to the Special Duties List, specifically to work on his engine designs.[41] He could now devote all of his time and energy to his turbojet engine and Power Jets Ltd.

     With Laidlaw, attention was refocused on the combustion chambers— now they were considering multiple, not single combustion chambers—and the problematic fuel delivery system. Whittle's intention was to inject vaporized kerosene into the combustion chambers to fire the engine, but was still having difficulty with fuel delivery and soot buildup. Furthermore, Whittle was worried he would stigmatize his RAF career by being placed on the "Special Duties" roster, and was pleasantly surprised when he was promoted to Squadron Leader (and left on Special Duties) in December 1937.

     The early months of 1938, the last full year of European peace, brought the reconstruction of the W.U. Whittle had overseen almost all of the construction, but he was becoming concerned about the quality of BTH input into the project. The BTH turbine blades were constructed based on existing ideas about steam turbines, that is to say straight from root to tip. In large, cumbersome steam turbines, this was both efficient and adequate, and the design followed the age-old maxim, "if it ain't broke, don't fix it." Whittle, however, was looking to improve the turbine for optimum performance from the smallest and lightest power plant. In a flash of brilliance, Whittle decided to twist the blades, from root to tip, to improve the efficiency of the "thrust vortex" as well as reduce the pressure on the end bearing. The improvement had two consequences: first, Whittle's engine was more fuel efficient as well as more powerful as improvements continued; second, Whittle created animosity between his company and its BTH host. Although it was brand-new technology, and there were no real "experts" in the field with years of experience, Whittle quickly found that a large proportion of the BTH engineers resented being told that they were wrong, even though Whittle turned out to be right.[42] Whittle filed for and received a patent, and when a new BTH industrial steam turbine was constructed based on Whittle's improvements, then tested, Whittle was proven correct.

Following modifications and rebuilding, the engine was ready for trials again in April 1938. The "new" engine incorporated a number of modifications. The impeller was improved and inlets were added for more air flow, the combustion chamber was redesigned based on Whittle/Laidlaw improvements, and it was finally complemented with a new turbine inlet and redesigned "twisted vane" turbine, proven to be more efficient.[43] Initial testing began on April 16, and continued for 2 weeks while Whittle and the engineers worked out the bugs in the system. On the 29th the redesigned engine was run up to a "modest" 8,200 rpm for "more than an hour."[44] Unfortunately, a large, oily rag was sucked into the engine ending the test abruptly and causing minor damage. Whittle relates, "I still retain a vivid picture of Crompton [one of the techs] standing frozen with a mingled look of horror and blank surprise."[45] The good news was that the new configuration was viable; the engine had been running for almost 2 hours when the unintended accident occurred. Interestingly, the measurements taken while the engine was running were significant. The engine had been run up to 13,000 rpm and had produced an estimated 480 lbs thrust. Thrust was only estimated because of the dangers involved, "It was rather a hazardous business getting a thrust reading, because it was necessary to go past the engine and note the reading of the spring balance which linked the test truck to a post embedded on the test room floor."[46] This illustrates the simplicity and informality of the birth of one of the greatest achievements in aeronautical engineering since the Wright brothers flew at Kitty Hawk. Spring scales and deserted foundries were the symbols of the financial strains felt by the young innovator. But Whittle had overcome these boundaries and persisted in manufacturing a working turbojet engine, even if it was only experimental.

Whittle, however, was depressed. He was worried that the lack of finances coupled with this latest setback would spell doom for his project. But he was assured by BTH, who indicated that they had come too far to quit, that money would be available. And, the new deputy director of Scientific Research, W.S. Farren, was unfazed by the accident, and continued to be supportive. Whittle was somewhat bolstered, but he recounts failing health because of stress and strain.[47] But Whittle doggedly continued work on the W.U. His next brainstorm resulted in the development of individual combustion chambers for the engine, ten in total, corresponding to the ten outlets from the impeller housing. The effect was a lighter and more compact engine. The combustion chambers were connected in sequence to aid in combustion, and aided in aspiration and efficiency. Whittle relates that the first combustion chamber setup—the scroll turbine inlet single combustion chamber configuration—was inefficient in combination with the other carefully designed parts of the original engine (impeller and turbine). His new combustion chambers would shorten the shaft, and thus shorten the engine's length. The individual, interconnected chambers would alleviate problems of thermal expansion and uneven heating, and the individual chambers were easier to inspect and test independent of the entire system.[48] This was the new configuration that was tried and proved successful.

Still, the financial crisis continued to haunt Power Jets; the company had trouble finding backing, in part due to the imposition of the Official Secrets Act by the Air Ministry, and in part to the failures of Falk and Partners. Whittle was committed as ever to his project, and believed in its viability, but he was beginning to wonder if, without financial help, he would be better served to go and serve as an RAF officer at a normal posting. By June 1938 the engine had cost a total of £9,000, but Power Jets needed funds for the new combustion chambers and a rebuild, and had only £1,200 in reserve.[49]

With the new configuration, the main new components were the multiple combustion chambers; the third W.U. rebuild began testing in October 1938. The incorporation of the ten reverse-flow combustion chambers shortened the engine and made it more efficient. The vaporizers injected gaseous kerosene into the chamber, and the igniter fired the fuel/air mixture for thrust. Compressed air from the impeller entered the combustion chambers and flowed to the rear of the chambers. The compressed air was mixed with kerosene vapor and ignited, increasing volume and heat. The high-pressure air/fuel mixture flowed back over the improved turbine, both turning the compressor impeller and creating thrust. Whittle was excited about his prospects. If he could gather the requisite funds, he felt that his engine could be a viable Air Ministry project. This sentiment was echoed by Bramson in a report that stated, "The feasibility of jet propulsion for jet aircraft has been, for the first time, experimentally established."[50]

In addition, the Air Ministry was willing to support the engine upgrade, and supported the rebuild and experimental bench tests for 20 hours at £200 per hour. The total Air Ministry infusion equaled £6,000. Indications of financial freedom came in the form of a secretary for Whittle and Power Jets, two night watchmen, an office boy, and a watchdog by the name of Sandy. Whittle was happy for the secretarial help; he no longer had to type reports and letters.

The end of 1938 brought a mixed bag of results. On the financial scene, it seemed as if Air Ministry assistance would finally alleviate Power Jets' funding woes. As far as the engine itself was concerned, the year had been important not for testing but for the improvements that would pay off in the future. It had been in all senses a rebuilding year, 1939 would be a watershed.

In February 1939, the deputy director of the Department of Scientific Research (DSR) felt obliged to inform Whittle that he needed to have concrete results. Whittle was up for review for his "special circumstances" and the DSR did not feel that he was contributing substantially in his line of development. Whittle, in turn, concerned about Air Ministry support, pushed himself and the project to its limits. Whittle withstood the pressure, the machine did not. After achieving 14,000 rpm in March, the compressor impeller failed in subsequent testing. Downtime followed as new parts were gathered, and time was against Whittle and Power Jets. Pushing the limits of existing technology, in June the engine was run up 14,700 rpm, 15,700 rpm, and finally 16,000 rpm.[51] The limiting stages were still the combustion chambers, but there was definite progress.

As the combustion chambers improved, and the rpms and heat increased, the W.U. team ran into unforeseen difficulties in regard to materials inadequacies. As the engine heat increased, the Stayblade steel used for the exhaust turbine blades began to prove unusable. Due to problems that Whittle did not understand, poor heat distribution in the exhaust focused the most heat and pressure on the roots of the turbine blades, which is where the failures occurred. Whittle searched for an improved metal for the heat and temperature of his turbojet and finally in a visit to Firth Vickers came across a new alloy designated Rex 78.[52] Hopefully, Rex 78, a highly experimental nickel-chrome alloy steel, would be the answer to the turbine blade problem.

In the face of deteriorating health, problems with the engine, and financial crises, the Power Jets team pressed on. One of the high points of the project was that there were a number of big-league supporters in Henry Tizard, the DSR's Dr. Pye,[53] and his deputy Farren. And, even though the engine was problematic, it seemed to have the ability to run when it needed to. When the director of the DSR (Pye) visited on June 30, 1939, to determine both the viability of the engine and the need for Whittle's presence at Power Jets—instead of as a needed Squadron Leader—the engine was run for 20 minutes at 16,000 rpm. The actual thrust output was not as high as predicted, but with the cumulative modifications the engine was at least approaching projections. Pye inquired whether Whittle was willing to sacrifice his RAF career for the project, and the answer was in the affirmative.[54] Pye was convinced, both by the engine's performance and Whittle's convictions, and promised Ministry support and an expansion of the program. Pye informed Whittle that the Air Ministry should buy the experimental engine to provide funds to Power Jets for needed replacement parts, and that the next step would be the development of a flight engine and airframe. Early next month the Air Ministry released funds for the purchase of the W.U. (version three), which would stay with Power Jets for further modifications. Further, Power Jets was contracted to build a flight capable engine based on their experiments for Britain's first turbojet aircraft. BTH remained under contract with Power Jets to provide manufactured parts for the engine.

Although Whittle did not secure the coveted contract for the airframe as well, he and his staff were pleased when it was announced that the contract would go to Gloster Aircraft Company. Whittle's old friend J.H. McReynolds was the Air Ministry Overseer at the Gloster Company and had made introductions between Whittle and the Gloster officials: George Carter, Gloster's chief designer, P. "Gerry" Sayer, their chief test pilot, and "others of their senior personnel."[55] The relationship between Power Jets and Gloster started off on a good foot, and continued in harmony.

Over the summer all fears were alleviated for the team at Power Jets. The initial drawings for the first flight engine were completed based on continued experimentation with the W.U. The new engine was designated W.1. Financial support finally came in from many sources, and as the old maxim states, "when it rains it pours." BTH offered a £2,000 investment, as well as another £2,000 (on top of a previous £3,000) from J&G Weir Ltd. The Air Ministry declared that the test runs by the W.U. were sufficient; Power Jets could thereafter run the engine at low speeds to perfect ongoing combustion problems rather than push the engine to maximum rpms and eventual failure. And finally, the Air Ministry, in accordance with DSR wishes, informed Whittle that he was to remain at Power Jets on Special Assignment for the duration. Not even impending war would take the innovator from his all-important work.[56] The corner was turned, Whittle's invention was a viable power plant, and the Air Ministry recognized the importance of both the technology and the engineer.

On the continent, and unknown in Britain, the Germans were making great strides in turbojet technology as well. On August 27, 1939, the first turbojet aircraft in history lifted off the field at Marienehe airfield in Germany. The engine was created by the young German physicist Dr. Hans von Ohain, the airframe by the aircraft designer Ernst Heinkel. The Heinkel He 178 flew a short circuit around the airfield on pure jet power and marked the beginning of a new era in aircraft technology. One week later Europe went to war when Germany invaded Poland.

As promised, in spite of war, Whittle remained at Power Jets. No one outside Germany was aware of the German program, but there was prescient concern within the Air Ministry that if the British had the technology, the Germans could not be far behind, and in fact may be ahead. Events would show that the Germans were indeed ahead of the Allies in turbojet aircraft technology.

Power Jets received the Air Ministry contract for the first flight capable engine, designated the W.1, as well as a contract for the development of the W.2, the next-generation aircraft engine, larger and more powerful. The W.1 was based on the W.U. in its third incarnation, only with significant weight reduction by incorporating new materials. The W.1 was designed to produce 1,240 lbs thrust and its successor, the W.2, would increase that estimation to 1,600 lbs.[57] Work started on the W.1 at Power Jets as Gloster began the design process of Britain's first turbojet, designated the Gloster E.28/39, affectionately known as the "Squirt" to its designers.

The interaction between Gloster and Power Jets remained cordial, and on a visit to Power Jets, Walker, from Gloster, remarked that Power Jets had been nicknamed "the Cherry Orchard" by the Gloster team. He explained that the atmosphere at Power Jets was reminiscent of a Checkov theater play in which "various characters would appear on the stage, say something quite irrelevant and then disappear again." Whittle asked what was meant by that and Walker continued, "A small boy comes through one door carrying a cup of tea; then you jump up, pick up a rifle and fire it through the window. Next, one of your directors appears, to ask whether he can afford to have a three-inch gas pipe put in; then the same boy comes through with another cup of tea—immediately a Power Jets employee entered to exclaim his excitement upon receipt of a 'luxury' ink blotter with the statement 'Rocking Blotters.'"[58] This incident solidified Power Jets' reputation as unconventional and erratic—not unlike Whittle himself! But, the project was also unconventional, and the erratic behavior aided the development of revolutionary outcomes.

Work on the W.1 continued into the new year while the company expanded. Power Jets grew to a staff of 25 in January 1940. In an effort to secure both extra funding and create an aircraft turbojet engine production center, Whittle wrote a proposal for expenditures for shop equipment.[59] The funds were not allocated, events showed that the Air Ministry did not want Whittle to produce turbojet engines on a large scale; Power Jets was to be the design consultant. But there were funds available for experimental research and design as the W.1 neared completion. Tizard visited in January 1939 and observed the experimental engine. He remarked that "a demonstration which does not break down in my presence is a production job," and told

Whittle to be very proud of his work.[60] In addition, Air Vice-Marshal Arthur Tedder examined the engine (in a different visit) and was excited about the possibilities. Whittle was able to exploit this enthusiasm and request test facilities and equipment for their experimental work.[61] Tedder promised all assistance he could muster, and later sent Whittle a note confirming his impression of the "fascinating and impressive job," and "I shall certainly feel even more than before that it is up to me to do all I can to help it forward."[62]

Fortunately for Power Jets neither of the official visitors realized the ongoing combustion problems. The team had been plagued by fuel vaporizing problems, employing 31 different types of vaporizers in the combustion chambers. But throughout, the team continued work on the engine, and had reached speeds of 17,000 rpm and 1,000 lbs thrust from the bench tests. Whittle's design team was getting very close to optimum proposed output in their experimental turbojet engine.

As the relationship between Power Jets and BTH soured, Whittle became concerned about Air Ministry indications of alternate production centers. Whittle was unhappy with BTH for a number of reasons. He was concerned that the "old timers" of the steam turbine company did not understand the complications of adapting the turbine for aeronautical applications. They did not have to worry about weight restrictions, Whittle did. Moreover, the BTH factory did not possess precision tools for manufacturing complicated impellers and turbines. Whittle recalls that the BTH machinists could not weld the thin, 1/64 inch, Staybrite stainless steel; only a personal challenge from Whittle directed at one of BTH's welders resulted in success. Finally, Whittle was dissatisfied with the relationship as a whole. He was angry that he had suggested improvements to turbines on a general level, BTH had used these improvements, and Whittle had received no recognition. Whittle was depressed that his Power Jets company continued to rely so heavily on the BTH corporation for money, parts, tools, and workspace.[63] Whittle wanted autonomy, and started shopping around to replace BTH.

Whittle wooed Rover. With Maurice Wilks, chief engineer of Rover, Whittle suggested transferring contracts from BTH to the Rover Company. Rover was adept at aircraft engine technology, and Whittle, with BTH concerns in mind, thought the Rover would be better suited to producing aircraft engine parts that required exact manufacture. However, the Air Ministry put an immediate halt to these discussions and told Rover to "cease and desist" talks with Whittle.[64] It was as if the Air Ministry wanted to maintain complete control over Power Jets. Later they reversed their decision and contacted Rover themselves, but for the moment Whittle was back to square one.

In a heated conversation in February, Sporborg of BTH made it clear that they knew Whittle was looking for other contractors and that they were angry. Sporborg cancelled all contracts with Power Jets and told Whittle that they would no longer work on the engine or its components.[65] It took an official order from the Air Ministry to get BTH to resume contract work for Power Jets, but the seeds of discontent had been sown.

In light of these crises, Tedder from the Air Ministry called a meeting at Harrogate on March 25, 1940; the new composition of the W.1 workforce was enacted. In attendance were Tedder, Pye, Tweedie, and a contracts officer from the Air Ministry; White and Whittle from Power Jets, and the Wilks brothers from Rover. Sporborg (BTH) was invited but declined and—tellingly—met with the Air Ministry separately.[66] Whittle was reassured when his engine was designated "war winning material" and given priority status by the Air Ministry. But there was tension in the air as the Ministry officials dictated the future of Whittle's turbojet manufacture. Whittle relates,

> Tedder said the purpose of the meeting was to reach conclusions which would enable development work to proceed as fast as possible. He was not expecting [a] production plant to be laid down yet, but development and design work should be done with production in view. To the great dismay of White and myself, he went on to say that the Ministry proposed to give direct contracts for development [of the] engines to the Rover Co. Power Jets would be maintained as a research and development organization and would be expected to co-operate intimately with the Rover Co.[67]

The Air Ministry officials could impose these circumstances because of the nature of Whittle's patents. As a serving RAF officer, he had registered his engine patents in cooperation with the Air Ministry and thus they were joint patents with "Agreements for User" clauses.[68] The Air Ministry had complete control over the patents and did not have to pay Whittle in return for developing the product; they were part owners. Whittle again, "...*the Crown* [British Government in the form of the Air Ministry] *had free use of Power Jets' patents and therefore he* [Tweedie] *did not see they had anything to offer in return for finance.*"[69] The Air Ministry—according to British patent law, Government power, and wartime constraints—could dispose of the contracts as they saw fit. And they did. Whittle and Power Jets were marginalized as a research and development facility with some say in the manufacturing process; Rover and BTH were given permission to begin production of first the W.1 and later the W.2 engines. Finally, the contracts for construction went directly to Rover and BTH, not through Power Jets. Whittle's company was cut out of the Air Ministry procurement loop except for R&D and consultation on the progress of manufacturing. Power Jets was to collaborate, but was no longer in control.[70]

In April, with the proposed engine development, the Gloster Company was awarded the airframe contract for a twin-engine design based around the improved W.2 engines. The Gloster F.9/40, later known as the *Meteor*, was envisioned as a jet fighter from the start and developed accordingly.

The war impinged on Power Jets again in May 1940. The Low Countries, France, and Norway were invaded; Neville Chamberlain lost his position as the Prime Minister and was replaced by Winston Churchill. The Air Ministry was immediately restructured to include the new Ministry of Aircraft Production (MAP) headed by Lord Beaverbrook (born in Canada as William Maxwell Aitken). Beaverbrook was instructed to streamline aircraft production and prepare for the worst. He curtailed long-term projects for immediate output, and achieved an incredible increase in aircraft output leading up to the Battle of Britain in August. Production figures for 1940 were 2,729 aircraft built between January and April, increased to 4,576 manufactured between May and August.[71] With increased production levels, Beaverbrook made it possible for the British to defend against German aggression during the Battle of Britain. But this had a serious impact on Whittle's development of turbojet aircraft engines. Whittle's project was obviously long-term and the RAF needed planes immediately. Within the new MAP, Dr. Harold Roxbee Cox was named the deputy director of DSR with regard to jet aircraft production. In addition, D.G. Tobin was named as the liaison between the MAP and the special arrangement of the three companies involved in the turbojet engine's development: Power Jets, Rover, and BTH.

Whittle met with Cox in June, and was granted test facilities and research equipment. Then in July Whittle was summoned to Lord Beaverbrook's office, for a very short meeting. Whittle's 3-minute audience was enough to convince "The Beaver" (according to Whittle) of the importance of the possibilities of the turbojet engine. The contracts were not severed. In fact, Beaverbrook assured Whittle that plans were still in effect for the development of the first Gloster experimental plane.[72]

Throughout the year, divisions between BTH, Rover, and Power Jets continued to widen. Each company became secretive and attempted to continue engine development on their own. Although Power Jets was supposed to be the final word on the development of the W.2 in each of these places, BTH and Rover both tried to distance themselves from Power jets. Whittle was incensed, he went to the MAP and argued that BTH had no experience with aircraft turbines, and Rover had no experience with turbines at all![73] Cox met with all the feuding parties and settled the argument with a directive that all three were to share information freely, and in all cases Whittle and Power Jets were to be consulted; after all, it was Whittle's engine. But, bad blood between the three continued. In an illustrative example, Rover complained of errors on W.2 technical drawings, when Whittle went to inspect the drawings for errors he found that Rover had removed all reference to Power Jets from the blueprints.[74]

Whittle was concerned with two things. He wanted to preserve Power Jets and he wanted to provide a turbojet aircraft for the defense of Britain.[75] He knew that BTH and Rover could not build the engine without him, but did not want to lose Power Jets to bickering. He made a strong case to Cox and the MAP that Power Jets should be the final consultation on all turbojet engineering questions. The MAP honored Whittle's request, and BTH and Rover were forced to comply. Whittle's other goal, regardless of problems, was to develop the engine for placement in the Gloster, to produce Britain's first jet aircraft. Whittle, in true fashion, pressed on in the face of adversity.

Power Jets continued development of the W.1 into the summer and fall of 1940. Funds were allocated for materials and tools, BTH grudgingly gave up more space at the Ladywood Works for expanded testing, in fact, a rented train car was hired to alleviate the lack of available space to the growing company.

In July the combustion chamber problem was finally solved by outside involvement. I. Lubbock of Shell Petroleum, who had been advising Whittle on combustion chambers for some time, had come up with an innovative design. The difference was in the controllable atomizing burner, which introduced fuel into the chamber in a "fine mist of liquid droplets."[76] The successful chamber was brought back to Ladywood, set up on the test stand, and fired for Whittle. Immediately Whittle was sold on the Shell chambers and began replacing all of his with the new design. He recalls, "... the introduction of the Shell system may be said to mark the point where combustion ceased to be an obstacle to development."[77] All the major components were ready for flight testing; it became simply a matter of assembly and minor modifications.

The first new engine was a hodge-podge collection of spare parts from the old W.U. and experimental parts for the proposed W.1. This contraption was labeled the W.1X, and was thrown together in order to conduct advanced tests. The mock-up was sent to Gloster to measure engine fit, and went in without difficulty. Another design shortcut, the W.1A incorporated the best of the W.1 and W.2 in one system. This engine was designed to test the feasibility of the proposed air-cooled turbine wheel (the W.1 was water cooled), as well as a new compressor intake arrangement.[78] The W.1X was intended to power the first Gloster E.28/39 prototype and Whittle intended the W.1A to power the recently approved second prototype. Meanwhile BTH was busy manufacturing W.2 engines under Power Jet's direct supervision and according to Whittle's standards. But the Rover team had modified their W.2 version in direct defiance of Whittle's wishes. Whittle submitted a redesign of the W.2 as the W.2B after recalculating for recent advancements. His final W.2B proposal was accepted, and the engine was earmarked for use in the Gloster Meteor (F.9/40) project. The W.2B was an upgrade to 1,800 lbs static thrust, but to be on the safe side, this was downgraded to 1,600 lbs thrust for use in an aircraft.[79]

The W.1X was returned to Power Jets from Gloster on December 11, 1940, for testing trials. The new combustion chambers were not ready—they were being built in-house—therefore the chambers were scavenged from the still present W.U. The configuration was similar, but there were significant modifications. The new exhaust turbine had more blades, 72 rather than 66, and they were attached to the turbine wheel by the "fir tree" design. Although initially criticized, this method proved more durable and efficient.[80] The first tests of the W.1X were promising. The engine was assembled and run up to 16,459 rpm, and according to Whittle, "the performance of the engine was very promising indeed."[81] Power Jets doubled their working engines, the added W.1X was only the second engine produced by Power Jets. The team was still working with the original 1937 engine when the W.1X was delivered.

The war impinged on Power Jets again that winter. On a Sunday daylight raid by a single twin-engine bomber—the bomber was probably lost, and the bombs missed their target—Whittle recalls that testing was thrown off when one of the frightened workers dropped and damaged one of the two remaining impellers.[82] Other than that relatively minor incident, Power Jets was and Ladywood were unaffected by Axis air raids. But the potential threat was enough to prompt Whittle to write a memo on the defense of Power Jets, including reference to underground storage and arms for the defense of the factory.[83]

The work continued into the new year 1941, as Power Jets increased in size. The lack of tools and machinery meant that Power Jets remained a consultant to other construction firms, but Whittle was optimistic about the continued experiments. In time Whittle got used to the constant interruptions from Gloster, BTH, Vauxhall, Rover, and MAP officials visiting and often asking the same questions. The tension was alleviated in a hilarious anecdote presented by Whittle. The commander in chief of RAF Fighter Command, Air Chief Marshal Sir Hugh Dowding, visited Power Jets to see the novel contraption. Whittle was uneasy about escorting his commanding officer around, and in the midst of engine testing, no less. Whittle walked Dowding outside because of the noise, and to see the product of the jet engine, thrust. The exhaust pipe was sticking out of the workshop, and the engine was at full blast. When Whittle pointed out the tailpipe, Dowding misunderstood him and walked into the jet's exhaust stream. Whittle explains the events, "Suddenly a mighty invisible force wrenched open his raincoat and sent him staggering across the concrete—his "brass hat" rolling away on the grass."[84] It quickly occurred to Whittle that the jet stream was both powerful and nearly invisible. Whittle was humbled and horrified as he helped his commander recover. Dowding was impressed and recovered well, joking about the incident only hours later. He must have been embarrassed himself, walking into the jet blast that everyone at Power Jets knew to avoid. But as Whittle states, "It will be many a long day before some of us forget how we nearly blew the Air Chief Marshal into the next county."[85]

Power Jets' inventory was reduced again in February 1941 when the original W.U. that had undergone multiple revisions and two complete rebuilds finally suffered terminal failure. The end was in sight, and with the W.1X, Whittle and the team decided to put the original W.U. through a series of low-speed endurance tests. At estimated cruising speeds, the W.U. was run for 8 hours at 14,500 rpm, and later for 10 hours at 14,000 rpm. The engine proved its worth and viability, and provided invaluable information that went into its successor, the W.1X.

The first W.1 finally arrived from BTH in February as well. It was not immediately tested, as bearing problems in the W.1X were still under investigation. However, it was assembled and sent to Gloster to assure fit in the prototype E. 28/39. The fit was near perfect and the day approached for the initial flight testing.

But, there were more Rover problems to overcome. Rover had been making their own modifications, in spite of both MAP insistence against and Whittle's continuing complaints, and problems were reaching their worst. When a meeting was held in February, it was finally decided to construct the W.2B engine specifically to Power Jets designs, and there was to be no deviation except for minor production efficiency. Rover took advantage of the final clause, and exploited their position to redesign a number of the main components. When Whittle finally caught word of this he exploded with rage and vented on the MAP. Whittle suggested that the Power Jets' drawings would be sent directly to the MAP, and they could distribute them as they saw fit.[86] Interestingly, this political wrangling concerned future engine developments; the first British turbojet aircraft had not yet flown, and the three companies were arguing over power plants for future fighter prototypes. The ideas (both airframe and engine) were sound, but no one even knew if they would work. There was concern at the MAP that the engine would be too powerful, and tear an inherently delicate airframe apart. The discussion spiraled downward and relations between Rover and Whittle became very jaded.

In the midst of the infighting, the Gloster E.28/39 was pronounced ready for flight by the beginning of April. The W.1 from BTH, used to check fit, had not yet been run and Whittle decided to use the W.1X for initial taxiing runs.[87] By April 7, 1941, all was ready. P.E.G. (Gerry) Sayer, Gloster's chief test pilot, mounted the revolutionary machine and prepared to taxi. The Power Jets team had set the throttle controls to max at 13,000 rpm in order to prevent damage and keep the plane from actually flying. To Sayer's disappointment, the plane barely moved. The grass was wet, and the engine did not provide enough thrust to move the plane at 12,000 rpm. At maximum governed thrust, 13,000 rpm, the plane crept along at a heartbreaking 20 mph.[88] Sayer was not convinced that the plane would fly at all, even after Whittle explained to him that the power band increased dramatically as rpms were increased above 13,000. Night fell and thus began the inauspicious start to the British jet aircraft program.

The next morning the throttle control was set at 15,000 rpm maximum. Whittle himself took the controls—he *had* been a test pilot—and taxied to around 60 mph. Whittle was overjoyed. He realized that there would be enough thrust as the engine controls were advanced, and the little plane was already proving to be a delight: low noise, little vibration, and excellent field of vision.[89] After lunch the throttle controls were reset to a maximum of 16,000 rpm, and Sayer took the controls once again. He was warned that this engine was "unairworthy," and had not been designed to fly. The W.1 was waiting for that distinction. Regardless, Sayer pointed into the wind and pushed the throttles forward. The plane picked up speed and actually left the ground for about 200 yards. Sayer "landed," turned around, and repeated this feat two more times. In all fairness, this was the first British flight of a turbojet aircraft. But Whittle insisted that the taxiing trials be halted and the proper engine installed, for "real" flight to take place.

The W.1X was removed from the E.28/39, and returned to Ladywoods. The W.1 was started and ran its 25-hour acceptance test. The outcome was that the engine, at 16,500 rpm, produced 860 lbs thrust. In one test the engine produced 1000 lbs thrust at 17,000 rpm. The MAP cleared the W.1 for installation and 10 hours flight testing. The engine was delivered to Gloster, fit into the plane, and preparations were made for the first official flights.

On May 15, 1941, the Gloster E.28/39, powered by the Whittle W.1 engine, officially made its historic first flight. The Gloster plane with the Whittle engine had been transported to Cranwell, an ideal airfield for flight testing. It was also very appropriate that Whittle's creation would return to the same airfield where he had come up with so much of his initial interest and intuition concerning jet-powered flight. The weather was bad in the morning but cleared up by evening for ideal flying conditions. Sayer taxied to the end of the runway, and was ready to go at 7:40 PM. He ran up the engine and released the brakes. The plane accelerated down the runway, and took off after a 600-yard run. Sayer climbed into the clouds but the observers could plainly hear the roar of the jet. Sayer returned for a perfect landing showing complete confidence in the aircraft.[90] Everything went smoothly, and Britain, in second place, entered the jet age.

The British history of turbojet development is a mixed bag of successes and failures. During the interwar period the British were thinking about advancing technology; there were amazing advances in the development of radar, the fighter command communications network, and development of fighter/interceptor aircraft. Whittle's turbojet idea did fall into the greater scheme of the "Defense of Great Britain," but the possibilities were not immediately recognized. Whittle made some of his fundamental postulations during the economic crisis of the Great Depression, but could not find funding for his revolutionary idea. Eventually, after supporting his research through private funding, and with the tacit approval of the Air Ministry in letting him continue experimentation, the viability of turbojet aircraft propulsion systems was recognized and funded through government sponsorship. But it took the threat of war and successful tests to convince the Ministry to support Whittle's engine program.

3

The Jet Comes to America

When General Henry H. "Hap" Arnold visited England in April 1941, the United States was still practicing isolationist neutrality. Officially, the United States remained out of the war and on the sidelines. To put the visit into context, the Germans were winning the jet race as well as the war on the continent. The French were defeated and Britain stood alone. Stalin was still on speaking terms with Hitler; "Barbarossa" was still in the future. Pearl Harbor was 7 months away. Arnold went to Britain to confirm the newest Lend–Lease act with regard to the Royal Air Force (RAF) and technological exchange. What he saw was the revolutionary Whittle engine powering the Gloster E.28/39; Britain's first jet airplane. The seeds of the American jet program were planted in Arnold's head; for he was a true believer in the marriage of airpower and technology. This visit, and the technological exchange that ensued, became the basis for the American jet program one-half year before the U.S. entry into World War II.

The story of the American turbojet program begins with a military official who pulled the program to its feet and ends with the American companies that produced the American jets with government funding. Henry Harley "Hap" Arnold, a West Point graduate (1907), became a very important airpower advocate as the chief of the U.S. Army Air Corps. He saw his first plane in Paris in 1909, returning to the United States the long way around from duty in the Philippines.[1] He was struck by the potentialities of aircraft in a military sense. But he also commented that this airplane at least seemed very fragile.[2] Arnold was again exposed to airplanes later that year. Back in the United States, on assignment at Fort Jay, Governors Island, near New York, Arnold saw and definitely read the accounts of the record-breaking American flights of the Wrights and Glenn Curtis. He also attended the "first international air meet ever held in America" in the fall, and witnessed the miracle of flight and experienced the danger and excitement associated with it.[3]

Arnold was desperate to escape the doldrums of the infantry and gain promotion, and tried many schemes and applications to transfer. He was not accepted by the cavalry; his biographer Dik Daso mentions that Arnold did not have the "Special Qualifications" or S.Q. when he graduated from West Point for consideration.[4] It may have stemmed from an incident between Arnold and the Chief of Cavalry just before graduation.[5] He was also awaiting transfer to the Ordnance Department, which promised fast promotion, but did not pass the qualifying exams in math and physics.[6] Arnold had also applied, on a lark, to the new Aeronautical Division of the Signal Corps, and was approved. When Congress passed a budget allowance for War Department "aeronautical pursuits," Arnold was selected as one of the first volunteers for the nascent air service. In April 1911 Arnold with his newfound friend "Dashing" Milling reported to Dayton, Ohio, for "instruction in operating the Wright airplane."[7]

In addition to flight training, Arnold went through an important "crash-course" in aircraft maintenance. The technology was so new that no one knew the intricacies of the aircraft; Arnold was given hands-on instruction in rigging and upkeep of the novel machines. He was adept enough that he could pass on the information to mechanics in the field, the first crew chiefs of the Air Force. It is noteworthy that internal combustion engines were relatively new as well, and there were few available who could repair such intricate technology. In addition, this was also before the introduction of tanks, or any other heavy military machinery that could have effectively "mechanized" the mentality of the U.S. military. By comparison, in World War II the average airman was familiar enough with machinery—cars, trucks, engines—that with the combination of the relatively simple mechanization in the form of trucks and jeeps, the U.S. Army could maintain its mechanical efficiency throughout the war. In 1911 few had experience with maintenance of engines, let alone airplanes!

After 28 flights, and a total of 3 hours 48 minutes instruction, Lt. Arnold was cleared as a pilot; one of the first two, along with Milling, in the U.S. Army.

He was an innovator in the air from the beginning. He suggests that he was the first to wear goggles, at least in the United States: as "the result of a bug's hitting me in the eye as I was landing my plane."[8] Arnold's pain and near disastrous one-eye landing convinced the young pilot and all of his colleagues to wear protective eyewear.

Arnold and Milling returned to College Park, Maryland, where they set up the first Army air base. The new service pilots taught others to fly, and set a number of records in the process for altitude, duration, and speed. They were also in charge of teaching the new maintenance section of mechanics who would be responsible for the upkeep of the planes. Arnold states that as he and Milling returned from Dayton, they labeled the parts of the aircraft on photos taken earlier, thus creating the phraseology of flight.[9] As their flight knowledge and proficiency grew, the new pilots also began experimenting with aerial roles. Riley Scott, one of the first trainees, was the first to develop and test a bomb aiming system from aircraft. Although he did not get much attention in the United States, he was awarded prizes in the form of cash at a French air show.[10] His aerial bombing experiments were not lost on the French or German participants and spectators who incorporated Scott's ideas into military planning.[11] At different times, and at different events, the military pilots experimented with firing rifles while airborne, testing radios, flying in movies, and offering rides to paying passengers.

Arnold was asked to testify to a congressional hearing on the high accident rates in the U.S. Army Signal Corps (Aviation Section), and speak to the relative strengths of other air forces.[12] Arnold was seen as the "expert" on both the state of the U.S. Army's Aviation section and equivalent services around the world. Arnold stated that the new technology was still in its infancy, and accidents were bound to happen, and that the Americans were still in the "instructional phase."[13] Arnold spoke to the development of other air services and was asked about whether the United States should have their own independent Air Corps. The proposal submitted by Lt. Paul Beck was rejected, as the consensus was the time was not yet ripe.[14]

At this point, Arnold asked to transfer from the Air Service. He was getting married and according to him, "in those days you didn't plan to continue flying after you were married—unless you were an optimist."[15] Arnold was reassigned to the 13th Infantry and returned with his wife to the Philippines in December 1913. By May 1916, as the war in Europe ground on, Arnold was assigned as the supply officer at the Aviation School, Rockwell Field, San Diego. Arnold was also promoted to captain. The school boasted 23 military aviators, 25 pilot students, and brand-new Curtiss JN "Jennys."[16]

As the war intensified, the U.S. Army reorganized their Aviation Division into Aero Squadrons. Of the seven squadrons, Arnold was selected to command the 7th Aero Squadron, dispatched to Panama.[17] Because of disagreements, Arnold was returning to discuss the matter with the General Staff in Washington, DC, when the U.S. declaration of war against Germany was announced. The United States was now at war, and Arnold wanted to do his duty in Europe, not Central America, and was determined to keep from returning to Panama. Arnold was not to return to Panama, but he did not venture to Europe either. He was assigned to the War Department's Air Division in Washington, DC, where he was an organizer rather than a combatant.

As American aviators flew in combat, Arnold fought in Congress. His organizing skills were rewarded with increased responsibility and subsequent promotion. The Air Division had to submit a proposal to the Congress to increase the size of their forces based on French suggestions. At the time, according to Arnold, the Aviation Section was composed of 52 officers and 1,100 men (plus 200 civilian mechanics). There were 130 pilots, of which only 26 were "really qualified." Finally, there were 55 airplanes, "51 of them obsolete, 4 obsolescent, and not one of them a combat type."[18] Arnold's plan called for a 1-year increase, by May 1918, to 8,000 combat planes in the field out of 20,000 total planes. Arnold's proposals were accepted and $43,450,000 was allocated in June for the manpower, and $640,000,000 was approved in July for the planned 22,600 airplanes and 45,000 engines for the American Expeditionary Force (AEF).[19] Arnold understood both the importance of production as well as the costs involved.

In order to solve the manpower crunch, 41 flight schools were set up to train pilots—25 schools in the United States alone. In addition, there were new ground schools, mechanic's schools, photo schools, and an Artillery Observation School. The planes were procured through the prewar mechanism, the Bureau of Aircraft Production, directed by Howard Coffin. By May 1918, the confusion over the name of the department was also settled, when the Aviation Section of the Signal Corps was designated the Air Service of the U.S. Army. Arnold enjoyed quick wartime promotion, and was named the executive officer of the Signal Corp's Aviation Section, and given the rank of colonel.

Although the war showed the shortages of American production, there were bright spots. From the *Liberty* engine to license building European engines, the Americans produced 32,000 engines in 18 months. But lack of airframe production was a concern for Arnold during and after the war.[20] His ongoing concern centered on the fact that no American-designed planes made it into the war, and American-built European planes were behind schedule throughout the conflict.

At the end of the war Arnold was reassigned away from DC and returned to Rockwell Field in San Diego as the district supervisor, Western District of the Air Service. He was put in charge of both demobilizing officers and enlisted men and keeping the base running efficiently. At Rockwell Arnold met and became fast friends with (then 2nd Lt.) James Doolittle. Doolittle made an impression when he bet a fellow airman that he could sit on the landing gear of a plane while it was landing. Without notifying the unsuspecting pilot, once aloft Doolittle climbed down to fulfill his bet. The pilot hesitantly landed, Doolittle won his bet, and Arnold grounded him for a month for stunting.[21]

Arnold's position was abolished in 1919, but he was promoted to the staff of General Liggett, and put in charge of all aviation in the western United States. Back in Washington, General Billy Mitchell was making a name for himself. Although he was not given command of the Air Service—that position went to Major General C.T. Menoher—Mitchell organized air competitions and bolstered the spirit of the postwar military aviators. Mitchell set the foundation for American commercial airpower with endurance and speed competitions. The competitions fostered the growth of new airports as waypoints for cross-country flight. The new airfields were set up near towns and were equipped with mechanics and refueling stations for the flyers. In 1919, the most abundant aircraft was the Curtiss JN-4 *Jenny*, which flew at around 130 mph, with endurance of 300 miles, but only during daylight hours. Consequently, new airports sprang up along the favorite East–West course from New York to San Francisco at 200 mile intervals.[22] The Americans profited from regular long-distance flights where pilots could reference landmarks to navigate. Flying over land in the United States was easier than over water, specifically the Atlantic, and European pilots did not fly the great distances on a regular basis that the American pilots had to deal with. American pilots consequently benefited from the geography of the United States in navigation and flying techniques. Further, the American plane manufacturers began to think in terms of long-distance and endurance for their designs, considerations marginalized by the Europeans who focused on speed.

The National Defense Act (1920) allowed the Air Service their own budget within the Army, and gave it autonomy in procurement. In addition, the rating of "Airplane Pilot" was established with 50 percent flight pay. Unfortunately, at the same time, Arnold's temporary wartime colonel rank was reduced, making him a captain. His assistant, Major Carl "Tooey" Spaatz, had earned major in combat and retained it by law. Thus, Arnold immediately became his assistant's assistant. In order to obviate an already confusing situation, Spaatz asked for and received an immediate transfer to another post, leaving Arnold West Coast Air Officer at the rank of captain. He was promoted to major a few months later.[23]

Mitchell's battleship bombing experiments are well documented; the emphasis of the exercises for Arnold was the importance of the role of aircraft.[24] In a number of experimental flights, in spite of Navy protests, planes bombed and sank a number of different types of ships. The point was that planes, with crews of at most a handful of men, and at insignificant costs compared to battleships, dismantled the Mahanian system of naval power. In one significant example, the "unsinkable" captured WWI German Battleship *Ostfriesland*, a veteran of Jutland, went to the bottom of the sea under a hail of Mitchell's 1,000-pound bombs. The importance of aircraft in the military was assured. The point was made, at the same time echoed by theorists such as Giulio Douhet, that the bomber was the apex of military technology, and that it was the one and only decisive factor for future wars.[25] Mitchell was quoted as saying, "There has never been anything that has come which has changed war the way the advent of air power has."[26] Airpower had paved the way for a new way of thinking in military minds. The leading supporters, including Arnold, defined the air component of the U.S. Army in future wars.

By 1924, a team of Americans flying Douglas *World Cruisers* had flown around the globe, the first American purpose-built bomber had been constructed, and Arnold was off to the Army Industrial College (AIC).[27] During his time at the Industrial College, Arnold came to the conclusion that aircraft should be produced solely at aircraft manufacturing firms, and that the auto manufacturers should be cut out of the loop. He wanted specificity in production, not diffusion of interests, and the auto industry had too many other concerns. Auto manufacturers could be relied on for subassemblies and small parts, but the overall manufacture should be left to dedicated aircraft manufacturers. Arnold indicates that this was an instructive and important realization for him and for the future of Army Air Forces development.[28] At the completion of AIC, Arnold was reassigned as chief of the Information Section. He returned to Washington, DC, as Mitchell's military career was reaching its terminus. Mitchell had angered too many traditional staff officers and became a sacrificial lamb.

Mitchell had also been reassigned, to Fort Sam Houston, Texas, reduced to his permanent rank of colonel (although most still called him by his wartime rank, general) and designated "Air Officer." Following two disastrous air accidents—an Army plane ran out of fuel and was lost on a trip from San Francisco to Honolulu, and a dirigible had broken up over Ohio in bad weather and 14 were killed—Mitchell focused his wrath on "nonflying men" in the military who were setting aviation policy even though they had no knowledge, experience, or right. Mitchell stated that "[the] terrible accidents to our naval aircraft are the direct results of incompetency, criminal negligence and almost treasonable administration of our national defense by the War and Navy Departments."[29] Mitchell of course was court-martialed, sentenced, and resigned his commission. The most important airpower advocate was gone, only his friends were left to carry on the fight.

In the midst of the Mitchell madness, Arnold was forced to make a life-decision. He had been one of four in the development of a new American airline, Pan American Airways. Arnold was slated to become the president, but decided not to resign from the Army in the face of hostility, and stayed to ride out the Mitchell controversy. He was reassigned to Fort Riley, Kansas, as the Commanding Officer of the 16th Observation Squadron. At the cavalry base, Arnold was given permission to "write and say any damned thing [he] want[ed]" provided he let his commander, General Ewing Booth, know first.[30] With a few planes, and more reluctant students, he instituted an aerial observation course for the young cavalry officers. The officers, in training to be cavalry observers, added aerial observation to their list of proficiencies. But the indoctrination was not completely error-free. Arnold was surprised at one point to see a very airsick cavalry observer in a plane trailing 300 feet of telephone wire. The pilot had flown too low, snagged the wires, but fortunately landed safely. One of Arnold's main tasks was observers' familiarization with aerial reconnaissance, and his pilots were not helping matters by flying too low and stunting. But overall his plan worked, cavalry officers were initiated into aerial observation and gained invaluable skills.

Arnold finally submitted an application for General Staff School at Fort Leavenworth. He expected to meet with resistance, but in the end completed the course with a desire to modernize outdated air policy taught at the school. His next assignment was at Dayton, Ohio, where he began to implement policy changes. Arnold's location until 1931 was beneficial to his outlook as well. At Dayton, Arnold was exposed to all of the newest improvements in aircraft technology and development of the time. He was on hand for developments in variable-pitch propellers, improved superchargers, brakes, airbrakes, and dive brakes, all-metal aircraft, biplanes giving way to monoplanes, and so on as the years and experiments progressed. He was on hand during the planning of America's first 200 mph bomber, the Martin B-10. But few still recognized the potential of the aircraft in war; fortunately, the few were determined to rewrite airpower policy.

In 1930 and 1931, Arnold was put in charge of annual Air Corps maneuvers. In 1930, they were held in Sacramento, California, and involved 250 aircraft. The next year, they were in Dayton, and the numbers increased to 700 aircraft and 1400 men. The exercise taught Arnold about the importance of supply and communication in the field. His findings were generalized to war mobilization plans that envisioned concentrations of 1,000 to 2,000 aircraft and corresponding men and support staff.[31] His transfer to the command of March Field, California, was enacted in the fall of 1931.

At March Field, Arnold was in charge of transforming the flying school into an operational air base that housed two air groups, one each bomber and fighter.[32] Arnold named Major Joseph McNarney as the commander of the Bomber Group, the highly decorated Major Frank Hunter was put in charge of the Fighters, and Major Spaatz became Arnold's Exec. The base was equipped with a motley collection of aircraft; for bombers Arnold used B-2, B-4, B-5, and B-6 aircraft, and for fighters primarily P-12s. With continued supercharger development, the Air Corps planes could fly progressively higher, and this, in addition to night flying, was what Arnold's men practiced. In an effort to find suitable land ranges for gunnery and bombing practice—the sea was off-limits because the Navy flatly said so—Arnold came across the dry lake bed near Muroc, a small nondescript California way station. In fact, Arnold was responsible for obtaining titles to the bombing range in 1939.[33] The importance of Muroc in 1932 was that it was a perfect training ground for Arnold's fighters and bombers. Minutes away from March by air, the site was the target of frequent training missions.

In 1933, Arnold was made commander of the newly christened 1st Fighter Wing, including the fighter groups all along the west coast. He added to his duties in November as the commander of the 1st Bomb Wing, incorporating the corresponding bomber groups. Thus, when the 1st Wing of the GHQ Air Force was established in 1935 on the west coast of the United States,[34] there were no substantial staff changes that had to take place. The reorganization simply meant that the 1st Fighter and Bomber Wings were under centralized control: under Arnold. He was promoted to the temporary rank of brigadier general, and had control over the bombers and fighters at March, Rockwell, and Hamilton Fields.

"Hap" Arnold was known for his experimental methods. In addition to gunnery trials with aerial machineguns and cannon, Arnold also had his "boys" try new bombing techniques and hardware. The West Coast Air Forces continued to work together, testing their aircraft and accessories in the California desert.

But, in January 1936 Arnold left his command, and the serenity of the West Coast, and returned to Washington, DC, as the assistant chief of the Air Corps under the chief, General Oscar Westover. Although Arnold protested the move—he insisted that he would rather remain a lieutenant colonel in California—he was reassigned and promoted. Also, to the benefit of the fledgling U.S. Army Air Forces, Arnold was put in charge of procurement and supply. He guided the development of the Air Forces into the upcoming conflict.

1936 was a watershed year. In Germany, Hitler remilitarized the Rhineland. A young physicist by the name Hans von Ohain who had recently finished his doctorate began work for Ernst Heinkel on Germany's first jet engine. In England, Frank Whittle formed Power Jets and continued development of his prototype turbojet power plant. The Spanish turned against each other in their bitter Civil War, the Italians invaded and bombed Abyssinia in their attempt at an empire, and the Japanese were expanding their Greater East Asia Co-Prosperity Sphere at the expense of Manchuria and China. In the United States, Arnold oversaw the first flights and acceptance of the Boeing YB-17, a very important four-engine American bomber prototype.[35] Although the first prototype crashed on its first flight because the ground crew had failed to "unlock" the flight controls, the plane's potential was realized and a number of test models (YB-17s) were ordered in January 1936. And, although the Army did not invest in large numbers initially, the development of the B-17, and the backing of Arnold, was an indication of the importance of the type. The B-17 and later four-engine bombers were originally designed as coastal patrol planes keeping in mind the Mitchell antiship bombing experiments. The planes were viewed as a complement to the oceans that served as natural barriers for American iso-lationism. Eventually, the planes developed into amazing vehicles of strategic airpower, but this role was initially unintended.

Arnold's most influential impact on the growth of the Air Corps was his dedication to research and development. He was introduced to the Hungarian Theodore von Kármán in 1935, and remained in close contact with the Guggenheim Aeronautical Laboratory at the California Institute of Technology (GALCIT). Kármán had emigrated from Hungary when he accepted the prestigious U.S. position, but had been trained in the German system of theoretical aeronautical research. As director of GALCIT, Kármán was on the cutting edge of practical and theoretical U.S. aircraft development.[36] By approaching civilian institutions and engineers, and connecting them with industry for production, Arnold created an intimate relationship between engineering evolution, aircraft production, and military procurement: this became known as the military–industrial–academic complex.[37]

Arnold was concerned with production in sufficient quantity; he did not forget the lessons of underproduction in World War I. But he was equally interested in innovation and development of new types and designs. While focusing on current designs and production figures, he continued to prophesy future designs including "some yet undiscovered power source, untapped or unharnessed"[38]; he of course was speaking of rocket and jet power. And in a demonstration of the interconnectedness of the military and civilian spheres, Arnold even asked Donald Douglas, of the Douglas Aircraft Manufacturing Company to write the foreword to his 1938 *This Flying Game*. Douglas was only one of Arnold's friends and contacts in the civilian aviation industry that he would turn to, and award with contracts, as America built up her air forces.

On March 1, 1939, Arnold was officially named the chief of the Air Corps. He had occupied the position since September 1938 due to another fateful air accident, in which Major General Westover was killed. In the spring, Arnold was promoted to the position, complete with rank. Major General Delos Emmons was named the GHQ Air Force Commander, but still subordinate to Arnold and the Air Corps. Hap Arnold was now in the position to shape the U.S. Army Air Corps as he saw fit. Fortunately for the nascent branch, Arnold was exactly the right person to marry R&D, production, and doctrine as he constructed the air service.

One of his first decisions was to bring together his scientists to report on aerial innovation and progress. The meeting was labeled the Committee on Air Corps Research and held at the National Academy of Sciences (NAS).[39] His intention was to refocus R&D and commit to training pilots. The first issue was due to recent reports from Germany citing aerial advances by the Nazis. The second consideration was in regard to the Nazis as well; the United States had to have pilots available in case of wartime. Arnold, true to form, revitalized R&D with financial investment second in spending only to training. Arnold favored GALCIT with funds and contracts when they eagerly supported Arnold's Jet-Assisted Take Off (JATO) program. The first JATO proposal was actually rockets (therefore, RATO), and was disregarded by MIT representatives as superfluous and far-fetched.[40] GALCIT got the R&D contract to develop JATO as their Project No.1, the program that directly fueled the incorporation of the Jet Propulsion Laboratory (JPL).

As a member of the National Advisory Committee for Aeronautics (NACA), Arnold was able to keep abreast of all current developments. He was also able to connect the NACA with his office through a liaison, Major Carl Greene, who went between NACA in Langley Field and the Air Corps Materiel Division at Wright Field.[41] But by the early summer of 1939, world war was imminent. Germany was threatening in Europe, and Japan was already advancing in the Pacific. Arnold had to balance adequate production and infrastructure with technological innovation for his air services. His solution was that

> The production of aircraft in quantity should not be delayed too long awaiting the perfect article, for never has there been an airplane put into quantity production when there was not an experimental airplane already in the air or just around the corner. The true answer probably is this: at a given time, when the necessity for sufficient aircraft to equip all tactical units arrives, put into production the best airplanes of the types required which are available, and thereafter, on that type, stop all changes and discontinue every improvement which would interfere in any way with the production of that type in quantity. The new experimental plane of higher performance should be rushed to early completion, thoroughly tested, and then it, too, should be put into quantity production, and that new and improved article should be ready to go to the fighting units as replacements for the older, inferior plane. There lies the middle ground. Sacrifice some quality to get sufficient quantity to supply all fighting units. Never follow the mirage, looking for the perfect airplane, to a point where fighting squadrons are deficient in numbers of fighting planes.[42]

Arnold was in a position to completely control the fate of the Air Corps, but he was willing to sacrifice quality for quantity. He based his paradigm on his memory of the lack of planes and pilots in the last war, and was determined not to repeat that mistake. But he was also open to and welcomed technological innovation in the air, as long as it was attainable, and would not adversely affect production.

One of the overarching problems Arnold faced was time. Planes, as complex systems, take a long time to develop. From conception to production usually took years, Arnold wanted no more than an 18-month turnaround. Even that time frame had to be extended by 6 months to give enough training time to pilots; thus, new aircraft, even under ideal conditions, were

2 years in the future. In the spring of 1939 this was acceptable, by September it was a cause for concern. Even the latest and greatest American designs were years in the making. Arnold cites examples of the B-25 (designed in 1938, not delivered until 1941), the P-47 (1936 and 1941, respectively), and Arnold's project the B-17, designed in 1934, flown in 1936, but not delivered to the Air Corps until June 1939.[43] He knew that he had to think ahead to build up the Air Corps for future conflict. Fortunately for Arnold, he had the benefit of time that others did not.

Between the start of the war in Europe and Pearl Harbor, Arnold worked to rectify America's lack of a viable air force. He was intimately involved in overseeing the increase in American aircraft production of both planes and pilots. He personally visited aircraft manufacturing plants and opened new training facilities. Meanwhile, as chief of the Air Corps, Arnold was also in charge of obtaining government funding for his service. By the end of June 1940, the financial fears of the Air Corps were put to rest. Along with contracts from the British, the U.S. government awarded Arnold $1.5 billion to "get an air force."[44] Now the roles were reversed. Arnold stated that "In years gone by we had all the time in the world but no money. Now we have all the money in the world but no time."[45] Under Arnold's direction, American aircraft industry was about to gear up for wartime production.

In the fall of 1940, Arnold gained an important ally in the new assistant secretary of war for air, Wall Street investment banker Robert Lovett. Lovett was the rational, grounded, facts-and-figures alter ego for Arnold's rearmament plans. Adding a practical air to the Air Corps, Lovett was responsible for making sure that Arnold's wishes could and should be carried out. Furthermore, they were both strong advocates for industrial efficiency and expanded training programs. Arnold admitted that Lovett was not only a grounding force, but also an important ally.[46] Further, Lovett was also an important mediator in the relationship between Henry L. Stimson, General George C. Marshall, and Arnold: secretary of war, U.S. Army chief of staff, and chief of the Air Corps, respectively.[47] Lovett mediated and advised on finances and contracts that went through the Air Corps offices as America prepared for wartime production.

A substantial portion of Air Corps funding went directly to research and development (R&D). Thus, with the knowledge of other "jet"[48] engineering projects throughout the world, Arnold contacted Dr. Vannevar Bush, chairman at NACA, to look into the problem. By March 1941, Dr. Bush had created the "Special Committee on Jet Propulsion" under the aegis of the NACA.[49] Although the NACA had investigated "jets" in the years leading up to 1940, it was determined that they were unsuitable for aircraft propulsion, and research had been discontinued.[50] But, fortunately for the then growing U.S. Army Air Corps as well as future American turbojet production, NACA was making significant progress in the theory and study of turbosuperchargers for conventional (piston) engines.[51] The committee was tasked with identifying the feasibility of turbine engines for use in aircraft, and suggestions for potential engine manufacturers. Arnold wanted to specifically avoid current piston-engine manufacturers because of a perceived conflict of interest and wanted to instead focus on supercharger experts at General Electric, Allison Chalmers, and Westinghouse.[52] By April the committee had developed a number of proposals on the potential of rockets, turboprops, and ducted fans, but was distracted by interesting events since their formation.

In the midst of the European war, the British, thanks in part to Lend–Lease, had been able to stave off German advances in the air. Arnold decided to venture to England to meet with his British counterpart, Air Chief Marshal Charles Portal, and discuss the events of the recent air war over Europe and the impact of American equipment. Arnold informed Portal that he wanted "to find a practical way in which the U.S. Army Air Corps could be of maximum aid to the British."[53] But it was the British who would aid and assist the Americans. Arnold went to visit Lord Beaverbrook who was in charge of wartime production. The two discussed production and delivery of aircraft in particular, and Arnold requested and was granted a number of British planes for American research. In the interest of cooperation, Beaverbrook at once offered to allow Arnold to inspect all current British projects. Among these were the joint projects of Whittle and Gloster, then in taxi trials. Arnold received permission from Beaverbrook to take plans and drawings for the revolutionary power plant back to the United States under one condition: utter secrecy. Arnold returned to Washington empty-handed, armed with the promise that all information on the Whittle engine and Gloster airframe would be supplied to the American Technical Staff in London.[54]

On July 22, 1941, a meeting was held at the British Ministry for Aircraft Production where the American technical advisors, Colonel A. Lyon and D. Shoults of General Electric (GE), were briefed on British turbojet development.[55] Colonel Lyon was Arnold's technical advisor in Britain, put there in order to keep Arnold up to date on British air technology development, as well as keep the Americans informed of the continuing aerial battles over England. Lyon was the "man on the ground" in place to be the eyes and ears of Arnold in England. Shoults was an engineer and was in England to advise the British on the proper use and care of the GE turbosuperchargers for the recently arrived B-17 bombers. His insight into the engineering aspects of turbosuperchargers was invaluable in assessing the importance as well as the viability of the Whittle engine. Three days later the Americans, with the addition of Major Brandt, the requested technical advisor to the project, visited the Power Jets facility and met with Roxbee Cox and Frank Whittle, who showed the Americans the revolutionary engine and its components. On the 28th, the men visited the Gloster Company to view the E.28/39 as well as the plans for the proposed F.9/40, the future *Meteor*.

By the end of July, Major Donald Keirn was sent to England as Lyon's deputy in charge of the jet development program. His visit to Whittle, and subsequent four-day analysis of the engine and engineering theory convinced him that the program was viable, and that the United States needed to pursue similar development. His recommendation to Lyon, upon return to London, was that the United States should build copies of the Whittle engine.[56]

Plans for the Whittle W.2B were brought to Washington, DC, and Arnold prepared to introduce it to specific manufacturers for development in the United States. At this historic meeting the government was represented by Major General Arnold (chief, Army Air Forces), Mr. Lovett (assistant secretary of war for Air), Brigadier General Carl Spaatz (chief of the Air Staff), Brigadier General Oliver Echols (chief of the Materials Division), Lieutenant Colonel Benjamin Chidlaw (Materials Division), and Major Brandt. The company chosen to develop the turbojet engine in this country was, unsurprisingly, GE. Its representatives included Dr. A.R. Stevenson, Mr. R. Muir, Mr. S. Puffer, and recently returned-from-England Mr. Shoults. At that point, Arnold laid the plans on a table and stated, "Gentlemen, I give you the Whittle engine. Consult all you wish and arrive at any decision you please—just so long as General Electric accepts a contract to build 15 of them."[57] At the same meeting it was decided to develop a twin-engine airframe due to the low predicted output of the engine, and that the airframe contract would go to the Bell Aircraft Corporation.[58]

These choices were, in hindsight, both simple and effective. GE was chosen for the simple fact that they had the most experience in the field. GE had been intimately involved in the development and manufacture of steam turbines, then later turbosuperchargers. Under the direction of Dr. Sanford Moss, the GE company excelled in supercharger development to the point that the turbojet was an uncomplicated evolution for the GE engineers. The turbosupercharger, then under development at GE, consisted of a centrifugal-flow impeller that would compress outside air and feed it into the cylinders of a conventional piston engine. Then, the exhaust from the engine drove a turbine that in turn drove the compressor stage. The purpose of the turbosupercharger was to compress the ambient air at high altitude (thus thinner) and force the compressed air into the cylinders of a conventional piston engine for better performance at high altitude. With this technical marvel, which had undergone significant development since World War I, the American Boeing B-17 Flying Fortress, sent to Britain under Lend–Lease as B-17Cs, flew at altitudes of 35,000 feet.[59] The only stage the turbosupercharger lacked to make it into a prime mover was the combustion cycle. But the GE plant had dabbled with this stage as well, and it was only a matter of time, according to both Constant and Young, before the Americans developed their own turbojet engines.[60] But they did not, and the British Whittle engine became the model that the U.S. jet program followed to fruition. Other interests influenced the decision for GE, not the least of which was Shoults. He had been involved in examining the engine and engineering since Arnold's initial England visit. He knew the Whittle engine better than anyone in the United States, and his company was rewarded. Finally, GE was not already involved in engine development for the war effort. They were building turbosuperchargers, but the production lines were running and there was a substantial amount of engineering brainpower "left over"—underused and available—for the development of the first of the GE turbojets. The GE plant at West Lynn, Massachusetts, was chosen as the production facility for the license-built Whittle engine.

The case for Bell Aircraft was also straight-forward. First and foremost, Larry Bell was a personal acquaintance of Arnold's; their friendship can not be taken lightly. Further, Bell's company was quite close to the West Lynn GE plant, and location was a consideration. As well, Bell was not at the time engaged in an important defense contract. His P-39 *Airacobra*, although innovative, was a disappointment to the designer and the Army, and had by this time been relegated to duties as a Lend–Lease aircraft only. This left Bell and his design staff necessary time and energy to develop a jet aircraft prototype. Furthermore, Lt. Colonel Chidlaw mentioned two other concerns: "Bell had a smaller but highly experienced and imaginative engineering staff, well experienced in fighter design."[61] The *Airacobra* was extremely innovative, and incorporated a number of fighter aircraft design enhancements that would later be incorporated into America's first jet. Further, "Bell had certain isolated facilities which could be made readily available to start this project under the strict conditions of the "SECRET" classification as imposed by General Arnold."[62] Last, but certainly not least, both Arnold and Chidlaw commented on Larry Bell's "tremendous personal drive and boundless enthusiasm in all matters relating to Research and Development," as well as Bell's assurance that he would personally oversee the entire project.[63]

The initial government contract requested three airframes from Bell Aircraft and 15 engines from GE, for the development of a prototype jet fighter for the USAAF. The British were notified that the program in the United States was about to begin, and the British in turn promised to send an entire engine, as well as one of their two Gloster E.28/39s to the United States for evaluation. Arnold had set in motion the American jet program; his influence was in getting the available technology and distributing the appropriate contracts to the best-suited manufacturing companies.

Thus, Arnold's influence was enormous in the appropriation and acceptance of jet technology in the United States. Although Americans had been working on turbojet-related technology in different forms, it is obvious that it was not available before GE was presented with the contract in September 1941. Arnold had recognized the importance of jet technology, and had been influential in bringing it to his shores even before the official American involvement in the war. Once he had implemented the American jet program through his influence, the story shifts focus to the designers at Bell Aircraft and GE.

Larry Bell was an aircraft designer. His fascination with aircraft construction—although he was averse to flying—began at an early age. His parents relocated the family to southern California to retire closer to their grown children; Larry Bell was 13 when the family took the train from Warsaw, Indiana, to the West Coast in 1907.[64]

Bell was interested from a very young age in aviation and airplanes. His first big exposure to aircraft was at the Dominquez Field Airshow near Long Beach in 1910. With his older brothers Vaughn and Grover, Bell saw his first airplane.[65] In 1910 airship balloons and dirigibles were still superior to most airplane designs, and this was illustrated by a race won over an airplane. But, the balloonists, and Bell, realized the potential of the heavier-than-air craft, and Bell especially was immediately taken with the concept.

When Bell's older brother Grover learned to fly—for $500 at the Glenn L. Martin Company in Los Angeles—then bought an old Martin biplane and went on the road as a traveling flyer, Larry Bell dropped out of high school to become his brother's mechanic. The Bell legacy almost ended in July 1913, when Larry's older brother Grover was killed in a landing accident; Larry Bell renounced aviation and went into mourning for his brother.

A close friend of Bell's, Dave Hunt, persuaded Bell to return to aircraft manufacture. Larry Bell and Dave Hunt became a team, manufacturing floats for seaplanes.[66] Pouring himself into his work, he once again relished building airplanes and eventually took a job with the Glenn L. Martin Company. Bell built aircraft and was quickly promoted within the company. He learned the fundamentals of aeronautical engineering on the job, even if he did not fly. His aversion to flying but competence in the technology is aptly illustrated in an interesting vignette:

> Although Larry was not a pilot and rarely flew, he knew enough about flying to teach the basics to a young Japanese naval officer who walked into the plant late one afternoon. "I told him all the pilots were out of town on exhibitions," Bell said, "but he persisted. And he had the necessary $500 fee." Larry took an old biplane that was parked behind the plant, put a used engine in it, and made a certified flier of the man.[67]

Bell became shop foreman at Martin and became involved in the choreography of the Martin flying team's exhibitions. In the famous "Battle of the Clouds" 1914 exhibition, the plan was to create an awesome spectacle. Bell wanted to show the crowd the effects of bombing from the air. His plan was for a two-day show with Martin planes dropping "bombs"—in the form of oranges—on a makeshift fort and soldiers. The fort was set up and painted to look like stone, Martin employees were dressed as soldiers and carried guns with blanks, and a fake cannon was in place to add to the spectacle.

The second day of the show produced the awaited "Battle of the Clouds." Martin dropped oranges, simulating bombs, and Bell set off black powder charges and dynamite to depict the smoke and noise of bomb damage. As the "battle" raged on, the fake cannon accidentally caught fire and there was a threat that the whole fort would go up in smoke. But when the dust settled, the crowd sat stunned and amazed at the exhibition—Bell's "Battle of the Clouds" was a huge success.[68]

Two men were utterly impressed by the show, and went to see Martin and Bell at their shop. Juan and Pedro Alcaldez were interested in buying a plane and bombs for Pancho Villa's triumphant return to Mexico. Martin set the price of the plane at $10,000—bombs extra—and the Alcaldez brothers opened a suitcase full of money.[69] Two weeks later a two-seat Martin airplane was shipped to Tucson, Arizona, to be the spearhead of the renewed Villa attack into Mexico. The Martin Company was questioned about the plane and its buyers, but denied specific knowledge and culpability. The plane was the first tactical and strategic bomber, and the revolution in Mexico continued with the use of airpower.

One year later, war broke out in Europe. The aerial battles of the World War I fed the evolutionary cycle of the newest form of technology committed to military strategy. Aircraft of all types, shapes, and sizes grew up in World War I while proving their worth as military hardware.

In 1914, Bell went to Martin to inquire about a recently vacant superintendent position. Martin argued that Bell was too young and did not have academic training, but that Bell would have choice on who he would work under. After contacting MIT, Bell met Donald Douglas, an aeronautical engineer. Bell began the interview with the forthright statement, "Mr. Martin has asked me to hire the man I'll be working for, and you're not going to see him unless you prove you know more about airplanes than I do and prove you're better able to run this company than I am."[70] Douglas impressed Bell, and Bell introduced him to the boss after a lengthy interview. Bell left, knowing he had hired his superior and was stuck as a shop foreman. The next morning, Martin announced that Douglas was to be named the chief engineer, and Bell was promoted to superintendent of the company.[71]

The Martin merger with the Wright Company went well for the duration of the war, as contracts poured in for engines. But, with no airframe contracts on the horizon, Martin and Bell set out to open a new plant in Cleveland. The new Martin works got a postwar contract for the MB-2 twin-engine bomber, well suited in range and reliability for a number of postwar roles.

In the 1920s, new faces came and went at Martin who became legends in the aircraft community. Douglas moved on after a dispute with Bell to form his own company in California. "Dutch" Kindelberger, the aircraft designer, worked for Martin, left to join Douglas, and later became president of North American Aviation.

Bell eventually became vice-president and general manager of Martin, and liaison between the company and Army in the development of the MB-2. Bell came into contact with General Billy Mitchell, the American bombing pioneer. Mitchell's ideas on strategic bombing were illustrated with Martin bombers on the captured German battleship *Ostfriesland*, which was sunk with aerial bombs. To the horror of the naval spectators, the mighty German battleship was sunk in a matter of minutes by wood and cloth airplanes dropping thousand pound bombs.

But there was growing tension between Martin and Bell. Larry knew that he would always be second place at Martin, and in 1925 decided to set out on his own. Although the 1920s were roaring, Bell did not find solid work for 3 years. In 1928, Bell was given an opportunity to buy into and run a small aircraft company in Buffalo, New York. Although his wife was not pleased, Bell knew that it was the chance to work in aeronautics and own his own company. Larry Bell jumped at the chance, and moved to Buffalo in July.

Bell began work in Buffalo for Consolidated under its president Reuben Fleet (Major, U.S. Army, ret.). Bell was put in charge (as vice-president) of the production of Consolidated aircraft including the PY-1 flying boat, the PT *Husky* trainer, the *Fleetster*, mail/passenger plane, and the *Husky Junior* sport plane.[72] But on September 13, 1929—a Friday—Fleet was seriously injured in an airplane accident and handed operational control of the company over to Bell.

Bell immediately began recruiting top aircraft specialists to build up the company. His first acquisition was Robert Woods from Lockheed Aircraft Corporation. Then Bell was granted the production contract for the YP-25 when it was dropped by the ailing Detroit Aircraft Corporation. Consolidated's *Fleetster* was in demand as a transport plane, and Bell's future looked bright. But as number two man, Bell continued to question his place. His break came when Fleet decided to move Consolidated to San Diego, for a number of reasons. Fleet wanted warm water for year-round seaplane operations, and also wanted to leave Buffalo behind. Bell took advantage of the break from Fleet, secured investors in Buffalo, and prepared to begin operations on his own. On June 20, 1935, Bell resigned from Consolidated and on July 10 Bell transferred his name to his new company, Bell Aircraft Corporation. Without contracts but with investors, Bell started his new life as an aircraft manufacturer.

At first, the Bell Aircraft Corporation literally depended on a wing and a prayer. The new Consolidated Aircraft in San Diego could not keep up with government orders for U.S. Navy seaplanes, and Bell was awarded a contract for outboard wing panels.[73] The over $800,000 contract kept Bell and his company in business. But it was not his own project.

That came in 1936 in the form of the YFM-1 *Airacuda*. The multiplace fighter proposal incorporated a twin-engine design and was armed with

37-mm cannon. With the conventional wisdom of the invulnerability of self-defending bombers, the Army had requested a heavy fighter with aerial cannon. Bell's preliminary design won the competition, but he still had to sell it to get a contract for construction.

The procurement order was issued, and Bell began manufacture of the XFM-1. The Army allotted $25,000 for the first prototype, and the Bell Company began construction on the novel aircraft. The *Airacuda* was a twin-engine heavy fighter/multipurpose aircraft. It was innovative in that the twin Allison 1,000 hp engines were pushers; the propellers were on the trailing edges of the wings. The two 37-mm cannons—originally antiaircraft guns from Colt Firearms (M1E1)—were incorporated into the front of the engine nacelles in a small compartment that could be manned. The cannon could be fired independently by gunners or fired simultaneously by a central fire control in the cockpit. For the proper weight distribution, the rear-facing propellers were connected to the engines by 64-inch drive shaft extenders, an important component to later Bell designs. The *Airacuda* was ready for its first flight on September 1, 1937.

Although there were initial teething problems, the XFM-1 was recommended to the Army who ordered 13 more prototypes. The defensive fighter, envisioned by Bell as a coastal defense aircraft, was first delivered on February 23, 1940. Thereafter the other 13 were built and sent out, but the *Airacuda* was already obsolete. The 13 aircraft were relegated to trainers as the United States prepared for war. In the final three produced, Bell incorporated a tricycle, that is nosewheel, undercarriage which would become one of his planes' trademarks.

By 1940, the *Airacuda* was too expensive, and the Army had purpose-built aircraft in the works instead of multirole aircraft. The Boeing B-17 *Flying Fortress* was coming off the production lines as America's premier bomber, and final tests were being completed on the North American P-51 *Mustang* fighter. The FM-1 *Airacuda*, already obsolete, was unnecessary.

The second specifically Bell aircraft was the "Model 4." Later known as the P-39 *Airacobra*, the plane was another innovative development of Woods and Bell. The plane was designed around a 20-mm cannon and two .50 caliber machine guns while other aircraft were only using .30 calibers. The low-wing, single-seat fighter incorporated other characteristic Bell features, such as a tricycle undercarriage and a set-back engine. The Allison V-12 engine was behind the pilot and a drive shaft provided power to the gear housing for the propeller. The gear housing was offset downwards so that the 20-mm cannon could fire directly through the propeller hub. The configuration allowed for a more stable aircraft with the engine over the center of gravity, and more accurate shooting with the cannon along the plane's centerline. The first *Airacobra* prototype flew in April 1938.

While the *Airacuda* and *Airacobra* were being developed, Bell witnessed the future of aviation. Larry Bell and his wife had sailed to Europe on

July 15, 1938, in the capacity of human intelligence. Bell, along with a number of other industrialists, had been asked by President Roosevelt to visit Europe and determine industrial capacity there.[74] Bell wanted to see what the Germans were up to in the field of aviation. Bell met with Ernst Udet of the German Air Ministry who promised a complete tour of German aircraft manufacturing plants. Bell was also scheduled to reunite with an old friend from Martin, Dr. Georg Madelung.[75] Madelung was well known in German aviation circles and was the brother-in-law of Willy Messerschmitt, the premier German aircraft manufacturer.

Bell was invited to visit the Messerschmitt aircraft manufacturing plant at Augsburg. By 1938, German military aircraft production was in full swing and Bell was impressed by the long and efficient production lines. He related that "Most impressive is the individual effort, the output, the organization, and the spirit and enthusiasm of the German workers. Production methods are far superior to anything in America or to any other country because they are doing things on a large scale that lends itself to progressive production methods. You get the feeling that they can do anything."[76] Bell was deeply impressed, and later configured his own production lines after the ones he saw in Germany. He later admitted that his factory was an exact replica of the Heinkel factory, "copied right out."[77]

Although impressed with the Germans, Bell was not as optimistic of the other countries' manufacturing capabilities on his European jaunt. His visits to Italy, France, and Britain were reported in a less favorable light compared to the Germans. The Italian designs and manufacturing were inferior to the Germans' but better than the other two western European countries. France was "in a 'pathetic condition'" and Britain was unprepared for "minimum defense requirements."[78]

Bell returned to the United States and gave written and verbal reports to his appointed government and military contacts. One of these audiences included "Hap" Arnold, the general of the Army Air Forces. In his official report he rated the European powers according to German proficiency. France at 1, compared to Italy (2) and Britain (5), with Germany setting the scale of 10.[79] Bell passed his concerns on up the chain of command to the president, who agreed that American production needed to be increased to face the possible German threat. This perception was echoed by Bernard Baruch, in charge of the War Industries Board, who used his idea of a German threat from Central and South America in order to garner support for the American aircraft industry.[80]

In the face of financial uncertainty, Bell visited the Anglo-French Purchasing Board, where he secured a $9 million order for two hundred P-400s, the European version of the P-39, for French buyers. The P-39 went into production, and the Bell Company was saved by an overseas government contract. With the fall of France in June 1940, the British took over the voided French contract, and the USAAF began to take interest in the P-39 for its own uses. The plane was a marvel of modern technology. Even with weight penalties of larger guns, self-sealing fuel tanks, and increased armor for the pilot, the P-39 was a good performer under 16,000 feet. Months before, when the Allison engine – equipped series P-39 was shown to USAAF delegates in January 1940, there was consensus that the plane was another excellent Bell design. Captain George Price, the Army test pilot, demonstrated the power of the plane and the durability of the plane became apparent when he had to make a "gear-up" landing, when the wheels refused to extend. The hardy P-39 not only survived with minimal damage, it was repaired and demonstrated to other officials two weeks later in Washington, DC. Price received the Distinguished Flying Cross for his piloting skills that saved the plane in its first dangerous flight.[81] In September the Bell Aircraft Company was expanded under the Emergency Facilities Contract Number 1 issued by the USAAF, and by August 1941 Bell was given a $75 million contract to produce 2,000 P-39s for the USAAF, on the condition that the plant could produce five aircraft per day.[82] Most of the P-39s were sent to the Soviets under Lend–Lease; the *Airacobra* fit well into Soviet tactical air doctrine.

But an infinitely more important meeting took place on September 5, 1941. Bell, with his chief engineer Harlan Poyer, was summoned to Washington at the request of Arnold. The meeting was short but decisive. The men were informed of British turbojet technology, and Bell was asked (personally, by Arnold) if he would build America's first jet airplane.[83] Bell's reply was simply, "When do we start?"[84] GE was to supply 15 engines, and Bell was initially contracted to build three airframes. Bell, Arnold, and D.R. Shoults, the GE representative, met later that day to discuss the project and its development. Shoults outlined the power plant and its projected capabilities, Arnold argued for a twin-engine design. Bell and Poyer began their journey back to Buffalo and set to designing America's first jet.

On their return, Bell secured additional but completely separate workshops at the Ford plant in downtown Buffalo (there was still a dealership on the street level[85]) and gathered his finest engineers to work on the project. The "Secret Six" swore not to divulge any information on the project, and the plane was even given a misleading name. The first American jet plane would be known as the XP-59A; the "A" added to the designation for an aborted Bell aircraft, a piston-engine heavy fighter design. Shrouded in mystery, the Secret Six began work on the XP-59A.[86]

There was much work to do. Literally as Bell traveled back to Buffalo on September 6, 1941, he began to sketch out his ideas for the new plane. The Secret Six were able to present a 1/20 scale mock-up proposal of the aircraft within 2 weeks, which in turn was presented to Arnold. The project was approved, and Bell Aircraft Company was awarded a fixed-fee contract for three planes for $1,644,431 on September 30, 1941.[87] Two stipulations of the government contract were that utter secrecy had to be maintained and that the airframe had to be ready within 8 months.[88]

GE was the natural choice to develop the first American jet engine. Under the direction of Dr. Sanford Moss, the design team was chosen and briefed. Moss was a graduate of Cornell, where he had developed his ideas on power plants for high-altitude flight.[89] After joining GE in 1903, he helped to develop aircraft superchargers. Initial GE work was in mechanical supercharging; Moss later developed the turbosupercharger that became famous during the Pike's Peak high-altitude tests in 1918.[90]

The premise behind the supercharger is that it is a mechanical device for compressing ambient air; fuel is added either before or after compression, and the mixture is forced into the pistons of a conventional engine. The purpose is to allow a conventional piston engine to operate efficiently even at high altitudes where air density is lower. A mechanical supercharger is a machine that is driven off the piston engine mechanically (through drive- or cam-shafts or belts) to increase high-altitude performance. A turbosupercharger, by comparison, is driven by hot exhaust gasses from a piston-engine exhaust, reducing mechanical losses. In the interwar period, GE was able to develop multistage mechanical and turbosuperchargers. Moss retired from GE in 1938 but returned when asked at the outbreak of war in Europe. He was responsible for the initial supercharged B-17 trials where the four-engine Boeing bomber equipped with turbosuperchargers flew at an amazing 315 mph at 25,000 feet altitude.[91]

The importance of the turbosupercharger and Moss' work was in the close relation to the innovation of turbojet engines. GE had already had to deal with centrifugal compressor impellers as well as turbines that had to withstand high temperatures and rotational speeds. GE led the field in materials analysis and implementation in the quest for high-temperature alloys for superchargers. Beginning in 1931, GE was the sole owner of Air Corps research contracts for high-temperature turbine nozzles and blades for superchargers; in fact GE had constructed a special hot gas stand specifically to test these components.[92]

The only component in the evolution from turbosuperchargers to turbojet engines as prime movers was the combustion stage. But, interestingly, even though there were independent assumptions and ideas, neither GE nor NACA had developed the idea or actuality of a turbojet engine in the interwar period.[93] And, although the main challenge remained the combustion stage, turbosupercharger development at GE was the key factor for Arnold's decision. GE was working with centrifugal impellers as well as turbines, thus was the obvious choice for America's jet engine designers. For the Americans, as with the other programs, the major problems lay in the development of the combustion stage of the turbojet engine. Further, Arnold did not choose leading piston-engine manufacturers because of his perception that they would be opposed to the revolutionary power plant in the extreme, and that it would be an unnecessary diversion at the very least.[94] Thus, the leading U.S. engine manufacturers, Pratt and Whitney, Allison, and others, were not invited to the developmental process.

One of the major fire walls in the development of the turbojet engine was the conception of the turbojet as a prime mover. Moss was as guilty as many others of considering the turbojet as an alternative to driving a propeller, a later development as a turboprop engine. The major misconception (or lack of conception) was that the turbojet engine—compressor, combustor, and turbine stages combined—could be an efficient prime mover in and of itself. The genius was in the simplicity of the engine as a power plant. Moss, as the head of the turbosupercharger division of GE—the one company that came the closest to developing the turbojet in the United States—did not envision the turbojet as a prime mover.[95]

But, at the same time, Moss and GE had made significant advances in metallurgy, and had already been working for years on the components that would later make up turbojet engines. The supercharger impeller, the compression stage, was very similar to the turbojet engine impeller. The engine impeller was larger, but most of the same engineering and manufacturing techniques could be transferred to the new technology. Further, the turbine was also similar, but once again the scale was larger. The contemporary supercharger impeller was 6 inches in diameter; the first GE turbojet engine, based on the Whittle drawings, had a 20.7-inch, double-sided impeller, as well as a 54-bladed, 14.2-inch turbine wheel.[96]

As mentioned above, Arnold was solely responsible for bringing the information to America and awarding government contracts to GE for the first United States-built turbojet engines. Planning began immediately at the Lynn facility. The GE designers designated the new program the Type I turbosupercharger, and the first engine was to be the Type I-A.[97] An enclosed test stand was constructed, and due to the secrecy was dubbed "Fort Knox." But the GE designers ran into immediate problems. The British data was incomplete, and their own experience told them that the design was flawed. The GE team, with the 6-month deadline looming, set at redesigning the peripheral engine components.

The GE team, including Truly Warner, was concerned about the engine control system for the GE I-A. In the original British blueprints, the pilot's engine controls were absent as the prototype engine was only a test model. In addition, the GE team reworked the inlet vanes, combustion chamber diffusers, and bearings from the original.[98] The team applied previous GE turbosupercharger experience to the new project, and in the end designed a better product than the British original.

But Warner wanted more—and current—British data, and requested an actual engine for analysis. Under Lend–Lease, and with the impetus of the "Top Secret" imperative, Warner approached Arnold about getting the latest British data and engine. By July Arnold had secured more data and an actual engine from the British on the condition that the program maintains utter secrecy. On October 1, 1941, a B-24 left Britain en route to the United States with a Whittle engine (the W.1X) and complete data and blueprints for the next Whittle design the W.2B.[99] The flight came to an interesting conclusion when American customs officials wanted to inspect the incoming cargo. The official military courier, Major Donald Keirn, refused with the explanation of "national security." The customs officials were content to count the number of crates coming in; the engine and data were transported to GE unmolested.[100] Accompanying the British technology were three technicians from Power Jets who contributed professionally to the American developmental process.[101] The British technicians included mechanical engineer D. Walker, Flight Sergeant King, and G. Bozzoni. Whittle reported that Bozzoni stated, "The first time I fly, I have to fly the ruddy Atlantic."[102] This is another simple indication of the novelty of flight as a whole; a key technician, knowledgeable in the development of the most advanced aviation power plant system conceived to date, had never flown!

With the actual artifact, and additional data, the GE team renewed their efforts on the project. Within 5 months, the GE I-A was ready for its first tests. On March 18, 1942, the I-A was rolled into "Fort Knox" for its first test run. The engine stalled out and for the GE team it was back to the drawing board. Over the next 4 weeks the combustion chambers were modified, and the team was ready exactly 1 month later. The GE I-A first ran on its own power on April 18, 1942, with the corresponding remarks from the test log: "... after many attempts Type I RAN."[103] However, teething problems continued; the Americans, like their British counterparts, still faced difficulties with the combustion chambers.

In June 1942, Frank Whittle came to the United States to consult on the American jet program. Traveling under an alias, Frank Whitley,[104] he viewed the GE engine under modification at the Lynn works. Whittle consulted Warner as the second I-A was under construction. Whittle's impressions were that the Americans tested his knowledge extensively—and were duly impressed—and that the Americans were in a much better financial situation than the British Air Ministry. He was especially impressed by the proposed $3 million test plant for turbojet components and GE's promise to produce 1,000 engines a month.[105] Whittle was convinced that the Americans were making great strides and had already adapted the British fundamentals for their own purposes. He returned to Britain in August, relaxed and refocused on the development of his own jet programs at Power Jets.

The Bell team was equally busy developing America's first turbojet airframe. In the development of the plane, there were a number of new considerations to be attended to. The jet aircraft was a novel complex system of military hardware, and the requirements were stringent. First, the plane was envisioned as a high-speed high-altitude fighter from the start.[106] The XP-59A would potentially fly at speeds of up to 500 mph, and altitudes of

25,000 to 50,000 feet. Thus, the Secret Six had to design an airframe that would cope with the demands of the projected performance as well as the comfort of the human pilot to fly it. The designers decided on a large wing area, approximately 400 ft^2, for a wing loading of around 25 lbs/ft^2. The pilot was to be enclosed inside a pressurized cockpit for his (and later her) comfort and safety, and the airframe was to be constructed of materials that could withstand low temperatures at high altitude.[107] Another great concern was the projected thrust rating of the GE I-A engine. The original Whittle W.1 gave only 860 lbs, and although the GE team was redesigning the British engine, the final figures were not available. The closest anyone could guess was an estimate of 1,250 lbs thrust, to which General Arnold said, "A two engine fighter should have potent characteristics."[108]

The Bell team worked from an 8$^1/_2$ × 11 inch rough sketch of the engine provided by GE, and literally drew an airframe around the proposed twin-engine design.[109] The plane was designed as a single-seat, twin-engine fighter prototype that incorporated many Bell characteristics. The XP-59A had a tricycle landing gear, and a fuselage strikingly similar to the production P-39 *Airacobra*. The engines were buried deep in the wing roots, side-by-side in the fuselage. The Bell team designed a straightforward, conservative airframe to include a number of variables. The wing had to be rather large because of the lack of information on the engine performance. Also, the large wing was necessary for high-altitude flight. Further, because of the high altitude, the cockpit was pressurized, with heating coming from air vented off the engines: for the pilot's comfort and safety.[110] The inherent problem was that the team had to decide on a set design early, and based ultimately on incomplete data. The airframe that was designed was good, but conservative. The plane was revolutionary only in the power plants it employed.

Further problems arose in the developmental stages of the XP-59A. In order to maintain utter secrecy, Arnold refused access to wind-tunnel testing. The Bell team had to design the plane based on purely theoretical and completely untested data. Whittle did offer information on potential thrust rates and expected temperatures, but the Bell designers were basing the entire design on theory. The record stated that, "Performance predictions for this aircraft (XP-59A) were based on estimated design performance characteristics furnished from England in lieu of United States engine test data. Unfortunately, neither the original nor the later production engines produced the output desired."[111] The lack of wind-tunnel testing meant that the airframe, and specifically the jet inlet nozzles, could not be tested for efficiency and performance. Arnold relented and let the team use the AAF wind tunnel at Wright Field (Dayton, Ohio), but this was a low-speed wind tunnel and the information provided, though helpful, was not conclusive.[112] Secrecy also prevented the team from consulting outside sources. Although NACA had studied submerged engines[113] and air intakes,[114] only the completed data was available to the Bell designers. Arnold forbid outside consultation, and the XP-59A was built based solely on the information available to the Secret Six. The problem was how to compensate for boundary layer turbulence: where to put the jet intakes, and what shape they should be. The Bell team made their best guess, consulted incomplete low-speed wind-tunnel data, and designed the intakes.

By January 9, 1942, the design was set, and construction of the Bell XP-59A began. The second floor of the onetime Ford dealership was turned into a workshop where specific, security-cleared Bell machinists were brought to build America's first jet. Some of the Bell workers across the city were concerned that their coworkers were "disappearing" from the plant, but with the recent declaration of war, the necessity was accepted.[115] Additional military guards were posted around the new building, windows were welded shut and painted over, and security checkpoints were instituted. In certain instances, workers on one part of the project were uninformed of their coworkers and concurrent programs within the same building. The "Super-Secret" designation was easy to understand in the case of the XP-59A.

By the end of the summer, GE was in the final stages of development of the I-A engine. Bell had nearly completed the first XP-59A airframe, and the two companies brought their products together in Buffalo for final assembly. But, in consideration for continued security, the decision was made not to use Bell's Buffalo test airfield for flight-testing the top-secret project. The completed aircraft would have to be relocated.

Before flight testing could take place, many factors had to be taken into consideration. The most important factors to the Army Air Corps—renamed the Army Air Forces in July 1941—were secrecy and good weather. Colonel Chidlaw and Major Swofford went around the country examining possible sites and finally settled on the Muroc Bombing and Gunnery Range in California. The location offered isolation, dry, consistent weather year-round, and an entire dry lake bed as a landing strip. The north end of Muroc was transferred to Air Materiel Command, and was renamed Materiel Center Flight Test Site.[116] In Buffalo, the former Ford dealership building had to undergo revisions to get the large plane out of the building. A hole was knocked through the wall, and the crated XP-59A was prepared for transport. The plane was loaded into train cars for the trip across the country. To avoid delays once in California, the engines were fitted into the fuselage in Buffalo. But there was concern about the mode of transportation. The engine designers worried about the rattle of the train, and it was decided to spin the engines slowly during the entire trip to protect the bearings. An air compressor was provided; the idea was to force air through the engines to keep them lubricated. At a constant 400 rpm the engine's oil system worked, and the plane was ready for the cross-country steam train trip.[117] Further, during the trip the level of security was so high that the railroad brakemen working the trip had to disembark rather than walk along the "top-secret" cars, necessitating full stops on a regular basis.[118] Nevertheless, the Bell XP-59A arrived at its new home on September 19, 1942.

The Bell/GE team worked feverishly over the next week to prepare the plane for flight. By September 26, it was ready for engine run-ups. The left engine was tested first. It would not start. One of the technicians had not removed the wooden air inlet plugs, and there was no air to the engine. The shame-faced tech "pulled the plug," and the engine roared to life. The right engine also came to life immediately; testing was off to a promising start.[119]

On September 30, Larry Bell made his appearance at Muroc. The Bell chief test pilot, Robert Stanley, prepared to make the first taxiing runs with the jet. Bob Stanley was uniquely qualified for his highly dangerous job. He had worked at Douglas Aircraft Company in the 1930s and had received his B.Sc. in Aeronautical Engineering at Cal Tech. He had been a test pilot in the Navy and at United Aircraft Corporation before joining the Bell team in 1940.[120] His expertise was invaluable in the jets' first flights. Stanley ran up the engines and made a number of low- and high-speed passes in front of the Bell and GE teams. He wanted to actually take off, but the request was denied by Bell. Bell wanted the "official government representatives" there first, and Stanley conceded.

On October 1, with Stanley at the controls, the Bell XP-59A was conducting taxi trials once again. The official crowd was still a day away, but the Bell sources record that the plane took off and climbed to heights of 25 and 100 feet in consecutive tests.[121] On October 2, Dr. Durand (Head of NACA), Colonel Craigie (chief of the Experimental Aircraft Section at Wright Field), and Major Heenan (British Air Commission) were in attendance, and Stanley officially became the first American jet pilot.[122] The XP-59A climbed to 6,000 feet and proved that the Bell project was viable. Stanley made a second flight and was amazed that "the speed in level flight at 10,000 feet was surprisingly high."[123] Colonel Craigie was the pilot for the third flight of the XP-59A, making him the second American jet pilot, and the first U.S. military jet pilot. Stanley flew the final flight of the day, but when he had troubles with the landing gear, he extended the wheels and landed. The XP-59A Number 1 did not fly again until the end of October. But on that historic day, America entered the jet age.

The Americans were the third contender in the jet race and the last to create a jet during the war years.[124] Following the British engine designs, GE fabricated a turbojet with uniquely American characteristics and improvements. Building on years of materials research and supercharger development, the GE team, led by Sanford Moss, improved on the British-designed Whittle W.1X. And, with American resources, industry, and security, GE copied the British technology and outstripped British performance. The Americans could boast a new level of efficiency for their centrifugal-flow turbojet design. Interestingly, it was only one year from the time the

W.1X left England for the United States until the American redesigned jet engine, the GE I-A, flew for the first time. This development is a testament to the ingenuity and diligence of the GE team in copying existing, albeit British, technology, while at the same time employing American techniques and research into the improved model.

The Bell XP-59A airframe was a novel improvement on existing aerodynamic design. While the Secret Six built on existing aircraft technology, there were substantial improvements that attest the inventiveness of the Bell team. The cockpit was pressurized, the first pressurized American design. The plane was designed to incorporate new power plants untested in the United States. Bell and his designers had only Whittle's word and their skills to determine the outcome of their design efforts. And the government secrecy restrictions hampered the team in their lack of outside information. But the plane in and of itself, while a vast improvement, only came into being after official government interest following on existing power plant technology. Bell Aircraft Company in the end was an excellent airframe designer, but the impetus for America's first jet came from outside influences.

Unfortunately for the Americans, even government and civilian research and development were not concerned about turbojet technology. Research in the United States focused on improving existing conventional piston-engine technology and making it as efficient as possible. There were rumblings of turbojet interest, but for the Americans, the technology was too theoretical for concurrent development in the closing years of the 1930s. Americans did not see the end of the usefulness of the piston-engine even as it was reaching the apex of its effectiveness.[125]

The single most influential element in the development of the American jet program was General "Hap" Arnold. He had traveled to Britain, had consulted the Air Ministry and Lord Beaverbrook, and saw the existing British technology. He was responsible for bringing the jet engine to American shores and assigning government contracts for the development of the American jet program. In the end, as James Young points out, America was "Riding England's Coattails."[126] The Americans did build and fly turbojet aircraft, but were years behind the Germans and the British, both of which were already fighting in the skies over Europe. The Americans benefited from British technology, and eventually surpassed British turbojet successes, but not yet.

This is not to say the Americans would have never developed turbojet technology. Most of the pieces were in place for natural evolution of jets. But the Americans were focused on improving applied technology. It took the catalyst of war to introduce Americans to the revolutionary technology.

Heinkel He 178 V1 (Germany). The world's first turbojet-powered aircraft. Powered by Hans von Ohain's HeS 3b engine. (Courtesy the National Museum of the Air Force)

Gloster E.28/39 "Pioneer" (Britain). The Allies' first turbojet-powered aircraft. Powered by Frank Whittle's W.1 engine. (Courtesy the National Museum of the Air Force)

Bell XP-59A Airacomet (USA). The first American turbojet-powered aircraft. Powered by a copy of Frank Whittle's British jet engine, manufactured by General Electric, the GE I-A. (Courtesy the National Museum of the Air Force)

Heinkel He 280 V1 (Germany). Heinkel's prototype twin-jet engine fighter which later lost the competition to the series production Messerschmitt Me 262. (Courtesy the National Museum of the Air Force)

Messerschmitt Me 209 V1 (Germany). The prototype Me 209, the proposed successor to the ubiquitous Me 109, and direct competitor to the Me 262. Seen here with propeller spinning prior to an early test flight. (Courtesy the National Museum of the Air Force)

Messerschmitt Me 262 V2 (Germany). The second prototype Me 262, with original tailwheel configuration. (Courtesy the National Museum of the Air Force)

Messerschmitt Me 262 A2a (Germany). A series-production Me 262 shown in bomber configuration. Note the ETC 503 bomb racks. (Courtesy the National Museum of the Air Force)

Messerschmitt Me 262 A2a (Germany). Close-up of bomb configured Me 262. (Courtesy the National Museum of the Air Force)

Junkers Jumo 004 turbojet engine (Germany). Series production German turbojet engine which powered nearly all of the German wartime jet aircraft. (Courtesy the National Museum of the Air Force)

Arado Ar 234 B (Germany). The German production jet bomber. First produced in 1944, the production of the Ar 234 allowed the Me 262 to be built exclusively as a fighter. (Courtesy the National Museum of the Air Force)

Heinkel He 162 Volksjäger (Germany). The last-ditch effort by the Heinkel Company to provide a viable mass-produced jet fighter for the collapsing Reich. Powered by either the Jumo 004 or the BMW 003 turbojet engine, the plane was intended to stem the tide of Allied airpower. (Courtesy the National Museum of the Air Force)

Messerschmitt Project P.1101 (Germany). An incomplete project that examined the theoretical benefits of swing-wing technology. Captured by the Americans and brought to the United States after the war, P.1101 became the design basis for the Bell X-5. (Courtesy the National Museum of the Air Force)

Gloster Meteor Mk I (Britain). Britain's first production jet fighter. The Meteor made its debut during the war, but was relegated to Home Defense and never saw combat against German jet fighters, although it was useful against German V-1 "Buzz Bombs." (Courtesy the National Museum of the Air Force)

General Electric GE I-A turbojet engine (USA). Based almost entirely on the British Whittle-designed Power Jets W.1, the GE I-A powered the Bell Airacomet. Built by a number of American and British companies, later versions powered the first generation of both American and British jet planes. (Courtesy the National Museum of the Air Force)

Lockheed XP-80a Shooting Star (USA). Lockheed's miracle jet fighter, designed and built in fewer than 180 days. The later P-80 became the first series production American jet fighter and was the victor in the first jet-to-jet combat during the Korean Conflict. (Courtesy the National Museum of the Air Force)

Bell XF-83 Airarattler experimental heavy jet fighter (USA). The ill-fated Bell Aircraft Company follow-on to the Airacomet, the XF-83 was doomed by poor performance and competing designs. (Courtesy the National Museum of the Air Force)

4

Jets at War: The Operational Record of the German Jets

The operational record of the German jet program is a mixed bag of genius and sheer idiocy. At their best, the German jets and their pilots showed proficiency and patriotism. At its worst, the German jet program was mishandled and misused. This chapter will outline German jet operations and their impact on the war. Although a full third of Me 262s were lost to ground accidents due to their unstable landing gear, and another third were lost in transport or from engine failure, there were a full third delivered to combat squadrons for aerial operations. This third—approximately 400 Me 262s and additional other jet types—was the foundation of the German jet force in the air against the Allies. Further, the Luftwaffe was the only air force to use jet aircraft in a hostile combat environment. The British did use their jets to a limited extent against German V-1 flying bombs, but the bombs did not shoot back! The Me 262s, as well as the Arado and Heinkel jets, flew against Allied opposition over German airspace. The Germans needed qualitative superiority to combat Allied quantitative superiority. In the end, the Germans developed their jet program out of sheer necessity, while the Allies had the advantage of time to develop advanced designs.

The Germans led the pack. Initial testing with the Heinkel centrifugal-flow turbojet engine and the He 178 turbojet aircraft were promising, but the Germans decided to pursue the more advanced and potentially more powerful axial-flow engine design. This engine, married with the Messerschmitt Me 262 twin-engine turbojet aircraft design, built the basis for jet aircraft testing in the heady days of the Third Reich, while the war was still under the German's control. The Me 262, designed from the beginning as an air superiority fighter aircraft, set the foundations for the German jet program during World War II.

All of the pilots to fly the Messerschmitt plane were enamored by the speed and maneuverability of the clean design.[1] The plane was a delight to fly, and Adolf Galland, the general of Fighters, among others, requested immediate production of the revolutionary weapon.[2] Unfortunately for the fighter general, and the Luftwaffe as a whole, the Me 262 was not yet ready for series production and the "bugs" were still being ironed out in the Jumo 004 turbojet engine design.

Galland had flown one of the tail-dragging prototypes (V3). Neither the airframe (even in its final design stages) nor the engine—which was still undergoing extensive testing—were ready for series production. Therefore, when Galland stated in May 1943, at an RLM meeting, to forgo production of the proposed second-generation Me 209, and replace all available Me (Bf) 109 production with Me 262, his statement was fantastic and baseless.[3] The RLM did choose the Me 262 over the Me 209, at a rate of 100 per month, but series production of the Me (Bf) 109 continued. The Me 262 was the choice of the RLM as the only jet fighter of the Luftwaffe, but even the RLM was not willing to take existing piston fighters out of the skies for the potential of the jet.[4] Galland only got 10 percent of the 1,000 jet fighters per month he requested for his Luftwaffe.

Requests notwithstanding, Messerschmitt was called before the RLM to give his opinion. In June, the RLM asked the aircraft manufacturer for his outlook on the future production of aircraft.[5] Messerschmitt stated that he would be unable to shift production capabilities to the new jet design before January 1944 due to limited capacity and shortage of workers. The requested first 100 completed aircraft were not projected before May 1944! Messerschmitt outlined that he would be in no position to produce numbers higher than 8 in February 1944, 21 in March, 40 in April, and 60 in May; the first 100 aircraft therefore might be delivered by May 1944. Messerschmitt proposed 60 machines per month delivered to the Luftwaffe between June and November, production figures rising to an estimated high of 400 aircraft per month by September 1945. He based his proposals on the production capabilities of two entire factories producing nothing but Me 262s.[6] Furthermore, it is important to note that Messerschmitt promised only airframes. He made no indication of coordination with Junkers for the power plants for the revolutionary aircraft. His figures were for Me 262 airframes alone, without engines.

It was not until later that month (June) that the first prototype to include a tricycle landing gear configuration with a nosewheel was tested. V5 was flown successfully, and the pilots reported better handling and better vision while on the ground.[7] However, the Opel-designed undercarriage continued to plague the Me 262 program throughout its operational lifetime. The lack of materials made it necessary to use hollow tube steel for the landing gear shafts rather than solid shafts. On the heavy aircraft, this caused frequent collapse, especially of the nosewheel, during landing and towing. The problem was never rectified, and numerous Me 262s were lost due to landing gear failure.

Testing was severely marred at the end of July when, in quick succession, two Me 262 prototypes (V4 and V5) crashed. Messerschmitt was down to two prototypes for testing—V1 and V3. The crashes led to a decision by Hitler for caution in aircraft production.[8] Messerschmitt, who took Milch's cancellation of the Me 209 program personally, called on Hitler for an audience. Messerschmitt met with the Führer and informed him that the Me 262 used more fuel than a conventional piston-engine aircraft, without clarifying for Hitler that the jets used low-grade diesel, fuel that Germany had in abundance.[9] Hitler, being uninformed at best, and often misinformed, ordered the resurrection of the Me 209 program. He wanted to make sure there were planes, no matter how obsolescent, for the Luftwaffe.[10] This order was followed, and supported in yet another RLM conference in August. It was decided that in addition to the 1,000 Me 262s that were to be produced each month, a total of 3,000 Me 209s and FW 190s were to be produced *as well*![11] Messerschmitt was expected to be able to produce both the Me 262 and the 209 in quantities that were unrealizable for either program, let alone both. But, the effects of the RLM decision were negligible. The dubious Me 209 program wasted scarce materials and manpower, as well as valuable time, but in the end the Me 262 program suffered from more obvious reasons—a lack of engines. Further, Hitler's strategy was appropriate: the Luftwaffe could have used the Me 209 if the Me 262 had been a total failure. And, it must be remembered that Messerschmitt was coming off a series of unfortunate decisions himself, among them the Me 210, a twin-engine multipurpose fighter. In addition, without engines for the Me 262— as yet unavailable from Junkers—the Me 209 program would still fly with conventional piston engines already being produced.

Me 262 production faced another significant setback on August 17, when the USAAF bombed the Messerschmitt works at Regensburg. Most of the manufacturing jigs for the production Me 262 were damaged or destroyed in a raid specifically intended to disrupt the Luftwaffe's aircraft supply.[12] Messerschmitt initiated a plan to disperse Me 262 production into forest factories to avoid the Combined Bomber Offensive (CBO).[13] This move both helped and hindered the Me 262 program. After moving the production facilities to the forest factories near Augsburg and Oberammergau in early 1944, plane manufacturing was safer from Allied bombing. But, because of the subsequent need to transport the assembled components for final assembly, the chaos in the German transportation network brought on by the CBO created bottlenecks and significantly delayed final assembly of the jets.

In November 1943, two important events influenced the future course of Me 262 development. The Me 209 program was finally, and officially, dropped, and Messerschmitt was ordered to channel all resources and efforts into the Me 262 program. In addition, November 26 was the first time Hitler saw the new jet aircraft. His reaction was unanticipated and caused quite a stir then, and continues to influence the record to this day. Hitler, upon seeing the Me 262 for the first time, exclaimed that this was finally the high-speed bomber that he had envisioned.[14] He inquired whether the Me 262 could carry bombs, and Messerschmitt responded in the affirmative. However, it is important to note that the Me 262 was still undergoing testing, and that no production models were forthcoming. It did not matter if it could carry bombs, or if the correct hardware was ready, the plane was not even ready for serial production. Messerschmitt worked on the bomb racks problem, but the question posed by Hitler was moot; testing on the prototypes needed to be completed to determine whether the airframe and engines were viable at all, even before it could be determined if the plane could be used as either a bomber or fighter. Incidentally, Hitler ordered that the Me 262 be produced only as a high-speed bomber until he changed his mind in November 1944 when the "true" jet bomber, the Arado Ar 234 became available in numbers. But even then the Me 262 was only just becoming available to operational units, and it was entering service as a fighter, contrary to Hitler's orders.[15]

The other half of the German jet program equation was also facing difficulties. The Junkers Motor Works (*Junkers Motorenwerke*) or Jumo was given the go-ahead for production of the Jumo 004 axial-flow turbojet engine in June 1943.[16] But Junkers faced a major roadblock; there was a shortage of raw materials for the construction of the delicate engines. Dr. Anselm Franz was in charge of the redesign of the Jumo 004 for production. Following the successful redesign based on materials restrictions, there were finally enough engines ready for service aircraft by spring 1944. The engines were fitted to awaiting airframes, and the Luftwaffe officially took over testing the new jet aircraft.

Erprobungskommando (testing squadron—shortened to *Ekdo*) 262 was formed in December 1943 but did not receive its first jet aircraft until April 1944.[17] The jet was Me 262 V8 (VI+AC). This refutes the claims of Manfred Boehme, John Foremen, and S.E. Harvey, who state that Ekdo 262 received 16 production Me 262s in April 1944.[18] There could not have been 16 Me 262s delivered because they had not yet been built. According to production figures presented by *General der Jagdflieger* (General of Fighters) Adolf Galland, the first nine production Me 262s were not even finished before the end of May 1944.[19] Although there were no Me 262s available for operations the day the Allies invaded the continent on June 6, 1944, output was increased and in June 26 Me 262s—with engines—rolled off the production lines. Manufacturing increased and Messerschmitt was manufacturing 124

Me 262s per month by the end of the year.[20] These completed airframes went from the Messerschmitt factory straight to operational squadrons.

Ekdo 262 quickly set to work ironing out the bugs in the new aircraft. Immediate concerns arose with regard to the Junkers engines. The redesign had saved valuable resources, but the engine's operational life span was only 10 hours. After 10 hours, the engines required complete overhauls, specifically with regard to high-stress and high-heat parts. The pilot reports continually criticized the poor performance of the Junkers engines at low speeds, especially at takeoff and landing.[21]

The Ekdo 262 pilots also suggested other improvements; this was not uncommon when new aircraft arrived for series trials to the Luftwaffe pilots. The plane was finally put through realistic flight testing, and unexpected problems arose immediately. Initially, the Me 262s were delivered with fabric-covered control surfaces. At speeds over 750 kmph, the fabric would flutter or bubble, causing the pilot to lose control.[22] Immediate action was taken at the factory to rectify the problem; therefore it is important to note that Messerschmitt himself commented that the plane was not ready for combat and needed more testing and modifications.[23] The plane was cutting-edge technology and had to be modified as problems arose, but it quickly became obvious that the plane needed further improvement before serial production could be initiated.

Ultimately, the German pilots focused on two areas of improvement for the plane. Unfortunately for the Luftwaffe, both problems were outside the sphere of Messerschmitt's influence. The weak undercarriage was one important concern. As noted, a full third of the Me 262s lost to accident could be attributed to the landing gear supplied by Opel. But, in the midst of shortages, there were no other alternatives. The second area of concern for the pilots was the engines. Junkers produced the best engine design with regard to the material constraints when the Jumo 004B-1 was "frozen" for production in summer 1943. And, the engine was continually modified to its highest tolerances with the 004B-4 and 004C models, delivered by the beginning of December 1944.[24] Modifications continued to improve the high-altitude and high-speed characteristics of the engine, but low-speed problems remained throughout. Eventually, the Luftwaffe had to allocate an entire Focke Wulf FW 190 *Geschwader* (squadron)—*JG 54*—to defend the jets as they took off and landed. An estimated 33 percent of all Me 262 accidents were attributed to engine failure or malfunction. Thus, almost two-thirds of losses due to accidents could have been avoided with more attention to these two vital components of the German jet. Further, there were more jets lost to accidents than to combat operations. The point is obvious that the plane was not yet ready for serial production but was rushed. But by the same token, it was the only option that the Luftwaffe had to combat the Allies in the air over Germany.

While Ekdo 262 was still testing the Me 262 to prepare it for serial production, Hitler once again interfered with the technological development. Incensed that his order to produce the new jet as a bomber was being ignored, Hitler reiterated his demand to produce the plane as a bomber only.[25] He went so far as to say that the Me 262 was to be addressed as a *Schnellbomber* (fast bomber), and any reference to the plane as a fighter would be punished. But it is important to note that Ekdo 262 was still only testing the prototype, and unarmed plane. The Luftwaffe pilots were still testing the viability of the aircraft alone, and had not embarked on weapons testing of any sort—as a fighter or a bomber. Also, there was no appropriate bombsight for the jet. All future bombing with the high-speed plane was done by guesswork. Messerschmitt, although he had initially confirmed the Führer's wishes regarding the jet as a bomber, had not up to May 1944 even addressed the issue of an appropriate bomb rack. It was only a coincidence that on the same day that Göring passed on Hitler's message that the jet was not to be discussed as anything but a bomber that the Me 262 first carried bombs. On May 28, 1944, the Me 262 V10 (the 10th prototype) carried a 250 kg bomb on an ETC 503 bomb rack along the centerline of the aircraft.[26] The installation of the bomb rack, and the added weight of the bomb, hampered the speed of the plane, the single clear advantage it possessed. But the plane—even with bombs—was still faster than anything in the Allied inventory. Hitler's intention was for the bomb-carrying Me 262 jet to be used as a nuisance bomber against the imminent Allied invasion of the continent. The plan was to have the planes drop bombs in the confusion of the landings and escape using their superior speed. Unfortunately for the Luftwaffe, there were no Me 262s ready for combat operations, in any form, when the Allied contingent of Americans, British, and Canadians waded ashore at Normandy on June 6, 1944.

In June 1944, as the Allies established a foothold on the continent, the Me 262 went into series production. The problems with the landing gear and engines went uncorrected; there was neither time nor resources. The Luftwaffe required a substantially superior fighter to combat the effects of the Combined Bomber Offensive and had to rely on Messerschmitt's creation no matter how flawed. Although it was not perfect, the Me 262 was constructed in the hopes that it would be a decisive weapon against the Allied bombers in the air and against Allied targets on the ground. The Me 262 was rushed into production in spite of its technological inadequacies because there was simply no other option. The Luftwaffe was desperate and had to gamble with any weapon that offered even the slightest potential of countering the Allied superiority in the air.

The Me 262, the fruits of the German jet program, entered production with a number of flaws: the engines were delicate; the landing gear was prone to collapse and caused frequent accidents; and the plane was brand-new technology that required pilot training. But, the Germans were able to put jets into production and into combat. And, the German jet was qualitatively superior to any Allied plane. Thus, the Germans entered the age of jet combat first, and had a large technological lead on the Allies in the summer of 1944.

By the time production of the Me 262 began in 1944, there was a lack of strategic raw materials for the highly demanding jet program. The scarce materials that made up the jet engines—chrome, molybdenum, nickel—were unavailable to the German war effort.[27] They had been gathered prior to the war,[28] but there was limited access once the war started, and the stockpiles were quickly depleted. In all fairness to Luftwaffe procurement, no one had any idea that these materials should be saved for the future jet program, which was still only in the planning stages in 1941. But by the time Albert Speer was appointed Minister of Armaments and Production in 1942,[29] material stockpiles were dwindling and production was inefficient. His implemented plan reorganized efficiency of German production at the same time as setting priorities for materials.[30] Further, the whole system was reconstructed once again in 1944 with the creation of the *Jägerstab*, or Fighter Staff.[31] Cooperation was increased, and German war production was focused on the production of fighter aircraft to defend the Reich from the Combined Bomber Offensive. Fighter planes received the top priority for materials, and the Me 262 was placed at the top of the pecking order. The jet program had the first priority over all scarce materials that were available.[32] But even the German jet suffered from a lack of materials. The Jumo engines incorporated substitute materials in production severely limiting operational life and efficiency.

Me 262 production was also hampered by a lack of skilled workers in Germany. Although there were ample unskilled laborers—drawn from the masses of noncombatant Germans, prisoners-of-war, and foreign laborers—there was a lack of skilled, technical workers in Germany. Skilled aircraft designers and machinists were in short supply as is indicated by Messerschmitt's constant requests for skilled laborers.[33] The lack of skilled workers had a detrimental effect on the final product. In many cases, the planes were flawed when they were delivered to their operational squadrons and required extensive modification and repair prior to combat.

Another problem faced by the Luftwaffe as a whole was a lack of fuel. But this did not extend to the jets. There were problems in transporting fuel for the jet aircraft; the CBO by 1944 had nearly crippled the German transportation network.[34] But there were ample supplies of fuel available throughout the war. The reason for this is that the jets ran on J2 (Jet 2) fuel: diesel. Bombing raids hampered fuel production,[35] but as opposed to high-grade aviation fuel there were stockpiles of J2 even at the end of the war. The *United States Strategic Bombing Survey* reports that there was still 100,000 tons of diesel in reserve at the end of the war.[36]

Another problem faced by the Luftwaffe in the closing stages of the war was a lack of pilots. However, the jet program did not suffer for need of experienced pilots, as has been argued.[37] The Luftwaffe on the whole was short of experienced pilots due to a lack of training, and high attrition, but the jet pilots (specifically in *Jagdverband JV* 44) were all experienced pilots under the command of one of Germany's greatest aces, Adolf Galland. Overall, the Luftwaffe pilots suffered because of Allied air superiority and the losses were made up by inexperienced crews.[38] The new pilots were spending less time in training, were severely inexperienced when thrust into combat, and flew aircraft that were outclassed (by spring 1944) by all Allied types. But this was not the case for the jet pilots, who were handpicked to be the foundation for the Luftwaffe's jet fighter group. While they did have to familiarize themselves with the new machines, they were all veteran combat pilots with years of experience and distinguished awards.

The biggest problem facing the German jet pilots was the Allies. The material superiority of the Allies contributed to the destruction of the Luftwaffe on a number of levels. The numerical superiority of the Allied fighters meant that there were going to be a lot of German fighters lost to attrition. This of course led to the lack of pilots mentioned above. In the final months of the war, the Germans were producing more planes than ever: between 2,500 and 3,500 single-and twin-engine fighter planes per month.[39] However, the western Allies (United States and Britain) alone were producing 9,000 fighters per month in the last full year of the war.[40] It must be remembered that there were only 1,624 jets of all types—and only 1,294 Me 262s—produced by the end of the war; all other Luftwaffe types and pilots were outclassed by the Allies. Clearly, the Allies were in command of the air through material superiority.

In addition to the fighters, the Allies were manufacturing 3,500 bombers per month.[41] The Allied bombers faced less opposition each day as German fuel was restricted and pilots were killed. The bombers became virtually immune from the defenders of the Reich in the closing days of the war through sheer numerical superiority.

In the midst of the defeat from the air Messerschmitt began series production of the Me 262 A-1. In the summer of 1944, manufacture of the jet began in earnest. The accelerated production schedule attempted to remedy problems in the airframe design as they were uncovered by Ekdo 262, but some of the problems continued without repair. Thus, series production began even before Ekdo 262 was done with initial flight testing; delivery of the first production Me 262s began even while flight testing continued.

Production centers for the Me 262 were almost as interesting as the plane itself. Messerschmitt's "forest factories" hid production facilities in numerous wooden structures for subassembly of the aircraft. One example was the plant at Horgau outside of Augsburg. Twenty-one wooden buildings, staffed by 845 workers, produced the tail and nose assemblies for the plane. The roofs of the buildings were painted green and covered by trees, making them invisible from the air. It was not until after the war that the Allies learned the exact location of the factory.[42] But the forest factories were vulnerable in other ways. The dispersed manufacturing centers relied more heavily on the fragile German transportation networks.

Other production centers were designed not to hide, but to withstand Allied bombardment. Two kinds of underground factories were used that were impervious to Allied bombing raids. The Germans initially used abandoned mines and mountain tunnels to relocate production to areas safe from Allied bombing. However, conditions in these workshops were poor at best; they suffered from a lack of heat, light, ventilation, and sanitation. One of the main problems was with the handling of materials and workers. In abandoned mines, vertical elevators were used to transport materials and workers to the shops. In the mines and tunnels that had horizontal entrances, there was a danger from cave-ins. Further, few of the underground factories were lined with concrete and dust and falling rock were a constant hazard.[43] Regardless of the conditions, the underground facilities were almost immune to Allied bombing attacks. Thus, due to its high priority status, the Me 262 was second only to the V-2 rocket to be moved to underground production facilities.[44]

In addition to "natural" facilities, there were man-made bunkers designed to house production. Three massive bunkers for use by the Messerschmitt works began construction near Landsberg am Lech. Code-named *Ringeltaube* (Wood Pigeon), the three bunkers were designed as facilities to house Me 262 production from start to finish. The bunkers were designed as multilevel, 1,000,000 square-foot production centers that could not only accommodate trains delivering materials but were also close enough to Autobahns for immediate flight testing of finished Me 262s.[45] It is interesting that the Germans initially dispersed production from larger facilities to smaller factories, specifically forest factories and underground facilities, but at the end of the war planned for the recentralization of production in massive bunkers. The Herculean efforts to centralize production in massive bunkers did not pay off for the jet program; no Me 262s were produced in the Landsberg bunkers, which were not even completed by May 1945. And, according to the *United States Strategic Bombing Survey*, the greatest achievement of the Allied bombing effort was in the response by the Germans to evade it. In the end the Germans wasted manpower and material building bombproof shelters for the production of war material. According to the USSBS, "The aircraft industry was blasted out of its well-planned plants in established industrial centers and forced to disperse to hundreds of makeshift factories all over Germany. It burrowed under the ground, fled to wooden sheds in the forests, and finally, at the end of the war, was in the process of covering itself with mountains of reinforced concrete."[46]

The production schedule for the Me 262s was originally set by Messerschmitt: the first 100 aircraft by the middle of May 1944 with 60 Me 262s a month thereafter until November, when an expanded production schedule would commence.[47] After November 1944, production increased to a maximum of 400 aircraft per month by September 1945.[48] However, due to a lack of engines from the Jumo factory, construction of the jet planes was severely curtailed and only nine production machines were built prior to the Allied invasion of the continent.[49] Incidentally, the first 100 Me 262s were not completed before the middle of August 1944.[50] The planes were not available because of a lack of engines and the extensive modifications advised by Ekdo 262; the testing group ordered specifically to find and suggest improvements to the novel weapon.

And even though it was ordered into service as a bomber, extenuating circumstances closed the door on Hitler's high-speed bomber concept.[51] There were no operational Me 262s—either as fighters or bombers—ready for June 6, 1944, for the plane was still in the testing phases. Further, there was neither a suitable bombsight nor weapons racks available: the Hitler order had been ignored. The plane eventually was fitted with a generic bomb rack, but was never more than a nuisance bomber even when it was used in that role.

The first combat squadron to get the new plane *KG(J)* 51— *Kampfgeschwader (Jäger)* for bombing group (fighter)—was formed on June 3, 1944.[52] The pilots, transferred from twin-engine Me 410 fighter-bombers, underwent transition training beginning on June 20. *KG(J)* 51 was a *Jabo* (fighter/bomber) squadron equipped with the new bomb-carrying Me 262s. With only two (of the original four) 30-mm cannons, and two 250 kg bombs, the role of *KG(J)* 51 was to provide tactical support for the German land forces. Although the bombing was not at all accurate, the pilots flew missions against targets such as bridges and supply lines of the rapidly advancing Allies. Other *KG(J)* units were formed before the end of the war, but most were in name only; *KG(J)* 54 was the only other *Jabo* Me 262 squadron in operation at the end of hostilities.

Other units equipped with the new jet, in addition to Ekdo 262 and *KG(J)* 51, included *Einsatzkommando Braunegg*. This unit evaluated the Me 262 as a reconnaissance aircraft.[53] Armed with only cameras, *Braunegg* used the Me 262 to take high-altitude and high-speed photos of the Allies. According to German records, *Einsatzkommando Braunegg* was in operation before the Allied invasion and took recon photos of the Allied buildup in England. However, these claims are refuted by the British.[54]

In the meantime, the Me 262 had been busy chasing enemy planes and making a name for itself. The first "kill" came on July 25, 1944, when an Me 262 caught and shot at a high-flying De Havilland *Mosquito* reconnaissance plane. The high-altitude, high-speed *Mosquito* was flying a routine photo reconnaissance flight over Germany from Britain to Italy. *Mosquito*s were used to gather photographic intelligence for bomb-damage assessment and target selection because they were high-flying and fast.[55] Their speed made them virtually immune to all contemporary German aircraft. On this day, the British pilot noticed a plane in his rearview, but thought nothing of it. When he noticed that it was getting closer, the British pilot began to dive to pick up speed. The Ekdo 262 Me 262 still caught up and fired on the British plane. The German, *Leutnant* Alfred Schreiber, lost the British plane in the clouds, assumed the plane destroyed, and submitted a "kill" claim. The British pilot limped his plane to an airfield in Italy, only to confirm the Allies worst fears that the Germans had developed an operational jet aircraft for combat. The encounter was the first Allied report of an engagement with the Me 262.[56]

By August 20, Hitler allowed one in 20 Me 262s to be built as fighters, and by September 20, Hitler finally agreed with Speer that the Me 262 production should be shifted back to fighters.[57] The change in attitude came as the first "true" jet bombers were coming off the production lines. The Arado Ar 234 series jet bombers were the high-speed bombers Hitler was looking for, and the Me 262 was released to perform its natural function as an air superiority fighter.

German jet pilots continued to harass the Allies in the air with piecemeal attacks on reconnaissance planes and lone bombers. The first Allied fighter did not contact a German jet until August 28 when American P-47 Thunderbolts attacked a *KG(J)* 51 pilot returning to base. The Me 262 was most vulnerable during landing, and the Americans were able to catch up to and shoot down the German jet. Pilots Joe Myers and M.D. Croy shared the first Allied victory over a German jet.[58] The fight between Allied piston-engine fighters and German jets had begun.

Because of the new Hitler order, and because of the increasing need for the jet, the first operational jet fighter squadrons were established in the Luftwaffe. General of Fighters Adolf Galland was given permission to form a jet fighter squadron on September 26, 1944, with the new Me 262s that were coming off the production lines. Galland formed the first jet fighter unit from members of Ekdo 262 and ZG 26 (*Zerstörergeshwader*—Destroyer squadron, the German term for twin-engine heavy fighter squadrons). The new unit was officially designated *JG* 7 (*Jagdgeschwader*—Fighter Squadron) but was initially named *Kommando Nowotny* for its commander Major Walter Nowotny. *Kommando Nowotny/JG* 7 was based at Achmer.[59]

Kommando Nowotny was instructed to continue testing the novel weapon without combat. But their grace period was cut short on October 7 with an air raid alarm. Although the Germans had only a dozen aircraft, and they had not developed high-speed tactics, Nowotny ordered the unit to scramble. The first operational sortie for the unit went badly for the Germans: three Me 262s were shot down in exchange for two Allied planes. The three Me 262s were caught by American P-51 *Mustangs* during takeoff, and the Americans took advantage of the jets' low takeoff speed. Three jets and one pilot were lost. Immediately after the fiasco, Nowotny requested fighter protection for the jet airfield, to cover the jets as they took off and landed. Nowotny's request was granted, and Focke-Wulf Fw 190s from JG 54 transferred to Achmer to provide fighter cover for the jets.[60] The removal of yet more fighters from the defense of the Reich was a necessary evil to provide protection for the jets. The benefit was that the Allies were reluctant to attack the jets that were protected by piston-engine fighters. The ruse worked; there was a substantial decrease in the number of jets lost to Allied fighters during takeoff and landing.

Over the remainder of the autumn, *Kommando Nowotny* was engaged in a pitched battle against the American bomber offensive. There were many teething problems with the new jets in addition to the questionable location of the twin airfields at Achmer and Hesepe. These airfields were located directly on the path of the American bomber stream into and returning from Germany, making them operationally effective for jet operations. The location was ideal for intercepting bombers, but the German jets were vulnerable to the accompanying American fighter escorts. And, as the bombers returned from their bombing runs into Germany, Allied fighters were often "cut loose" to attack targets of opportunity on the return trip. The preferred targets in this category were German jets and airfields.

On September 11, 1944, the first major combat between Me 262s and American heavy bombers took place. Up to this point, the jets had only attacked lone bombers or reconnaissance planes with any regularity. On that day, a handful of Me 262s joined piston-engine Me 109s and Fw 190s in an attack on the "Bloody Hundredth," the USAAF's 8th Air Force 100th Bomb Group. The Americans lost a total of 24 aircraft compared to 15 German piston fighters and no jets.[61] At this point, there was a growing Allied concern regarding the German jets. Although there were few jets in operation, Allied intelligence was unspecific on the capabilities of German jet manufacture or the number of available aircraft.[62] The Allies became concerned with the threat of the German jets and their impact on Allied air superiority. According to the commander of the British 2nd Tactical Air Force, Air Marshal Sir Arthur Coningham, "German jets could wash away our great air superiority tomorrow."[63] The Allies were anxious about the qualitative superiority of the German jets, while the Germans themselves were having trouble keeping more than a few dozen jets operational each month.

Kommando Nowotny did well combating the American air effort until November 8, 1944. On this day, Major Nowotny took off with one other pilot to intercept American bombers returning to England. Nowotny's wingman, Schall, was shot down but parachuted to safety. Nowotny, however, was not as lucky. After downing two American planes, he was last seen diving through the clouds and straight into the ground. However, due to conflicting reports, it is unclear whether Nowotny succumbed to Allied fighters or simply lost control of his plane.[64] In any event, the leader of *Kommando Nowotny* was dead. After a month of fighting the unit recorded 26 victories for 26 losses in combat—hardly a sterling record.[65] The squadron was immediately returned to the training grounds at Lechfeld for retraining and reassignment.

By November, Hitler released the Me 262 solely for fighter duties, but still stipulated that the jet be capable of carrying at least one 250 kg bomb. The order was expressly ignored by Messerschmitt and the operational fighter squadrons. In the end, this controversial directive had little impact on the operational life of the German jet. The Hitler order was not detrimental to the Me 262 as has been argued. The decision was irrelevant in the end; the operational Me 262s had been split between bomber (*KG(J)* 51) and fighter (*Kommando Nowotny*) groups, and neither had been particularly successful. *KG(J)* 51 was not equipped with Me 262s in any number to have any impact on the Allied invasion at Normandy; they were simply too late. Furthermore, without a proper bombsight, combined with a pitifully small bomb load, the jet as a bomber was virtually useless. According to Fritz Wendel, Messerschmitt's chief test pilot, "In level flight, the Revi [gun sight] was useless for accurate bombing. Pinpoint targets could not be hit. *Kommando Schenk* [the name of III *Gruppe KG(J)* 51] was therefore unable to claim any tactical successes."[66] By comparison, the fighters were not faring much better. Ekdo 262 and later *Kommando Nowotny* had been credited with only 40 "kills."[67] With limited numbers of jet aircraft available, and the numerous losses to accidents and combat, the Me 262 was not the decisive weapon that Hitler had envisioned as a bomber, nor the decisive weapon that Hitler got in a fighter. The Germans did not possess the machines to turn the tide of the Allied air offensive.

After a brief respite, *JG* 7 dropped its interim nickname *Kommando Nowotny*, and was reassigned. *General der Jagdflieger* Galland assigned *JG* 7 to Lechfeld to counter the Allied threat from the air. Gathering experienced fighter pilots from *JG* 3, *JG* 6, and members of *Kommando Nowotny*, the new *JG* 7 was reestablished on November 19, 1944.[68] Buildup continued through November and December, although Me 262 production was far behind proposed schedules. By the end of November, the squadron still had only 11 Me 262s for operations. Therefore, it was decreed that there were to be no engagements with escorted Allied bombers.[69] The unit was only allowed to attack unarmed reconnaissance planes. Losses of machines and pilots due to accidents continued to mount to the dismay of the unit commander, *Oberst* Johannes Steinhoff. During December alone, ten Me 262s were destroyed and five damaged in accidents with the corresponding loss of four pilots.[70]

During the last month of 1944, the Luftwaffe was busy reassigning pilots to jet squadrons. Beginning with bomber groups, pilots were being transferred for jet familiarization training. Bomber pilots were the first to be relocated for a number of reasons. Their previous multiengine training made them ideally suited to the twin-engine Me 262. Further, bomber construction had virtually ceased in the shrinking Reich and was replaced by fighter production. Finally, high-octane fuel required by the bombers was in short supply, while J2 diesel was still plentiful. Although five bomber squadrons were reassigned to jet training units (*KG* 6, 27, 30, 54, and 55), none were operational for months due to lack of available jet planes. *KG* 54 was not operational until February 1945; only one *KG* 6 *Gruppe* was operational by April 1945 and was named *Gefechtsverband Hogeback* after its squadron leader *Oberstleutnant* Hermann Hogeback. The other three *Geschwadern* (27, 30, and 55) were not operational with jets before the end of the war.[71]

Other jet-training units were set up to train raw recruits in jet operations. *Ergänzungs Jagdgeschwader* 2 (*EJG*—fighter-training squadron) was formed to train pilots at Lechfeld in jet operations. *Hauptmann* Horst Geyer commanded the training unit from the end of October 1944 until January 1945 when it was taken over by Major Heinz Bär. Bär later disbanded the training unit when he joined *JV* 44 (*Jagdverband*—fighter association), led by the charismatic but recently dispossessed Adolf Galland. *Ergänzungsgruppe Kampfgeschwader* 1 (*EKG*—bomber-training squadron) was also set up at Lechfeld to train Me 262 bomber pilots.

Further, there were two Me 262 reconnaissance units formed to take advantage of the high speeds of the jets for photography. *Kommando Braunegg* was a *Gruppe* in *Nahaufklärungsgruppe* 6 (*NAGr*) based at Münster-Hahndorf until February, when the unit went through a number of relocations until the end of the war. In addition, 1./*Versuchsverband OKL* (*Oberkommando der Luftwaffe*—Luftwaffe High Command) was formed as a special duties unit equipped with the most technologically advanced German and captured Allied aircraft for testing. This unit was amalgamated into *NAGr* 6 in March 1945.[72]

There were a number of Me 262 squadrons formed before the end of the war in a last-ditch effort to stem Allied air superiority. In addition to the above-mentioned *JG* 7, which is dealt with in depth by Manfred Boehme,[73] there were additional squadrons formed as jet fighter units. 10./*NJG* 11 (*Nachtjagdgeschwader*), also known as *Kommando Welter*, was a night-fighter squadron that employed the Me 262 A-1a and B-1a/U1 (two-seater) in night operations. From November 1944 to the end of the war, more than 160 sorties were flown by the 25 Me 262s that were operational with this squadron. *Kommando Welter* amassed 48 aerial victories against a loss of five aircraft and the pilots and radio operators. The unit focused its fury on the high-speed British *Mosquitos* that flew Pathfinder and reconnaissance missions over German airspace. *Welter* moved a number of times in the closing months of the war; finally forced to use Autobahns as airfields as the Allies overran German airfields.[74]

In an effort to protect industrial targets, one *Industrie Schutz Staffel* (*ISS*) squadron employed Me 262s in the defense of German industry around Lager-Lechfeld. The unit was ordered to protect industry in the immediate vicinity of its airfields.

Finally, one jet fighter unit was formed as the foremost jet fighter squadron of the Reich. *Jagdverband* (*JV*) 44 was formed in February 1945 from the best the Luftwaffe had to offer. General of Fighters Galland had been Göring's scapegoat for the failure of the Luftwaffe to withstand the Allied CBO. Galland had been demoted and shunned by the *Reichsmarshall* for his failure. But, as a favorite of Hitler's, Galland gained audience with the Führer to make his case. Galland's complaints about Göring went unheeded by Hitler, but Galland was allowed to form his own fighter squadron in the closing days of the war. Hitler went so far as to allow the former General of Fighters to handpick his men for the ultimate defense of the Reich. The formation of *JV* 44 echoed Baron Manfred von Richthoffen's formation of *Jasta* 1 in 1916. Galland gathered the best of the best, a "Squadron of *Experten*" to form the ultimate jet-fighter unit for a final stand against the Allies. The role call was the elite of the Luftwaffe fighter corps and included *Obersts* (Colonels) Heinz Bär, Johannes Steinhoff, Günther Lützow, and Gerhard Barkhorn. All had been *Geschwadern* commanders and had amassed extraordinary victory tallies and decorations. Although they realized that the end of the war was near, there was general consensus among the 17 *JV* 44 pilots that it was a privilege to fly the Luftwaffe's finest fighter, even in defeat. Many of the pilots came to the unit without transfer orders, some from retirement or leave, in an effort to become the first jet-fighter pilots in history.[75] *JV* 44 began operations on March 31, 1944, from the Munich-Reim airfield. These experts embarked on the final stages of the air war over Europe.

Outfitted with as many machines as they could find, and funneling the aircraft straight from the factories, initially there was no lack of machines. Until the end of the war when there were more jet pilots than available planes, *JV* 44 had the highest priority on aircraft and supplies. Fighting bravely until the last, *JV* 44 was responsible for the destruction of 50 Allied aircraft in its short 34-day operational history. And, even though Galland went to the hospital after being wounded on April 26,[76] *JV* 44 continued operations until it was overrun by the Allies on May 3.[77]

However, the Germans were only able to mount piecemeal jet counterattacks against overwhelming Allied air superiority. Even on the most active day for the Me 262, April 10, 1945, only 55 Me 262s were available against an attack by over 2,000 Allied aircraft.[78] The Luftwaffe had been hopelessly outclassed by the material superiority of the Allies. In the end, it was as Galland stated to his pilots, "Militarily speaking the war was lost. Even our action here cannot change anything. I shall continue to fight, because operation with the Me 262 has got hold of me, because I am proud to belong to the last fighter pilots of the German Luftwaffe. Only those who feel the same are to go on flying with me."[79] Needless to say, they all did.

The operational exploits of the Me 262 have been documented in detail by John Foreman and S.E. Harvey in their book *The Me 262 Combat Diary*.[80] Through research in the relevant documents at the Public Record Office in London, England, they have compiled an accurate account of the Allied planes shot down by Me 262 pilots. In addition, they outline the number of Me 262s lost in combat in the closing months of the war. Compared to Me 262 claims of 446 Allied planes downed between July 26, 1944, and the end of the war, the Allies (British and Americans) claimed 190 Me 262s destroyed in combat operations.[81] Therefore, according to the claims (which are quite accurate on both sides), the German jet pilots were able to shoot down 2.34 Allied planes for every Me 262 lost in combat. However, the Germans only produced 1,294 Me 262s in total.[82] This is compared to the Americans, who were able to build 49,761 aircraft between January and June 1945 alone.[83] The figure is indicative of the amazing material superiority of the Allies over the Germans, and their ability to outproduce the Germans at will. The Germans were hopelessly outclassed in aircraft production even though they possessed the technological edge with jet aircraft. There were not enough planes of any kind, let alone jet aircraft, to counter Allied production capabilities. But, even to the end of the war, the Me 262 was a potent weapon in the hands of capable pilots. The Germans had the technical edge, but little else.

In September 1944, another German jet program entered operations. The Arado Ar 234 *Blitzbomber* was introduced into the Luftwaffe inventory as the first purpose-built jet bomber. The Ar 234 was a twin-engine (and the later Ar 234-C was a four-engine) high-wing jet bomber. The first prototypes and series Ar 234-A models made use of a jettisonable takeoff trolley and landing skid, rather than retractable undercarriage, to conserve weight. The later Ar 234-B was fitted with retractable tricycle landing gear. The jet bomber could carry 1,500 kg of bombs, and flew at a top speed of 461 mph (742 kmph). The Arado project was built around the Jumo engines as well, and later versions carried the rival BMW 003 axial-flow turbojets for power. The final version of the Ar 234 to see operational service was the Ar 234-C, a four-engine jet bomber, with more thrust, higher payload, and slightly higher top speed.

The Ar 234 was delivered primarily to *KG 76* for daylight operations against Allied targets. Its most important contribution to the war effort was the bombing of the Bridge at Remagen on March 7, 1945. In the first instance of combined jet operations, Me 262s from *KG(J) 51* flew fighter cover for the jet bombers while they bombed the bridge.[84] The Ar 234 was used until the end of the war as both a nuisance bomber and a high-speed photo reconnaissance plane. Invulnerable to Allied piston planes due to its high speed, the Ar 234 perfectly suited these roles. Known units to receive the Ar 234 jet bomber included *KG 76*, 1*(F)/ Aufklärungsgruppe 5*, 33, 123 (Photo reconnaissance), and 1*(F)/* 100.[85] Only *KG 76* used the Ar 234 as a bomber; all other squadrons used the jet for aerial photography.

Interestingly, in the closing stages of the war, the Heinkel aircraft company designed, tested, and put into operation a last-ditch jet fighter for the Luftwaffe. The He 162 was proposed in September 1944 and designated *Salamander*, named for the creature with a mythical ability to live through fire.[86] The plane was given the official RLM designation *Volksjäger*— "Peoples Fighter." The He 162 was a developmental wonder, going from paper to reality in a matter of weeks; the first prototype flew on December 6, and the RLM immediately ordered planning, preproduction, and production of the improvisational fighter. Heinkel was able to mount the BMW 003 axial-flow turbojet on top of the mostly wooden aircraft and thus the plane was easy to construct. By the end of the war, only 116 He 162s were constructed, the entire production line.[87] Only 37 He 162s were delivered[88]; only one squadron, *JG 1*, was issued He 162s that were operational before the end of the war. Incidentally, *JG 1* surrendered a mere 4 days after receiving their first complement of He 162s.[89] Because of its novelty, the He 162 was forbidden from engaging Allied aircraft and only one combat report exists. An American P-51 Mustang pilot, flying the most advanced American fighter of the war, reported that the He 162 he encountered was very maneuverable and faster than his mount.[90] The plane was a mastery of mass production and design, the He 162 was built using a minimum of scarce materials and an abundance of wood and plywood products. It was easily built and reportedly easy to fly; hence the official RLM designation *Volksjäger*. The point is that Heinkel had developed wonderful jet fighter designs; they were simply rejected by the RLM. When he was again called upon at the end of the war, Heinkel was able to throw together an excellent design within the boundaries of wartime constraint that could have been used very effectively. But, his early and by far more important jet design was refused.

There were additional projects in the works for the future of the German jet program. Designs abounded and a few radical new prototypes existed in the mock-up and testing phases. Messerschmitt had developed a variable-sweep–wing jet aircraft (Project 1101) that was captured intact by the Americans. The Horton/Gotha team designed and built a flying wing, the Ho X, which was in its final stages of testing as another jet bomber. The Germans were well into the developmental stages of the engines and airframes that would eventually replace the Me 262 in combat; but the end of the war in Europe came before the Germans could make further jet programs operational.

In efforts to capture the products of the German jet program, the British, Americans, and Soviets were pitted against each other; programs were instituted on all sides to capture the technological resources of the defeated Reich. In the end, all of the victorious powers were able to gain scientific knowledge from the Germans as the world began the cold war. But it is interesting that the Germans also aided the Allies by handing over important technical drawings, information, and, in cases, undamaged equipment. For the most part, the Germans preferred to be captured by the Americans over all others, and this also facilitated the Americans' quest for German technology. The Americans, through German action and amazing organization, were able to gather important technical material and personnel for the benefit of the U.S. War Department.[91]

By the end of April 1945 in Europe, there were no illusions about the end of the war. The Allies were pressing in from all sides of the shrinking Reich and some hard decisions had to be made. In the last days before the German surrender, Adolf Galland decided to handover *JV* 44 Me 262s to the Americans. In an effort to contact the advancing American forces, Major Wilhelm Herget volunteered to fly a Fiesler Fi 156 *Storch* ("Stork" liaison aircraft) to contact the Americans and surrender. Herget was shot down by ground fire and no surrender was arranged.[92] As the Americans advanced on the *JV* 44 airfield, the crews destroyed their planes.[93] No *JV* 44 jets were turned over to the enemy.

However, other German jets found their way into Allied hands. Four *KG(J)* 51 Me 262 pilots, unwilling to become prisoner to the Soviets, decided to fly from their airfield at Zatec, north of Prague, and return to German soil. Two of the pilots made it to the American Zone of Occupation; one flew to Fassberg, where he surrendered to British forces. The last of the four, Wilhelm Batel, flew to Lüneberg Heath, close to his hometown, crash-landed his Me 262, hid for the night, and made his way home. A few days later he gave himself up to British authorities.[94]

Under similar circumstances two *KG(J)* 54 pilots also preferred American capture to Soviet imprisonment. They flew from Czechoslovakia to Austria on May 8 in order to surrender to American forces.[95] Finally, the ground crews of *NJG* 11 (Me 262) and *JG* 1 (He 162) lined up their aircraft on the tarmac at Leck in Schleswig-Holstein for takeover by British forces.[96]

For the Germans the war was over. But the most amazing story of technological development was still in its infancy. During the war, the Germans had been able to engineer first the centrifugal-flow then later the axial-flow turbojet for use in combat operations. Messerschmitt and Heinkel had designed and developed jet airframes for use by the Luftwaffe as combat aircraft. The Me 262 was mass-produced and went into combat, regardless of its imperfections, against the Allied Combined Bomber Offensive.

The reason behind the German success was twofold. First, the German jet designers were better trained from the beginning. Men like Ohain and

Franz, Messerschmitt and Heinkel, had developed their skills in the German technical schooling system and were intellectually capable of developing high-technology weapons systems. The Germans could and did strive for the most efficient and effective jet aircraft, and made them operational before the end of the war. The design and construction of the first combat jet aircraft is a tribute to the training and education of the German physicists, engineers, and technicians.

Second, the Germans needed the jet program to reach fruition. They were relying on aircraft, although good, which were not qualitatively better than Allied models. By spring 1944, with the introduction of the long-range North American P-51 *Mustang* (with drop tanks to escort the bombers for entire missions), the German models could compete but not overcome. This was because of two obvious factors. One, German pilots had been lost to attrition; in Germany there was a strong but small cadre of top aces and the rest of the German pilots were young and inexperienced. The Combined Bomber Offensive had worn away the Luftwaffe's pilots to the breaking point.[97] Second, although the German piston-engine aircraft (Me 109 G8 and G10 and FW 190 A-8 and Ta 152) were almost as good as the Allied models, the Germans did not have the same production capabilities as the Americans. The Americans could simply build more fighters. The Germans needed to design, produce, and commit a substantially superior fighter to combat the Allied CBO, and the overwhelming numbers of escort fighters over Germany. Thus, in the exigency of the Second World War, the Germans developed the Me 262 jet fighter along accelerated lines, inspired by the viability proven in the Ohain He 178 prototype.

The Germans needed a substantially superior fighter to make up for shortcomings in both men and machines, and during the war developed a symbol of German technical ability, the Messerschmitt Me 262 jet aircraft.

5

Britain Catches Up

May 15, 1941 was an important day for the British. The Gloster E.28/39 *Pioneer* (called *Squirt* by Whittle and the Power Jets team) flew for the first time powered by Frank Whittle's W.1 engine. But, for Britain, the war was not going well. Britain had defended against the Luftwaffe and persevered through the Battle of Britain, and the Ministry of Aircraft Production (MAP) was busy procuring aircraft for retaliation against the Germans. But British military doctrine concentrated on offensive bombing campaigns in the form of heavy, multiengine bombers, at the expense of development of high-speed, high-altitude fighter interceptors. Perceptions of the day (in all countries) were that the offensive was the decisive doctrine; heavy bombers were the ideal weapons platform. The Avro 683, later the famous *Lancaster*, was in the final stages of development and became the definitive aircraft of RAF Bomber Command.[1] The Supermarine *Spitfire* was in its fifth permutation, the Mk V, with a new engine it had marginally better performance than the Mk I or II, but the addition of 20 mm cannon to supplement four .303 caliber machine guns meant that the new *Spitfire* packed a bigger punch.[2]

But with the threat of the Luftwaffe over England removed, the British began to build up Bomber Command. British interest was on bombers, not fighters, and the revolutionary Whittle/Gloster turbojet project was relegated to distant second at best. But, both Whittle and Gloster pressed on, confident that their new project would soon become important to British military planning and procurement.

The *Pioneer* took flight in May 1941, 19 months after the first German jet. Popular British consensus was that this was in fact the first jet flight; the German project was still unknown. However, initial reactions were similar. The British, like the Germans earlier, considered their first turbojet project as purely experimental. The Gloster E.28/39 *Pioneer* was intended to test the viability of the turbojet as a prime mover for aircraft; in Britain Gloster was preparing plans for an operational jet aircraft. But for the time being, the *Pioneer* was the culmination of British turbojet technology.

The flight reports for the first 17 flights of the *Pioneer* were laudatory. Jerry Sayer, chief Gloster test pilot, and others commented on the stability of the airframe and the relative quiet and lack of vibration of the turbojet engine. In his first flight, on May 15, 1941, Sayer reported that the plane was a delight to fly. The *Pioneer* was prepared at Cranwell, an RAF airfield with a concrete runway, for test flights. Earlier taxi-trials were conducted on grass fields where the underpowered plane had problems with the natural surface. At Cranwell, the *Pioneer* was loaded with 50 gallons of fuel and Sayer started the engine. The new Whittle W.1 was run up to 16,500 rpm, Sayer released the brakes at 7:40 PM, and the plane began to roll. At about 600 yards, relying on "feel" rather than gauges, Sayer lifted the plane from the runway. He retracted the landing gear at 1,000 feet altitude, and flew the plane for 17 minutes. After a perfect landing, he was warmly greeted by the onlookers, a mix of Gloster, Power Jets, RAF, and Air Ministry personnel.[3] The *Pioneer* reached 240 mph on the first flight, and flew to an altitude of 4,000 feet. The first British turbojet flight was a success.

Over the next 13 days, the *Pioneer* continued flight testing powered by the Whittle W.1 centrifugal-flow turbojet engine. On the 16th, Sayer took off with 81 gallons of fuel for a 24-minute flight. According to the flight report he reached a top speed of 280 mph at 16,500 rpm. The flight log also notes that "the firm's estimated figure based on the airframe drag and engine thrust data was [a top speed of] 290 mph."[4] As test flights continued, higher speeds were recorded, the plane reached higher altitudes, and it was given a thorough examination. Whittle records that the *Pioneer* reached speeds approaching 370 mph at 25,000 feet altitude, at engine speeds of 17,000 rpm.[5] This figure conflicts with the pilot's reports of the first flights, but the high-speed flight was also at high altitude, and the engine's rpm restrictors has been set higher for testing purposes. Whittle commented that he attributed the high speeds attained—higher in fact than contemporary British fighters—to the excellent performance of both his engine and Gloster's airframe.[6] Sayer reported control surface problems with the unresponsive rudder and the overresponsive elevator, but admitted these were probably characteristic of the plane itself and were in any case easily rectified.[7] On May 28 testing was suspended when the engine failed during flight. The W.1 in the *Pioneer* had logged 10 hours 28 minutes flight time; consensus was that it was time to disassemble the engine for examination. The seventeenth flight of the *Pioneer* was the last flight of the year for the British jet program. In the first 17 flights the *Pioneer* had proved the viability of the turbojet engine for use in aircraft.

The main problem faced by the early turbojet aircraft was extremely limited range. Early turbojet engines were especially thirsty for fuel, and had high consumption rates. Thus, it was important to carry ample fuel. The *Pioneer* was equipped to carry a fuel load of 81 gallons, for a maximum take-off weight (MTOW) of 3,690 lbs. But, even with a maximum fuel load endurance was limited to 56 minutes.[8] Thus, even at full speed, the plane had an operational radius of only 100 miles. Improvements had to be made on both the engines and airframe to make the British turbojet operationally viable.

Early turbojet aircraft were designed with three considerations. Speed was the primary concern, and second-generation designs focused on increasing top speed. Turbojet aircraft speed was dependent on thrust from the engine(s). Unfortunately, all early turbojet engines were severely underpowered. Thus, British aircraft designers turned to twin-engine design to achieve high-speed flight. But, this hampered the second consideration: weight. Added engines meant added weight, which had a detrimental effect on top speed. In order to keep weight down, all unnecessary weight was deleted from the airframe; limitations were put on fuel capacity. The British designers developed a twin turbojet-engine airframe that was fast and relatively light, but the sacrifice was fuel capacity. The plane's range was limited in order to maximize speed and reduce weight—the ongoing battle for all aircraft design and particularly planes with turbojets. Thus, designers were in a conundrum, how to maximize range without sacrificing speed. The Gloster Company, which had designed the experimental *Pioneer*, thought they had the answer with the F.9/40.

Gloster developed and submitted a design study to the MAP in August 1940 for a twin-engine turbojet fighter.[9] The turbojet airframe was designed to house the engines in nacelles in the middle of each wing, a similar design to many conventional twin piston-engine planes. The setup allowed for a number of different power plant configurations, it was unclear at the time where the engines would come from and what type they would be. The plane incorporated tricycle landing gear and a high elevator tailplane to maximize the effectiveness of the turbojet engines' jet thrust. The Air Ministry issued requirements in November in response to Gloster's proposals requesting additions to the design, including six cannons, new pilot's seat arrangement, and room enough in the cockpit for a pilot in a pressure suit.[10] Gloster agreed to these terms in principle and planning continued. Gloster secured an order from MAP on February 7, 1941, for the production of twelve F.9/40 twin-engine turbojet "Gloster Whittle aeroplanes."[11]

The choice of Gloster to construct the first British turbojet airframe is in and of itself important. Gloster had good designers, but most importantly, Gloster was not designing anything new. Their prewar fighter designs (the single-engine F.5/34 and twin-engine F.9/37) had been rejected by the MAP, and Gloster was building Hawker Hurricanes as a subsidiary of that company. Gloster had been bought out by Hawker Aircraft Ltd in 1934 in answer to a government move to reduce the number of aircraft manufacturing firms in Britain in order to increase efficiency, concentration of innovation, and ease of production. Hawker took the first step and acquired Gloster in order to expand Hawker production facilities. Gloster was therefore a Hawker company, but had independent R&D offices and still retained the Gloster name. When Whittle approached Gloster in 1939, and established a working relationship with designer George Carter, the stage was set for Britain's first production turbojet aircraft.

Likewise, Gloster was an excellent choice for Britain's second turbojet airframe. The contract for Britain's first operational combat jet aircraft was awarded in February 1941 while significant improvements were planned for the power plants. The British jet program was ordered for further investigation before the first British jet had even flown. The initial contract was for twelve series-production aircraft for testing. Gloster began to retool for the potential production of 80 F.9/40s per month. The plane was designed as a single-seat, twin centrifugal-flow turbojet engine fighter aircraft for the RAF.

But, Gloster was not the only company courted by MAP. In early 1941 discussions were initiated with de Havilland, Armstrong Siddeley, and the Metropolitan-Vickers Electric Company (better known as Metrovick).[12] Armstrong Siddeley worked toward axial-flow turbojets and later led in British turboprop development. Metrovick was also working on axial-flow turbojets, and later produced excellent engines for the MAP. De Havilland was the first to benefit from the MAP contracts, and also the first to impact British turbojet development. With the benefit of Whittle's work, de Havilland began work on a 3,000 lb thrust–centrifugal-flow turbojet engine labeled the Halford H.1. De Havilland had successes where the Whittle-Rover relationship lagged. Meanwhile, de Havilland was also working on conventional piston-engines as well as airframes; turbojet manufacture was secondary.

In April 1941, U.S. Army General "Hap" Arnold visited Britain in order to cement ties with the British. The U.S. Army Air Forces general was particularly interested in technological exchange. When he learned of the turbojet program in Britain, he was immediately interested and secured rights for bringing British turbojet technology to the United States.[13] He did, and the American jet program was based directly on the efforts of Arnold and the technology of Whittle.

In May, Gloster and Whittle proved they had a successful airframe-power plant combination with the first flight of the E.28/39 *Pioneer*, and the MAP sent a letter of intent to Gloster for an additional 300 production F.9/40s.[14] The turbojet aircraft was a reality in Britain, and the MAP was ready to move to the next level: production jet aircraft for combat operations. The F.9/40 airframe was accepted as viable, and Gloster began work on the development of the original preproduction series order.

But, there were substantial delays in the British turbojet program, delays that were inherent in the development of turbojet technology. The Gloster airframes were built with relative ease. They did incorporate new design technology, but the Gloster planes were not a radical departure from British airframe development. The conservative design was for ease of construction, and not highly theoretical, but it was a good design based on the potential of high-speed turbojet flight. The F.9/40 engineers had to take into account that they were constructing a new aircraft, one designed for speeds in excess of existing technology, but there were few major theoretical leaps in the Gloster airframe. New components included nosewheel tricycle undercarriage and a high elevator surface, both incorporated to deal with the new propulsion units. But Gloster did not deviate from established airframe design; there were no substantial delays due to airframe construction.

The delays in the British turbojet program came from the developmental lag in Whittle's engines. Following the successful bench tests with the W.1, it was decided by consensus that the engine needed to be modified and improved. The W.1 produced 860 lbs. thrust; it was agreed that the output was too low for the next generation of turbojet aircraft. It was back to the drawing board for the British turbojet designers.

Turbojet engine production had been denied to Power Jets Ltd and the British jet program relied on Rover for engine production.[15] One of the major problems was that Rover was not manufacturing engines according to Power Jets' design parameters. One of the concerns at Rover was that the engine, the W.2B, was not performing up to standards. There were problems in the combustion stage of the new engine design, and both Whittle, in charge of his Power Jets team, and Rover had differing ideas concerning the new engine. Whittle's answer was to modify the individual combustion chambers; Rover's idea was to use larger, annular (straight-through flow) combustion chambers.[16] Ongoing friction between Rover and Whittle meant that development consistently fell behind, and the new centrifugal-flow turbojet model, the W.2B, was not ready even as Gloster was finishing its preproduction F.9/40 airframe. Rover continued to insist on design changes in order to secure a potential postwar monopoly on British turbojet contracts, while Whittle attempted to maintain Power Jets control over the entire program. Eventually, a new company agreed to undertake engine manufacture, and allow Whittle design authority over the W.2B centrifugal-flow turbojet engine, but for the time being the competition continued with disastrous results.

The MAP was impressed with the flight of the *Pioneer*, and offered contracts for the initiation of the British turbojet program. The MAP was interested in procuring turbojet aircraft, and set production figures at 500 airframes from Gloster and 1,200 engines from Power Jets/Rover beginning immediately with projected results by early summer 1942.[17] Thus, the British had the potential to lead the world in turbojet production. But, the answer from Gloster was that airframe production based on MAP requests would take until spring 1943, and there was no answer from Rover on the question of 1,200 engines. MAP interest in exploring turbojet potential was not matched by realities of production. Thus, although there was a complete shift in official government interest by 1941 in favor of turbojet aircraft, British industry became the limiting factor in the development of jet aircraft.

Whittle showed his concern immediately after the first flights of the *Pioneer* when he argued for immediate refinement of the W.2B design.[18] But MAP favored Rover, an established company. In a time when support was needed, Whittle was left out in the cold by the British government agencies. MAP allowed Rover to alter engine designs and marginalized the inventor's input.[19] Conflicts continued throughout the year, and there was no resolution in sight at the end of the year when Pearl Harbor was attacked and the Americans officially entered World War II.

By December, the first Allied axial-flow turbojet ran successfully, two new turbojet airframes were under development, and two new centrifugal-flow engines were in the final developmental stages. The latest breakthrough in Britain was the Metrovick F.2 axial-flow turbojet. Based on practical applications from axial-flow steam turbines, the Metrovick team led by Dr. D. Smith worked to develop a viable axial-flow turbojet for aircraft. The engine, with a nine-stage axial-flow compressor and a two-stage turbine, ran in December. With minor modifications over the rest of the year it produced 1,800 lbs thrust by November 1942.[20] Although promising, the Metrovick project did not reach fruition until well into 1945 with the F.2/4, a 10-stage compressor and single-stage turbine axial-flow turbojet rated at 4,000 lbs thrust for an installed weight of 1,725 lbs.[21] The two airframe projects were the Gloster F.9/40, still in development, and the de Havilland DH.100 jet airframe. Both were given the go-ahead in 1941; the Gloster was the first to fly. Finally, two centrifugal-flow engines were also under development: the higher-profile and troubled W.2B Whittle/Rover project and the overlooked de Havilland turbojet engine project, the H.1. With government interest and funding it was only a matter of time before the British became viable turbojet contenders.

In early 1942, British turbojet development began to pay off. In relative obscurity, the de Havilland H.1 was run for the first time. This centrifugal-flow engine was developed according to information provided from MAP on the Whittle engines, and was built and tested within twelve months of the original contracts. De Havilland was busy with their own piston-engine production and aircraft manufacture, but they were also very eager to get into the jet race. The H.1 as tested in April 1942 produced 3,000 lbs thrust, demonstrating Whittle's original W.2B projections.[22] But, even with the first de Havilland H.1—later given the official designation *Goblin*—there was still no airframe for the engine, and there were too few (literally one Gloster E.28/39) for flight testing. De Havilland continued development of all of its projects; the *Goblin* program was neither prioritized nor neglected.

By April, flight testing was also resurrected. *Pioneer* tests continued with moderate success and with a new engine. The new W.1A, successor to the W.1 and precursor to the W.2B, was installed in the *Pioneer*, and new performance data was gathered. Sayer, still the Gloster chief test pilot, recorded 430 mph in high-altitude flight.[23] But problems developed with the engines. Whittle was not satisfied with the Rover workmanship on the flight engine or the new W.2Bs being delivered. His impression was that shoddy workmanship would lead to accidents at best, and contract cancellation at worst.[24] His fears were realized when Sayer made a dangerous landing in the *Pioneer* when turbine blades failed in flight in March. Sayer survived, and brought the plane safely to the ground, but the engine was damaged and testing was suspended.

It was around this time that Whittle discovered that Rover was secretly developing their own engine design. Whittle's W.2B design had been forwarded to Rover for production, but they had also enjoyed complete autonomy from MAP with regard to actual development. Rover had underhandedly redesigned the combustion cycle, and renamed their secret project the B.26 engine. This was the final issue that split Whittle and Power Jets away from Rover for good. Whittle was furious that his designs had been altered, and was also frustrated that his own Power Jets company had been cut out of the information loop.[25] Rover had been given autonomy and exploited it for their benefit.

Frustrated, and incensed with his treatment, Whittle was happy to travel to the United States, under orders from MAP, to help the Americans with their turbojet program—after all, it was based on his research and innovation! In June 1942, with little encouragement about the situation at Rover, and under too much stress, Whittle went to the United States. Whittle was able to visit the General Electric (GE) facilities where his engine design was being copied as the GE I-A turbojet. He recalls pleasant interaction with the engineering staff at GE, and enjoyed his discussions.[26] Whittle was also invited to Bell Aircraft in Buffalo to see the first American jet plane under construction. Although Whittle does not give any indication about his reactions to the American plane—it was much different than any of the British designs—he does mention that there were three airframes under construction with "considerable speed and enthusiasm."[27] Whittle's U.S. trip was full of official visits and interaction with aircraft and engine-manufacturing firms, which after time only added to the stress he was feeling. Fortunately, Whittle was able to rest for a few weeks on the California leg of his trip; much needed rest in a deceptively peaceful environment. Whittle hints at the lack of wartime concerns around his newfound California friends, including an expatriate British dancer named "June."[28] His American trip concluded with a final trip through Washington, DC, and astonishment that the Americans were willing to put more time, money, and effort into turbojet research and development, and that the "Americans were generally astounded at the parsimonious attitude of the MAP toward the work of Power Jets."[29] By the summer of 1942, the Americans were able to devote more materials and financial resources to the development of turbojet engines based wholly on the original Whittle Power Jets' designs. Whittle returned to Britain just before the first American jet flights at Muroc; he was not in attendance to see his dreams fulfilled in America as they had been previously in England.

In Whittle's absence, the Gloster airframe had moved ahead to testing. The engines were not ready for first flights in June, and only taxiing trials were conducted. The Gloster F.9/40 had been given the official designation *Meteor*, and trials began in July to test the airframe's suitability. But continuing dislocation between Power Jets and Rover delayed the British jet program substantially. Taxi trials were carried out with W.1A engines; neither Rover nor Power Jets had completed any flight-worthy W.2Bs. Sayer, the test pilot for the *Meteor*, cautioned against using the underpowered engines for flight testing.[30]

In fact, it was not until September that the first W.2 series engine ran. The W.2B made at Rover, with annular combustion chambers and renamed the B.26, began bench tests that month. The Power Jets' W.2B, which incorporated parts manufactured at Rolls-Royce, also ran for the first time in September. One other company was involved in W.2B production, but even the Vauxhall program was behind schedule.[31]

Power Jets began bench tests of the W.2/500, the next progression in the Whittle/Power Jets developmental timeline on September 13, 1942, according to Whittle, "exactly six calendar months from the date on which we had begun the drawings."[32] Initial results were outstanding. The engine produced thrust according to predictions, a full 1,800 lbs. And, at 835 lbs dry weight, the output was more than 2.15 lbs thrust per lbs weight.[33] But bench testing was different from flight tests, and the best thrust after further modifications was 1,600 lbs.

In the interim, the Power Jets–Rover relationship was at a standstill. Neither side was communicating, and turbojet manufacture in Britain was in jeopardy of failure. Consequently, in one of the important instances in history, a dinner meeting was held between Ernest Hives of Rolls-Royce and S.B. Wilkes of Rover in November. Rolls-Royce had been manufacturing components for Power Jets who lacked shop space. Rolls-Royce, and Hives in particular, saw potential (and money) in turbojet engine manufacture well into the postwar period, when it came, and called an informal meeting to discuss the matter with Wilkes. At the momentous occasion, in one sentence Hives offered Wilkes, "Give us this jet job and we'll give you our tank-engine factory in Nottingham."[34] Wilkes saw an opportunity for Rover to not only increase engine production, in the conventional sense, but also a chance to avoid Whittle and Power Jets. Hives looked to solidify relations with Power Jets, and expand their wartime—and potential postwar—manufacturing. The deal was struck, Rover was out, and Rolls-Royce saved British turbojet manufacturing from death by apathy.

Later that month, the W.2B engine flew for the first time, embedded in the tail of a Wellington bomber. The plane was configured to house the engine for flight tests, and the W.2B performed adequately, but not up to design. In the Wellington test flights, the W.2B only produced 1,250 lbs thrust in the existing configuration.[35] It was back to the drawing board as Whittle and the Power Jets team redesigned the impeller for better efficiency.[36]

The transfer of manufacturing from Rover to Rolls-Royce was immensely important and virtually immediate. As the year ended, Rover had a mere 57 hours testing completed on their version of the W.2B (B.26). By the end of January 1943, Rolls-Royce had logged nearly 400 hours bench test time for the W.2B after taking over manufacture.[37] And, the relationship was better between Rolls-Royce and Power Jets than Whittle could ever imagine.

Unfortunately for Whittle, there was interference from on high. Air Marshall Sir Wilfred Freeman at MAP was concerned about the working relationship between Whittle and Rolls-Royce. Freeman was of the opinion that the turbojet program in Britain was a waste of time and resources, and had considered ending the entire program when he took over his new post.[38] Freeman's concern was in the power dynamic between the two companies: Power Jets and Rolls-Royce. He wanted Rolls-Royce to be in charge of future production of the W.2/500 and subsequent designs, but did not want Whittle to exercise control over the larger company. Whittle was told to "think it over" for the weekend, and dismissed. Whittle had discussions with Rolls-Royce and the Committee on Research and Development (CRD) representative Roxbee Cox that weekend to discuss matters. It was decided that Rolls-Royce would be in charge of production, but there would be and "engineering liaison," that would be "so close that any blame or credit was carried jointly."[39] At the same time Power Jets would maintain control over experimental R&D with regard to turbojet development. The MAP agreed to the terms as set forward by Power Jets and Rolls-Royce; W.2B production at the new facility, and in a new sense of cooperation, began in January 1943.

In March, *Pioneer* flight testing continued with the second prototype. The Gloster plane was fitted with a Rover-built W.2B engine for further flights. Problems with the Rover engine allowed only ten flights that month, with two aborted flights because of mechanical problems. When a Rolls-Royce built W.2B was installed in April, performance of the engine was substantially better.[40] On April 17, the *Pioneer* was flown from Edgehill to Hatfield for a demonstration for Prime Minister Winston Churchill. For safety reasons, two *Spitfire* Mk Vs and a Hawker *Typhoon* escorted the *Pioneer*. The jet pilot, John Grierson, reported that he lost the *Spitfires* altogether and had to "throttle back" (reduce speed of) the jet just so that the *Typhoon* could keep up, which was running at full throttle.[41] Although Whittle comments that he had no record, Whittle understood that "the Prime Minister was duly impressed."[42] An unnamed observer at Hatfield recorded a more interesting anecdote: as the *Pioneer* raced past at 400 mph, "Churchill turned his head so fast that his cigar fell out of his mouth."[43] The prime minister was impressed and excited about the plane; another pilgrim was converted.

Engine development under Rolls-Royce went more smoothly than earlier. One simple indication was the 100-hour endurance test on the W.2B performed in May 1943. Using Whittle's suggestion from two years previous, which had gone unheeded by Rover, the turbine blades were twisted to 5° to increase efficiency and combustion. The increased turbine efficiency was illustrated during the disassembly of the engine after the endurance test; the engine did not suffer major degradation during the test.[44] The engine produced 1,600 lbs thrust for the entire 100-hour test and survived, no small feat. Whittle exchanged a congratulatory note with Rolls-Royce regarding the successful tests and although Whittle thought that the W.2B was nearing its performance limits of 1,600 lbs thrust, the Rolls-Royce team speculated that it could be pushed to 1,700.[45] Rolls-Royce was intent on providing justification for the 100-unit contract for W.2Bs as issued by the MAP. By the end of the next month, June 1943, Rolls-Royce had once again type-tested the W.2B for 100 hours, this time at 1,700 lbs thrust. But, Whittle and Power Jets were intent on closing out the original MAP contract and initiating production of the W.2/500: the next generation turbojet engine which was designed to produce 2,000 lbs thrust.

While Power Jets and Rolls-Royce were discussing the relative merits of the in-production W.2B versus the potentially better yet untested W.2/500, their work was overshadowed by other programs. Although the Whittle engine was still the staple of the British jet aircraft program, the MAP was interested in actual aircraft and less interested in potential. The Gloster F.9/40 airframe had been prepped and was ready for flight; all it awaited was engines. The conservative elliptical-wing design planned for the installation of the engines at mid-wing, one on either side of the oval cross-sectioned fuselage.[46] This installation allowed for alternate engine packages as Gloster did not know when or what type of engines would be forthcoming. The configuration led to ease of conversion between various engine arrangements.

The Gloster plane was readied for engine installation and prepared for ground testing. The first engines were Rover W.2Bs (official designation *Welland*), left over from that company's production lines since taken over by Rolls-Royce. The engines were not considered airworthy, and the newly named *Meteor* was kept on the ground. The Gloster *Meteor*, powered by the *Welland* engines, began taxi trials in July 1942. At this point the engines were not providing enough thrust for actual flights, Gloster and the British jet program awaited flight-worthy engines.

As time passed, the MAP was not assured that Rolls-Royce/Power Jets would deliver turbojet engines on time. The ministry began to court other engine manufacturers. Thus it was on March 5, 1943, the first flight of the *Meteor*, that the plane was powered by de Havilland H.1 engines.[47] To fit the larger de Havilland engines, the center section was widened, and the fifth Gloster prototype (designated F.9/40H) was flown by Michael Daunt. Daunt was made chief Gloster test pilot after Sayer's fatal crash a year before. As well, Daunt is remembered by Whittle in an interesting side note: Daunt walked too close to a running jet intake one day and was nearly sucked in. Afterwards, wire mesh screens were fitted over intakes to avoid accidents. The screens were affectionately named "Daunt Stoppers."[48]

De Havilland had been busy by order of the MAP. Having been offered a contract in 1941, De Havilland had worked toward the completion of the H.1 turbojet engine. Similar in configuration to the Rolls-Royce/Power Jets W.2B, the H.1 was rated at 2,000 lbs thrust at the first *Meteor* flight in March 1943. Renamed the *Goblin*, the engine was an immediate success. Unfortunately for the British jet program, de Havilland's production facilities were inadequate for extensive turbojet engine production. De Havilland's focus was diffused by many projects, and their jet engine production suffered. On the other hand, turbojet engine design was highly successful. By September, the *Goblin* was upgraded to 2,300 lbs thrust, and continued to be improved throughout the war.[49] De Havilland will be revisited as one of the successes and potential leaders in British turbojet design and development.

The other British turbojet design team was located at Metropolitan Vickers—Metrovick. They had also been approached by the MAP and had been working on a new engine design. The Metrovick team decided on an axial-flow compressor for their turbojet engine. The axial-flow turbojet offered more potential in efficiency and thrust, but also promised more problems in development. The axial-flow components had to be machined to higher tolerances and also made to be able to withstand higher temperatures and torsion speeds. But Metrovick was successful; by December 1941 the Metrovick F.2 ran on the test stand. It was a nine-stage axial-flow turbojet engine and the first Allied axial-flow type.[50] In November 1943, Metrovick F.2 engines powered the third *Meteor* prototype, F.9/40M.[51] The engine produced 1,800 lbs thrust, comparable to the contemporary German Jumo 004 axial-flow turbojet engine. The *Beryl*, the first in the Metrovick "precious stone" series engines, was not immediately chosen to power the *Meteor* project for most of the same reasons as the de Havilland *Goblin*. Metrovick was still facing developmental problems and production facilities were lacking. Although the engine was improved, it was not selected as the ideal power plant for the British jet program. Interestingly, the F.9/40M *Meteor* carried the axial-flow turbojets underwing, the same basic configuration as the German Me 262. It is uncanny how similar the two look from head-on views.

The Power Jets/Rolls-Royce team was still the main contender to develop and produce British turbojets. Under the direction of Whittle, and incorporating the industry of Rolls-Royce, the W.2B was still the MAP's preferred choice for production turbojet engines. By June 12, 1943, the first *Meteor* prototype, DG202/G, was flown with Rolls-Royce W.2B engines. The Rolls-Royce designation was used, and W.2B/23 delivery began early in October 1943. The engine, in the official records as the *Welland I*, produced 1,600 lbs thrust for 850 lbs weight.[52] Rolls-Royce concentrated on delivery of production engines rather than an entire redesign which of course was Whittle's goal. By the end of *Welland* production, 100 contracted engines, the design, production, and procurement triad had to decide on current production or future potential.

Subsequently, Power Jets was in stagnation as a simple R&D outfit while Rolls-Royce was growing. With the acquisition of the Rover plant at Barnoldswick, Rolls-Royce was the biggest turbojet producer in Britain. Thus, Rolls-Royce felt that they could determine their own course of action—and production. In separate MAP contracts, Rolls-Royce decided to continue production of the *Welland I*, the erstwhile Rover B.26/Power Jets W.2B, and incorporate design modifications of their own.[53] Although concerned, Whittle was nonetheless powerless to override MAP or Rolls-Royce. And, by this point, Whittle and Power Jets were receiving R&D funding heretofore unrealized; Whittle was actually content with his marginalized position.[54] Whittle's Power Jets was being overshadowed by the production facilities at Rolls-Royce; it was an unforeseen harbinger of events to come.

Morale remained high at Power Jets. Under R&D contracts, Whittle worked to satisfy the British Air Ministry. When reports from Germany suggested high-technology weapons based on rocket and jet power, Whittle turned his attention to include theoretical pulse-jet designs. Further, he was constantly working to raise company morale. In one instance he had a *Meteor* fly over Power Jets at lunchtime. And, Whittle can also be credited with the innovation of turbine automobiles! A test engine was lashed to a truck (lorry), and the turbojet truck was demonstrated with wild excitement. Whittle remarked, "I would have given a lot to have seen the effects on the general public of a run of our jet-propelled lorry along a public highway."[55]

Throughout the summer and autumn of 1943, *Meteor* flight testing continued with the different engine packages. The Metrovick F.2 *Beryl* showed promise, but was still years ahead of its developmental time. The Metrovick team continued refinement of their axial-flow turbojet in anticipation of its eventual viability. The de Havilland team also continued improving its *Goblin* engine; de Havilland had other ideas for its use. They were concentrating on building their own complete jet package, a de Havilland engine and airframe combined. By the winter of 1943, Rolls-Royce was the production center for the British turbojet industry while Gloster remained the first choice for jet airframes. By the new year 1944, the eight Gloster *Meteor* prototypes had been completed and tested and the first production *Meteors* were becoming available.

The first production *Meteor* was flown in January 1944. The production version was similar to the prototypes but incorporated production Rolls-Royce W.2B/23 *Welland* engines as well as four 20 mm cannons. The first flight corresponded with the first flight of the American Lockheed XP-80, later the famous *Shooting Star*. Like the first *Meteor*, the first flights of the XP-80 were also powered by the de Havilland H.1, the American GE engines were not ready for production. The British had loaned the Americans one of the two completed de Havilland H.1 turbojets. The first production *Meteor* was sent to the United States in February in exchange for a Bell XP-59A *Airacomet*, then under flight testing in the United States.

The exchanged *Meteor* was part of an initial order for 20 production aircraft. With the production of the first 20, Britain's—and the Allies—first jet fighter unit was created. No. 616 squadron was equipped with Rolls-Royce-powered Gloster *Meteor Is* as the first Allied jet unit. Based initially at Culmhead, the first *Meteor* reached its squadron on July 12, 1944. No. 616 was moved quickly to Manston for Home Defense, where the *Meteors* replaced Spitfire Mk VIIs. The jet fighters took up residence in the direct path of the German V-1 flying "Buzz" bombs, in the hope that the fast jets could catch and kill the unmanned pulse-jet cruise missiles. The plan worked, and in a stunning display of daring and speed, Flight Officer Dean disrupted the flight path of a V-1 by tipping the wing of the missile with his own jet's wing. The date of the first Allied jet victory was August 4, 1944.[56] The pilot's report read: "F/O Dean took off from Manston at 1545 to patrol inland area under Kingsley II (Biggin Hill) Control. At 1616 hours a Diver was sighted at 1,000 ft near Tonbridge on course of 330°, at speed of 365 IAS. Dean dived down from 4,500 ft at speed of 450 mph, and attacked from dead astern; his 4 × 20 mm cannons failed to fire owing to a technical trouble now being investigated, so flying level alongside the bomb, Dean maneuvered his wing tip a few inches under the wing of the flying bomb and by pulling upwards sharply he sent the bomb diving to earth 4 miles South of Tonbridge."[57] Furthermore, Flight Officer J. Rodger filed another "kill" claim on a V-1 later that same day. Rodger's kill claim was reported as, "F/O J.K. Rodger sighted a Diver at 1640 hrs. near Tenterden on course of 318° at 3,000-ft speed 340 mph. Attacking from astern Rodger fired 2 bursts of 2 seconds and saw the Diver crash and explode, 5 miles N.W. of Tenterden."[58] Needless to say, No. 616 squadron was excited about the viability of the *Meteor* as was evidenced by these first two successes.

By February 4, 1945, *Meteors* had been assigned and moved to continental Europe under the operational direction of the 2nd Tactical Air Force.

In an interesting incident, the Germans bombed the No. 616 Squadron *Meteor* airfield at Moelsbrock. The Germans dropped fragmentation bombs on the airfield hangars damaging one *Meteor*.[59] This incidence was important because the bombing Germans were flying Arado Ar 234 jet bombers; the first reported jet vs. jet raid. But by the end of the war there had been no aerial contact between Axis and Allied jet aircraft, the historic first jet combat would have to wait.

In the meantime, back in Britain, the de Havilland Aircraft Company was hard at work to compete with the Gloster/Rolls-Royce project. Their first engine offering, the H.1 *Goblin*, was bench-tested and then flight-tested in the *Meteor* F.9/40H. But de Havilland was not satisfied to produce engines for other aircraft; their reputation was in airframes not engines. The de Havilland company, with branch offices all over the world, was an internationally acclaimed aircraft-manufacturing firm. Renowned for their Model 98, better known as the *Mosquito*, the de Havilland company produced some of the best airframe designs before the war. Concentrating primarily on commercial and training designs, de Havilland made a name with planes such as the *Albatross, Dragon, Dragonfly*, and the *"Moth"* series of trainer aircraft.[60] Once de Havilland had determined that they could produce their own engines they were interested in competing for the MAP contract for a turbojet interceptor.

The model designation was DH.100, the hundredth de Havilland design since the company's inception in 1920. Later called the *Vampire*, the de Havilland fighter was designed as a single-engine turbojet aircraft. But, that is where the convention of this revolutionary aircraft ended. Building on experience from the construction of the *Mosquito*, the *Vampire* was a marvel of modern engineering. The mid-wing airframe had a central pod fuselage set between twin tail booms. The pilot's compartment was made from wood and plywood, taken directly from the *Mosquito* design. The pilot sat forward of the wing leading edge, giving him excellent visibility. Behind the pilot, embedded in the fuselage, was the *Goblin* centrifugal-flow turbojet engine. In order to maximize thrust, the de Havilland designers created an airframe that would incorporate the shortest jet tailpipe. Instead of a long conventional fuselage, de Havilland built the twin tail boom aircraft with a short central fuselage pod. The trademark elliptical British wings were all-metal construction with the engine intakes at the root of the wings where they joined the fuselage. The tail booms were connected by a high set elevator; designed to provide stability and avoid jet exhaust.[61]

Production of the airframe was slower than the Gloster *Meteor*, but the first *Vampire* prototype was ready by September 20, 1943. By this time the *Goblin* engine was producing 2,300 lbs; substantially better than the contemporary Rolls-Royce W.2B/23.[62] On that day, the first completely de Havilland turbojet aircraft flew: the *Vampire* prototype powered by the *Goblin* engine. The plane was smaller and lighter, but powered by only a single engine (as compared to *Meteor*'s two), the performance figures were no better than the Gloster aircraft.

In January 1944, when de Havilland had only two flying engines in stock—and in airframes—a request came from America for the most powerful engines in the British inventory. The Americans were on the verge of a breakthrough, but needed a more powerful engine. GE was producing I-14s and in the final testing phases of I-16s, but the more powerful I-40 was not yet a reality. In a gesture of true Allied cooperation, one de Havilland H.1 *Goblin* was sent Stateside for the first flight of the brand-new Lockheed XP-80 single-engine turbojet fighter prototype. Then later, when the Americans asked again, the second flight-worthy *Goblin* was also sent to the United States. The Americans in time developed an adequate engine design for their requirements, but it is not too much to say that the American jet program piggybacked directly on the British development of turbojet aircraft.[63]

Nonetheless, de Havilland went ahead with production, under contracts from the MAP, and began building production *Vampires*. The production interceptor incorporated four 20-mm cannons, a single *Goblin* engine, and was ready for service by April 20, 1945, when the first operational de Havilland *Vampire* F.1 was delivered. Forty *Vampire* F.1s were eventually delivered with 2,300 lb thrust *Goblin* engines, later *Vampires* were equipped with *Goblin IIs* which had been upgraded to 3,000 lb thrust.[64]

The British made a number of other exciting advances in the field of turbojet technology. The Gloster *Meteor* F.9/40 EE227, the eighteenth production *Meteor*, was sent to Hucknall for installation of yet another engine configuration.[65] The airframe was fitted with two Rolls-Royce RB.50 *Trent* engines, basically a *Derwent* engine incorporating a shaft-driven propeller; the world's first functioning turboprop.[66] The first flight of the *Meteor* turboprop was September 20, 1945, admittedly after the war, but indicative of the progress of British turbojet engineering.

The British put one turbojet aircraft into combat operation before the end of the war, added to one experimental type—two prototype Gloster E.28/39 *Pioneers*—and had one ready by the end of the war; the British built three types during the war. The British relied on Whittle's centrifugal-flow turbojet design for all of these aircraft and subsequent military turbojet designs; the British were able to develop excellent centrifugal-flow turbojets, but lagged in developing axial-flow types. But the importance of the British turbojet program extends beyond the shores of the United Kingdom; the British Whittle turbojet program was the basis for the American turbojet program as well. The Americans literally copied Whittle's centrifugal-flow turbojet designs, and the GE product formed the basis for the American jet program.

In January 1944 the secret was announced to the public. The press was informed of the joint British-American turbojet program and the existence of Allied turbojet fighters. This announcement was intended to inform the public of Allied technological superiority in addition to their material superiority.

But Whittle was concerned about other issues. He was of the opinion that the entire British turbojet engine development and production should be nationalized and taken over by the British government. He wrote to the MAP and argued that the purpose of turbojet technology was best suited to government development and funding, and that all turbojet engine technology should be funded by the government. His argument was that the MAP and British government had been almost exclusively responsible for turbojet funding during the war, and that it only made sense that it fall under government jurisdiction for the future of not only R&D but also production.[67] His advice raised hackles as can be assumed; companies like de Havilland and Rolls-Royce saw future profit potential in turbojet development and production. But the MAP was interested in an exclusive, government-funded R&D facility, and chose to nationalize Power Jets alone. Whittle was angry that he could not establish a commercial merger that would be financially beneficial to the Power Jets team (as well as his personal interests) and was equally afraid that Power Jets Ltd. would fail in the immediate postwar period due to lack of interest. During the war both money and material were available for accelerated technological evolution, after the war Whittle feared that the pace would slacken.[68] He argued for complete nationalization of the technology, but the MAP disagreed. Whittle argued against nationalizing Power Jets alone, but his opinions went unheeded.

The MAP offered to buy out Power Jets Ltd. but at the same time threatened to take over the company without recompense. The Power Jets board met and decided to accept the offer against Whittle's wishes. He had requested arbitration to determine the value of the company in the face of imminent takeover. But Whittle was once again overshadowed by the government—Power Jets Ltd. was nationalized on April 28, 1944, for the purchase price of £135,563 and 10s.[69] As an RAF officer, under the employment of the British Government, Whittle was not entitled to any of the money. Whittle actually argued that he did not deserve any of the money; it was a conflict of interest as well as the fact that any share that went to Whittle would only reduce payments to the other shareholders. But, Whittle's most vehement argument was that he would take no money as a protest of the nationalization of Power Jets.[70] In response, at least implicitly, was Whittle's promotion to air commodore in July, while Whittle recovered in hospital from overwork and stress-related illnesses.

Work continued at Rolls-Royce after the Allies invaded the continent. In 1944, Power Jets (Research and Development) Limited, the new name given to Power Jets, began development of the W.2/700, the latest design. By the end of the year, it was producing more thrust (2,290 lbs), had better specific fuel consumption (less than 1.042 lbs/lb thrust per hour), and was more reliable than earlier designs (successfully completed a 150-hour test run). The W.2B was making strides of its own; Power Jets had passed a 500-hour bench test with the engine between major overhauls.

Although the W.2/700 was not chosen by Rolls-Royce for production, components of the latest Rolls-Royce design, the *Nene*, were based directly on the experimental work at Power Jets. By the end of the year the new Rolls-Royce engine produced 4,500 lbs thrust for 1,600 lbs weight. When the first *Nene* ran on October 28, 1944, it superceded the GE I-40 and de Havilland H.1 *Goblin* as the most powerful turbojet engine in the world.[71]

Unfortunately for the British, the *Meteor* was no match for the German Me 262. The Germans relied on more streamlined and higher-wing loading airframes, and thus the Me 262 was faster, but less maneuverable. The *Meteor* was slower, had shorter range, and less firepower, but it was still the first Allied turbojet aircraft. The *Meteor* did not face the German jets in combat, but the Allies won; in the end turbojet aircraft did not change the course of the war. By the end of the war, the British had one airframe in production and another on the way, as well as three turbojet engine companies hard at work to develop more powerful jet engines. When Whittle was informed just before the end of the war that Rolls-Royce was going to concentrate exclusively on turbojet engines and drop their conventional piston-engine manufacture, he was relieved that his invention would not fade away without the pressure of war.

The Air Ministry had waffled on the development of the turbojet engine in the 1930s. But taken in context, this does not seem so odd. In the interwar period, there were other things that caused more concern for the British government in power than theoretical potentialities. It must be remembered that Whittle was not an academically trained engineer before his invention was proposed. He was an RAF test pilot who happened to be good at working with his hands. That he got time off for Cambridge and retained his regular RAF salary was impressive in the grand scheme. His turbojet engine experiments and theories did pay off, and the Air Ministry was interested in funding the project after the successful flight of the E.28/39 in 1941. But, the development of British turbojet technology, even though impressive in the midst of war, still fell behind both enemy and ally.

The British Air Ministry acquired a package deal in the final years of the war when it completed the takeover of Power Jets Ltd. The British government finally realized the potential of turbojet aircraft and acquired an R&D establishment of their own. Because Whittle was a government employee, and the government had virtually funded the entire project, the takeover was both easy and justified. Whittle's invention thrust the British into the jet age, at a time when Britain was being eclipsed as a world power by their ally, the Americans.

Finally, it is interesting when a single conversation can define generational barriers. In October 1945 Whittle was invited to fly the RAF's latest and fastest airplane, the *Meteor F.3*. Whittle had begun his RAF career as a training pilot in 100-mile-an-hour biplanes, but was the inventive genius behind the Allied turbojet engine program before and during World War II. He was brought out to witness the world-speed record attempt and allowed to fly test runs for publicity. He recorded flights of 450 mph during the record-breaking weekend when Group Captain H.J. Wilson set the world speed record flight at 606 mph. When asked by his son what speed he had flown, Whittle replied 450 mph. His son, 11 at the time, disappointedly replied, "What, only 450?" Whittle recounts that his son told a friend the next day, "He only did 450 you know, and they will do 600—he must be out of practice."[72] The world was entering a new era, led by the younger generation.

6

The Americans Take the Lead

On October 2, 1942, the Bell XP-59A officially took to the skies. The Americans entered the jet age 3 years behind the Germans and a year later than the British. But the Americans benefited from both background knowledge and years of British experiments. The Americans did not have to build the engine from scratch; they picked up a working model from Frank Whittle's Power Jets Ltd. And background turbosupercharger development fed improvements in the original. But the Americans began behind the power curve, and needed time, industry, materials, and research to catch up to the leaders. Fortunately for the Americans and their jet program, they had all of these—in spades.

The October 1 flight had been a success when Robert Stanley, Bell chief test pilot, rose to 25 feet. But Larry Bell, his boss and contractor for America's first jet plane, deflected Stanley's requests to fly the plane. Bell was waiting for the officials from Washington to come to Muroc for the first official flight the next day. Interestingly, Stanley filed a flight report for October 1, and logged his impressions. He reported that the plane left the ground, attained 25 feet altitude, and the controls were "satisfactory." In his high-speed taxi trials Stanley considered the plane solid and responsive.[1] America entered the jet age with a whisper, following on the heels of the Germans first and the British second.

The next day the officials from Washington were in attendance. Dr. Durand (Head of NACA), Colonel Craigie (chief of the Experimental Aircraft Section at Wright Field), and Major Heenan (British Air Commission) were in attendance, and Stanley recorded his first "official" jet flight. This time he took the XP-59A to 6,000 feet and attained speeds of 160 mph. His flight was cut short due to an oil pressure warning in the right engine, later attributed to a faulty gauge and not a broken pump. Stanley's one concern was high cockpit heat, due to faulty ventilation and the hot air coming from the engines.[2] His overall impressions once again were that the XP-59A was a stable, capable airplane.

Test flights continued that day as the first U.S. military pilot took to the skies in the XP-59A. Colonel Craigie, in attendance as an official government representative, requested a test flight. His late afternoon flight was also successful; the military had officially tested the new jet plane.

The final flight of the day was with Stanley at the controls once again. There were problems with the landing gear—they would not lock up—and Stanley decided to extend them fully and land. He did, and test flying was over for the day. Although the XP-59A did not fly again for the rest of the month while it was fixed and modified, America had entered the jet age.

The first XP-59A underwent significant changes throughout the rest of the month. The landing gear was repaired for operations, a new pair of engines was sent out from General Electric (GE), and an observer seat was added. In place of the gun mountings—absent on the prototype—a small observers seat was installed in the forward fuselage.[3] A small windshield provided protection from the wind, but the observer's cockpit was open-air. The reason for adding the additional seat was to allow an observer to monitor the speed and functioning of the aircraft as the test pilot flew. In addition, the modified XP-59A was the first two-seat jet aircraft in the world.

With the repairs and modifications completed, the XP-59A was again ready to fly. On October 30, with the project engineer Edgar Rhodes in the observer cockpit, Stanley once again began test flights with the jet plane. With the addition of the observer, testing continued while additional information and measurements were gathered. In addition, the first XP-59A Service Instructions Manual was ready for the next series of test flights.[4] The initial service instructions were a cursory examination of the plane as a whole, and the proposed required maintenance of the airframe and engines. One thing that was obvious from the first service manual was that there was concern over the reliability of the engines; the manual specifies daily visual inspections as well as 25-hour complete inspections of the power plants.[5] The test engineers found out quickly, however, that the engines had to be maintained even more frequently than they had initially envisioned, often with complete rebuilds after 10–15 hours.

The next two prototypes were finally finished in Buffalo and shipped to California. Airframe two was at Muroc by January 4, 1943, but awaited engines. The new Bell test pilot, Frank Kelly, was finally able to fly the assembled number two on February 15. Unfortunately, the defroster malfunctioned, and Kelly was forced to make a blind landing. Because of his skills the plane was safe, the defroster was fixed, and he flew safely and without mishap the next day.[6]

The ad hoc nature of the first American jet test program was illustrated by another incident with the second prototype. Stanley repeatedly reported stiff rudder controls at high speed, but the Bell designers on-site could not come up with a quick fix. One day Stanley,

> landed and taxied in fast, directly at the open hangar. He turned the aircraft and stopped abruptly, then boosted the jet engines briefly, blowing exhaust and dust on the Bell men working inside. Stanley got out of the cockpit and climbed up on the XP-59A's elevator. "Jack Russell," He shouted to the crew chief. "Bring a hacksaw out here." Without hesitation, Russell brought out the saw. Stanley cut a few inches off the top of the rudder, squaring off the rounded edge. He threw the excess pieces of rudder and the saw to the ground, walked back to the cockpit and taxied away for takeoff. "Works much better that way," Stanley said later.[7]

It must be remembered that in addition to his duties as an accomplished test pilot Stanley was also a trained aeronautical engineer; his opinion was accepted even among the designers.

The third prototype was shipped disassembled to Muroc by February 21, but it too lacked engines. The Bell company had fulfilled their contract for three prototypes, and based on the viability of the airframe design were awarded a new contract. The USAAF contracted Bell for an additional nine series-production airframes under the new designation YP-59A. By the time of the first flight of the XP-59A in October, the engineering designs were almost complete on the YP series. As XP testing continued, modifications were proposed and accepted, and work began on the YP-59A series in late fall 1942. The date set for the delivery of the first YP-59A was February 28, 1943.[8] But, because GE was still retooling for the next generation turbojet engine, and Bell was having difficulty with airframe modifications, the first YP-59A was not ready until June 12, 1943.

In the new year 1943, GE was developing the I-14 and I-16 turbojet engines. The same basic designs as the I-A, the two were improvements on the original. Both were designed with higher power ratios in mind; the main improvements involved increasing the impeller size thus increasing the compression ratio. These improvements resulted in an overall increase in the thrust output of the engine, from 1,250 lbs in the I-A to 1,400 lbs in the I-14 and 1,600 lbs in the I-16. The I-16 was later redesignated J31.[9] In January 1943 the Army met with a representative from GE to discuss the possibility of a 3,000- to 4,000-lb thrust engine, and by March GE was asked to submit a proposal for a centrifugal-flow turbojet design to comply with the requests. The GE team came up with the design for the I-40 (later designated J33), an improvement on the I-16. The J33 was once again a larger, more powerful version of the original centrifugal turbojet designs, and further could be constructed relatively quickly, based on acquired knowledge and materials. GE also proposed the TG-180, an axial-flow design, which arguably had more potential thrust, but was also admittedly further in the future and would require substantial developmental time.[10] The proposed TG-180 engine began development at the Schenectady plant while I-40 (J33) construction began at the West Lynn facility.

The I-14 was first to be delivered to Muroc for flight testing. The new engine included design modifications in the turbine and casing, and produced 1,400 lbs thrust. But the most improvement was seen in the I-16 (J31). I-16 construction began in January 1943, and the first engines were delivered for flight testing that summer. Two 1,600-lb thrust I-16s powered a fully armed YP-59A to 46,700 feet at 405 mph in July.[11] Production at the West Lynn plant focused on the more powerful I-16; 241 engines were eventually built (in addition to 21 I-As and 9 I-14s). But of course the Army wanted more speed; this required more thrust.

Testing with the XP-59A, and later YP models, continued in the California desert. More Bell, Army Air Forces, and Navy pilots were added to the test flight program. In addition to Stanley and Kelly, military types and civilians took their shot at becoming jet pilots. The first Army pilot was Colonel Craigie, who flew the jet on October 2, 1942. The first Navy pilot was invited to Muroc and flew the XP-59A, still in testing, on April 21, 1943.[12] The Navy pilot, Captain Fred Trapnell, was delighted with the jet, and he echoed the Navy's interest in jet aircraft. During the war a number of Navy pilots flew the XP-59A and later YP-59A, and the Navy acquired three for testing purposes. Trapnell related another indicator of the secrecy of the project,

> I found myself in a group discussing rumors then emanating from Europe, of a weird and wonderful means of propulsion—without a propeller. The discussion became quite intense and very inaccurate, to say the least. I was supposed to be the most knowledgeable of those present but I had to sit silent and act dumb. I couldn't say that I not only knew about it but had flown one. I was forbidden to say a word.[13]

The Navy showed immediate interest and inquired about jet planes for themselves. The Navy received two YP-59As in November 1943, which were sent to Naval Air Station at Patuxent River, Maryland. Earlier that year, the Navy procurement Board had approached Ryan Aeronautical Company and McDonnell Aircraft Company for proposals for carrier-based jet aircraft. The results were the XFR-1 *Fireball* and the XFD-1 *Phantom*. The XFR-1 was powered by a hybrid combination—both conventional piston and jet engines—a Wright *Cyclone* in the nose and a GE I-16 embedded in the fuselage. The *Phantom* was a pure jet fighter, powered by two Westinghouse 19b engines.[14] But the Navy also started with the XP-59A.

New airframes and engines were delivered to Muroc and the XP-59A began trials as a jet fighter aircraft as initially designed. The jet was intended to be a high-speed interceptor and packed a punch with its weapons package. New test models were outfitted with two 37-mm cannons and three .50 cal machine guns in the nose.[15] But, the new jet was not a very stable gun platform; there was severe buffeting when firing the guns. Armament was scaled back to a single cannon and three machine guns in the final four YP-59A models.

As XP-59A testing continued, both Bell and the Army realized that it would not live up to the potential that was hoped. Even with the I-16 (J31) engines, the top speed of the XP-59A was only slightly over 400 mph at altitude. Concurrent conventional piston-engine fighters were flying faster and as high; by comparison the North American P-51 *Mustang* was flying faster (437 mph), almost as high (ceiling 41,900 ft), farther (operational range 1,300 miles with drop tanks), and was also coming off the production lines in quantity (by the end of 1942 more than 50 each month and rising).[16] The XP-59A was an exceptional airplane for its revolutionary technology, but was quite ordinary in its performance capabilities.

Nonetheless, the Army set up an experimental jet-test squadron. On November 20, 1943, the 412th Fighter Group was instituted and was assigned to begin transition to jet aircraft.[17] Under the oversight of the 4th Army Air Forces, the 412th familiarized with jet planes and prepared the next generation pilots for post–piston-engine flight. Colonel Homer Boushey was named commander and the unit was assigned to Muroc. The initial Army contingent included 20 enlisted mechanics and one engineering officer for familiarization with jet maintenance.[18]

Interestingly, there were a number of hilarious anecdotes that surrounded the nascent jet program. In early 1943, the Muroc "dry" lake flooded after severe rainstorms. Flight testing was scheduled immediately after the bad weather cleared, but the landing area was still unusable. The plane was towed to an alternate airfield for operations. In order to maintain secrecy, a dummy propeller was fastened to the nose of the shrouded plane to make it appear that it was a conventional aircraft. For flight the "dummy" wooden propeller was removed, then refastened after the plane landed. Several early pictures show the shrouded jet plane with the fake propeller.[19] The hijinks continued: on the occasion of their first jet flight, Army Air Forces pilots would snap off the propellers on their flight badges. The propeller-less "flight wings" were an inside joke among the Army pilots and an instant way of recognizing other "jet jocks."[20] Another indicator for the entire flight test program, civilian and military, were the black derby hats worn by the group. Initially brought back to Muroc from a city trip, the hats soon marked the Bell employees and test pilots in the desert. They could recognize each other instantly in town where desert clothing (presumably shorts) and bowler hats would stand out.[21]

Test pilot Jack Woolams used his bowler hat and an old Halloween mask for the ultimate joke. A group of P-38 *Lightning* trainees were flying over the desert when they were joined by a strange plane—without a propeller! And even if that was not strange enough, it was being flown by a gorilla, wearing a bowler hat, and smoking a cigar! The "gorilla" waved and dove away from the astonished trainees.[22] Woolams had established fuel for rumors for months to come.

And, the pilots and crew were still learning how to act around the new plane. The jet exhaust was of particular concern because it was a brand-new phenomenon; unfortunately people often forgot. Norton relates the story of a Bell Company inspector, E. Fischer, who was not paying attention:

[Williams] weighing two hundred pounds, walked into the jet approximately four feet behind the nozzle while the aircraft was operating at rated power. It lifted him approximately three feet in the air, tumbled him end over end approximately three times, and he made a face down landing on the concrete surface.[23]

One quickly learned to watch one's step around the "business end" of jet power!

In the autumn of 1943, the Army reciprocated the technological exchange with the British. The third production YP-59A was shipped to England straight from Buffalo. Kelly was the assigned test pilot, and along with one Bell and one GE representative went to England with the plane. The first flight of the Bell YP-59A in England came on September 28, 1943.[24] The plane was turned over to the RAF for evaluation; in exchange a new Gloster Meteor was promised. The Gloster did not arrive in the United States until February 1944.

The British were equally unimpressed with the American jet. A new coat of paint was applied, a national insignia and registration number (RJ 362/G) were added, and the YP-59A was given the name *Tollgate*, perhaps an indication of the Lend–Lease agreement that brought it to British shores.[25] Over the next year, the British tested the YP-59A, but it did not live up to expectations. After extensive testing, by the middle of 1944, the Bell plane was virtually abandoned and given over to Rolls-Royce; British reports stated that the plane needed over 200 modifications, of which only 60 had already been made. British consternation was confirmed when they cancelled an initial request for six additional YP-59A planes; after flying the YP-59A they even politely informed the AAF that a promised production P-59A was unnecessary.[26] The British did not want to deal with the same problems that the Muroc test group was facing; they had their own jet design to consider.

The British had been working on a new jet aircraft design, the Gloster F. 9/40, the *Meteor*. Although the British development has been discussed elsewhere, it is important to note that the Americans benefited once again from British technology. In exchange for the unimpressive YP-59A, the British reciprocated with a *Meteor*. In early February 1944 the Americans had a chance to put a *Meteor* through its paces, and were duly impressed with the new British design although it did not outperform the YP-59A to any great degree.[27]

Back in the United States, another chief test pilot took over the XP/YP-59A program in October 1943. Alvin "Tex" Johnston arrived at Muroc to assume flight testing from Jack Woolams.[28] As well, by the end of the year, the plane received its official nickname—*Airacomet*.[29] Flight testing included high-speed trials, high-altitude attempts, and airframe performance checks. Jack Woolams achieved the high-altitude mark of 47,600 feet before he left the base in September.

One immediate problem was the poor spin characteristic of the prototype. The original Secret Six did not have the benefit of high-speed wind tunnels to test their design, and its performance was found lacking in reality. The wind-tunnel test model finally underwent testing, and NACA delivered its wind tunnel test report to Bell by late 1943.[30] It was decided that the series production P-59A would incorporate a ventral fin under the tail to correct instability problems.[31]

Johnston also encountered problems with high-altitude jet flight. At altitude, the plane's speed corridor was only 12 mph. In other words, the plane's low-speed and high-speed stall limits were very close; thus the pilot had to work hard to maintain safe speeds. In one instance, when Johnston tried to throttle back to slow for descent, the plane did not respond. His solution was to cut the left engine—the right was the source of both cabin heat and pressure—and reduce speed through controlled engine failure. His pilot skills paid off, he brought the plane in safely. In the after flight report, the problem was discussed, and GE rectified the issue with the first jet-engine-altitude-compensating fuel regulator.[32] The problem was that the engines were drawing fuel from the tanks too quickly. The regulator compensated for the draw from the fuel-hungry engines as well as high-altitude flight where less fuel was required.

The shroud of secrecy surrounding the *Airacomet* was lifted on January 7, 1944. In newspapers across the nation, the Bell jet plane was announced to an eager public.[33] Although mislabeled as a "rocket"[34] the papers reported on the development of the "U.S.–British Mystery Plane."[35] Although pictures were not out until the next month (February 10[36]), the secret was revealed, and press coverage was thorough.

The new YP-59As, sporting GE I-16s, were put to combat testing beginning in February 1944. The jet was tested against the AAF's hottest model fighters—the P-47 *Thunderbolt* and P-38 *Lightning*. For 2 weeks, test and military pilots put the *Airacomet* through its paces in mock combat trials.[37] The jet's performance was lacking; it was not even as fast as the conventional fighters. The P-47 and P-38 were faster in level flight and also had better dive capabilities. The only apparent advantage was that the YP-59A, with greater wing area, could turn inside the piston-fighters with a smaller turning radius.[38] The flight test evaluations echoed the mediocre performance characteristics of the jet. The reports concluded that the future production P-59A was not a suitable combat aircraft, but would be valuable as a trainer and for experiments.[39] The Army decided the fate of the *Airacomet*; it was novel and useful, but virtually obsolete immediately.

Spin tests were concluded, and by mid-1944, the entire testing program was returned to Buffalo. Only dive testing was left to perform. The XP/YP-59A program at Muroc was disbanded as the Army received its new jet aircraft, the Lockheed XP-80 *Shooting Star*.

At Buffalo, the test team found that the plane had serious undercarriage and tail problems in high-speed dives. The undercarriage problem was finally identified and rectified with gear-up locks, which secured the gear in flight.[40] The tail problems were attended to with supports for the tail unit. But, in one eventful dive test Jack Woolams had to bail out after the tail ripped off in a high-speed dive. One indication of the speed came when he opened his parachute and the forces ripped his boots from his feet. He landed safely, but had to walk a mile and a half in his socks, in November snow, to a farmhouse to report the accident. One of Bell's new helicopter projects rescued Woolams from the farmhouse.[41]

Production P-59A *Airacomet*s were delivered to the Army for continued testing. Particular changes were made that affected the performance and operations of the test aircraft. The tail unit was strengthened after Woolam's accident, and a speed governor was installed to prevent the plane from flying faster than Mach 0.7. Further, new pilots were instructed specifically to refrain from attempting high-speed flight; the plane was not suitable.

The *Airacomet* was turned over to the Army's Fighter Flight Testing Division (FFT) at Wright Field, Dayton, Ohio, in October 1944. In an interesting sidelight, the first American woman to fly the jet was Ann Carl (in the WASPs—Women Air Force Service Pilots—and the only woman test pilot then in the Army Air Forces). She recounts how the plane was a delight to fly, and that her first flight was exciting but uneventful.[42] Her conclusions were indicative of the majority of *Airacomet* test pilots: the plane was a marvel, but with its long takeoff run and landing requirements, and poor overall performance compared to contemporary piston-engine fighter designs, the jet would be relegated to training. The official Army Air Forces report stated that "Even though a combat airplane did not result from the development of the X and YP-59A airplanes, it is considered that the development was worthwhile since it proved that the principle of jet propulsion for aircraft was sound and practical."[43] In October 1944, the

Army's order for 100 production P-59As was reduced to 39 aircraft. Bell wrangled an additional 11 out of the Army for a total of 50 production airframes.[44] Including the XP-59A and YP-59A models, Bell produced 66 *Airacomets* for the Army. The last P-59B-1[45] was accepted on August 27, 1945,[46] and remained in active service until November 1949.[47]

GE began development of the I-40 (J33) centrifugal-flow turbojet engine in June 1943, as the XP-59A was undergoing trials.[48] The I-40 was a larger version of the I-A through I-16 engines, and was designed to meet the Army's request for a higher thrust engine. The GE team, led by Dale Streid, designed the I-40 as the first 4,000 lb thrust jet engine. Concurrent development at Schenectady on the proposed 4,000 lb thrust TG-180 axial-flow engine was also in the works, but the designers admitted that the axial-flow engine would require more developmental time; and it did.[49] The I-40 was a centrifugal-flow configuration, only larger. The most significant change was in the combustion stage, the GE team decided to employ annular (straight-through) chambers rather than reverse-flow types (as were seen on the I-A, I-14, and I-16).[50] The 14 straight-through combustion chambers were made of wrapped Nimonic; a heat-resistant alloy that allowed for higher temperatures inside the engine thus higher thrust. By incorporating new materials and methods, and building on existing design, the I-40 was ready for testing as early as January 1944. By February, the new GE engine was bench-tested at 4,200-lb thrust, exceeding design promise. America's second-generation engine was ready for flight by June 1944.

Larry Bell also refocused his attention. His design team had come up with a good airframe, but its performance was lacking. Bell turned his attention to new jet projects for immediate development to supplant the *Airacomet*. Bell's first answer was a high-altitude, high-speed, long-range heavy escort fighter to protect bomber streams over Europe. The XP-83 was the natural evolution of this dream. In early 1944, as the limitations on the *Airacomet* were being fully understood, Bell undertook development of the XP-83. Robert Woods was the design engineer and he incorporated a number of P-59A characteristics into the new airframe. The XP-83 was intended to house the newer, more powerful I-40 (J33) engines from GE in a twin-engine configuration similar to the P-59A. The twin engines were designed for 4,000 lbs thrust each; Woods therefore designed the airframe larger and heavier. The single-seat twin-engine fighter incorporated hydraulically assisted control surfaces as well as a dive-recovery flap system to overcome dive problems found in the *Airacomet*. The Army decided it was a good design and ordered two prototypes in July 1944. The larger XP-83 was designed for larger engines, more fuel, and bigger armament.[51]

Unfortunately for Bell, the XP-83 was a fuel-hungry aircraft, and range figures were disappointing. And, although the flight manual suggests flying at lower speeds to conserve fuel,[52] the range of the twin-jet engine fighter was limited to 747 miles at full power and 1,750 miles at best endurance. These figures included auxiliary "drop" tanks with 150 gallons each—extra weight and accessories that would hamper performance further.[53] Top speed of the XP-83 was 522 mph, a vast improvement on *Airacomet* figures, but lacking nonetheless. When Woolams flew the XP-83 prototype for the first time in February 1945, the Bell test pilot found the speed good but not great, and reported that the maneuverability was marginal at best. The USAAF also tested the XP-83, and echoed Woolam's concerns. The Army paid for the two prototypes, but did not order production P-83s for their inventory.[54] The first prototype crashed in 1946 and the second was scrapped in 1947 ending the XP-83 program.

Bell's second attempt to replace the XP-59A was the "Venus Project." Contract number W33-038 AC 6636, the Venus was designed as a jet attack plane, with heavy armament for ground-attack missions. The four-engine high-wing jet was designed to meet Army Air Forces specifications (R-1800-E) from May 1944 for a ground attack aircraft. As stated in the Army requirements for

a high speed, low altitude, attack airplane. The tactical missions of this airplane are:

1. The destruction by machine gun fire, cannon fire, rockets, bombs, and torpedoes of military targets on land and sea in support of air, ground, or naval forces.

2. Medium range reconnaissance in support of air, ground or naval forces. The reconnaissance function of the airplane shall be considered as secondary and no bombardment characteristics shall be compromised to this end.[55]

Thus, the plane was designed as a four-engine jet attack aircraft to be built at the Bell Georgia plant. The provisions for ground attack included either eighteen .50 caliber machine guns (model T25E-3), or eight .60 caliber forward-firing machine guns and two .50 calibers in a tail barbette. The bomber version was designed to carry twelve 500-pound bombs or any combination up to 6,000 pounds. Interestingly, in the design proposal, "Provisions [were] made for carrying one 12,000 lb "Tall Boy" bomb."[56] Other configurations employed torpedoes, rockets, or cameras, according to Army specifications. But one of the limitations of early jet power was high fuel consumption at low altitude and Bell's ideas were good but unnecessary. The Army disregarded the close air support jet; the Bell project was stashed away.[57] The project was a bust, and Bell turned his attention to specifically experimental aircraft and his new passion: helicopters.

The next American jet plane was not from Bell, but from another source. The Army approached the Lockheed Aircraft Corporation on May 17, 1943, and asked for a design proposal for the Army's next generation jet fighter.

General Franklin Carroll, the head of the Army Air Forces Engineering Division, opened discussions with the promising Lockheed designers.[58] Lockheed's brilliant designer, Clarence L. "Kelly" Johnson, had been intimately involved in designing some of the most remarkable prewar airframes, including theoretical interest in a jet aircraft.

"Kelly" Johnson had come to Lockheed by way of University of Michigan. While testing a twin-engine transport model in the University's wind tunnel, Johnson suggested improvements to the control surfaces. The talented young aeronautical engineering student was hired upon graduation and quickly reshaped the Lockheed design team.[59] Kelly's twin-engine fighter designed P-38 *Lightning* secured his position in the firm and Lockheed's importance to the Army air effort. But he became equally important for his contribution to the American jet program.

As early as 1940, Johnson, along with Hal Hibbard, Lockheed's chief engineer, contemplated the problem of compressibility in the air. The two invited Nathan Price to construct a twin-spool axial-flow turbojet for a radical new aircraft design. The L-1000 axial-flow engine was designed to be a 16-stage twin-spool (contra-rotating impeller stages in cascade) with annular combustion chambers and four turbines (one impulse-stage followed by three reaction-stage turbines).[60] The highly complicated and heavy (1,235 lbs) engine would produce a projected 5,100 lbs thrust at sea level,[61] far more than contemporary theoretical designs. The L-1000 was designed to power the Johnson/Hibbard proposed L-133 airframe. Also a radical design, the L-133 was a twin-engine turbojet constructed with stainless steel and configured with the elevator controls at the front of the plane, canard style. The stainless steel construction was to deal with high temperature at high speeds; the canard configuration was to overcome compressibility problems at speeds above the projected 625 mph.[62] The unique design also featured wingtip stabilization jets using air rerouted from the jet engine in lieu of conventional control surfaces.[63] Unfortunately for Lockheed, the L-133/L-1000 project was refused citing the importance of the current conventional piston-engine projects in development.[64] But Lockheed's talent for designing unconventional aircraft was considered when it came to America's second jet aircraft.

Lockheed had been let in on the Bell XP-59A secret in late 1942, and was given technical data on the latest British engine as early as March 1943; design drawings of the de Havilland Halford H.1B *Goblin* centrifugal-flow turbojet. The Army's initial inquiry was presented in May, and the Lockheed design team, led by Johnson, began work on initial estimates. The formal proposal was submitted 4 weeks later at Wright Field and the contract was accepted on June 14.[65] The clock started, and Lockheed was tied into a 180-day developmental window for the XP-80 airframe. The design was based around a single 3,000 lb thrust (proposed) de Havilland *Goblin* centrifugal-flow turbojet engine—simply because the *Goblin* was ready—and was projected to be a frontline 500 mph fighter jet. Work began immediately on the first prototype, and the new airframe began to take shape.

The XP-80 was designed as a novel single-engine turbojet fighter. The plane had a low-wing with a laminar-flow wing section. The aircraft was purpose-built for speed. The engine was embedded in the fuselage, and wind-tunnel tested air intakes were placed in front of the wing's leading edge along each side of the fuselage. The streamlined bubble canopy housed a pressurized cockpit for the lone pilot. The prototype had no armament, but production called for six .50 caliber machine guns in the nose.

The XP-80 design and team were also sequestered; America's second jet aircraft was kept very secret. The team was settled in a tent next to a plastics factory, and when the wind was right—or wrong—the stench was almost unbearable. The design studio for the XP-80 was without a name until one fateful day when a phone call came in. Jokingly referring to the smell of plastics, and referring to the backwoods still in the "L'il Abner" comic strip, designer Irv Culver answered the ringing phone with the greeting, "Skonk Works."[66] Lockheed's Skunk Works became the project center for the development of ultrasecret aircraft.

The new housing was situated close to the Lockheed main plant in Burbank, California, but was completely autonomous. A machine shop was bought out, for the necessary tools, and the proximity to the Lockheed wind tunnel allowed the Lockheed team to conduct tests on the airframe components. Johnson set to work with 23 engineers and 57 machinists to build the XP-80 prototype. Work began on the XP-80 in earnest (and on the official 180-day clock) on June 24, 1943. Johnson decided that the team was going to work 10-hour days, 6 days a week to develop the prototype Lockheed jet airplane.[67]

By the nineteenth day, the wind tunnel test model was ready for trials. Johnson notes that the wind tunnel test model was "unusually detailed" so that the design team would not have to make substantial changes.[68] The plan worked, the wind tunnel test model was adopted as the basis for the first prototype with no modifications. As with the Bell XP-59A, the Lockheed team did not have an actual engine to work with. Wright Field provided drawings and performance estimates, but the designers had to develop the airframe without ever having seen the engine. One benefit Johnson mentions is that the aircraft's peripheral equipment provided by other government contractors—guns, radio, wheels, tires, etc.—were delivered early in the program, thus one less worry for the design team.[69]

In another great leap of faith, Johnson decided to incorporate an untested wing design from NACA. Developed as a high-speed laminar-flow wing section, the design was unsuited to low-speed (read: propeller-driven) flight. Johnson decided to put NACA high-speed wind-tunnel testing data to the test, and incorporated the new wing into his jet airplane design.[70] The selection of this predesigned wing section gave Lockheed a "tremendous advantage as far as schedule was concerned."[71] Johnson cross-checked his figures with those of the NACA design testing, and was confident in the high-speed capabilities and potential of the wing.

The control surfaces were redesigns of the P-38 *Lightning*'s partially hydraulically boosted system (the elevator and rudder were mechanical, but the ailerons were hydraulically boosted); the XP-80 was designed to have great maneuverability even at high speed. The fuselage was built for ease of access to the central engine; the front and back halves of the airframe separated for engine repair and replacement. The wing and fuselage were ready for test fitting by Day 83.

The project took on a hectic pace, and the self-imposed stress began to take its toll on the design team. Work loss-rates began to climb, but Johnson reiterated the time constraint to his men as the plane started to take shape. The plane was finally assembled in November, and the team conducted unsophisticated stress tests on the airframe. The assembled plane was suspended from the ceiling, and "a complete load of fuel was pumped in and out, and the entire craft was shaken to test flutter modes. Complete brake tests were run before the plane moved an inch. We almost pulled down the shed during tests of the cockpit canopy release mechanism."[72] The plane was deemed solid, mated with a wooden engine mock-up and moved to Muroc. On November 16, 1943, the airframe, at Muroc, was accepted by the Army Air Forces. The airframe was ready; the test flights would have to wait until suitable engines were ready. Airframe development had taken 143 days.[73]

Initially, the Lockheed team contemplated using GE I-16s as power plants for the XP-80, but they were deemed inadequate. The plane would have to wait for the *Goblin* engine for flight tests, and the delayed GE I-40 engine program for production.

The first engine arrived on November 17, 1943. The de Havilland Halford H.1B *Goblin* centrifugal-flow turbojet was installed in the XP-80, affectionately dubbed "*Lulu Belle*."[74] The first engine was run up to 8,800 rpm, and both inlet ducts collapsed. They were built to withstand the pressure; Johnson cited a structural failure. Unfortunately, the engine was damaged beyond easy repair when it was determined that the impeller had cracked. Structural modifications were completed while the Americans waited for the requested replacement engine.

On December 28, the second engine arrived, and on January 8, 1944, the XP-80 prototype, America's second jet airplane, flew for the first time. Johnson's Lockheed team had done an amazing job in designing America's second-generation jet fighter plane—an aircraft that was specifically designed to be a frontline jet fighter.

Unfortunately, the de Havilland *Goblin* engine was in short supply. The second model in the United States was literally taken out of a British prototype jet and sent to the Americans in a gesture of good will. There would be no more forthcoming. The Americans had to depend on their own designs for the future of the XP-80 program.

The first flight of the XP-80 was less than awe-inspiring. Milo Burcham, the Lockheed chief test pilot, took the controls and took off. The landing gear failed to retract, and the power-boosted controls were too sensitive. The first flight lasted a mere 5 minutes.[75] The faulty gear switch was replaced and the second flight of the day was spectacular. Burcham demonstrated the agility and speed of the new jet with daring and grace; all were impressed. Interestingly, the Bell plane was immediately eclipsed. Tex Johnson telegraphed Bob Stanley with the news, "Witnessed Lockheed XP-80 initial flight STOP Very impressive STOP Back to the drawing board STOP Signed, Tex"[76]

During initial testing the plane proved its worth to the air effort; the Goblin-powered XP-80 flew to 502 mph, almost a full 100 miles faster than the XP-59A. Further testing exposed weaknesses in the plane, unanticipated because of the novelty of high-speed flight. Improvements were made as GE neared completion of the I-40 program.

The engine program at West Lynn continued and the first I-40 went to the test stand in January 1944. By February, the I-40 was producing 4,200 lbs thrust, 200 pounds over design.[77] The plant began production and delivered the first engines to Lockheed for installation into the XP-80 in May. The American engine was bigger, and the slightly modified and heavier plane with the GE I-40 was designated XP-80A. The all-American Lockheed XP-80A, powered by the GE I-40/J33 engine, flew for the first time on June 10, 1944. America finally had a viable jet aircraft for combat operations.

GE lived up to its promise, delivering 300 J33 engines before the end of the war, based on completion schedules from the combined West Lynn and Syracuse plants that worked on the government program together.[78] GE had finally come into its own as the American production center for turbojet engines.

But, even with GE production in full swing, military procurement demanded more. The GE engine license was farmed out to Allison—a division of General Motors in Indianapolis—as early September 1945, where thousands of J33s were eventually built.[79] The shift from conventional piston-engine development was decided by the end of the war.

XP-80 testing continued to improve the design as XP-80As were prepared for initial trials. The wingtips of the XP-80 were modified for stability, and the XP-80A underwent further modifications. The GE powered XP-80A required a wider wing and longer fuselage; airframe weight also increased from 8,916 lbs to 13,780 lbs. Internal fuel capacity was raised and drop tanks were fitted for better range. Of the two XP-80As built for trials, one crashed and one was refit with a second seat, behind the pilot, for an onboard observer.[80]

The XP-80 was a success, and 13 service-test aircraft were ordered on March 10, 1944.[81] Designated YP-80A, the new plane was sent to a number of test facilities for extended analysis. Unfortunately, Milo Burcham, the chief test pilot for Lockheed and first to fly the XP-80 prototype, was killed in the maiden flight of YP-80A number three. Regardless, the production version, the P-80A *Shooting Star*, was ordered as early as April 4, 1944, when the Army requested two batches of 500 planes.

The P-80A became the first production combat turbojet aircraft for the U.S. Army Air Forces. In June 1945 an additional 2,500 jets were ordered to combat the Japanese.[82] But following V-J Day, the second order for 2,500 was cancelled, and the original order was reduced from 1,000 planes to 917. However, the P-80A did make its mark on the Allied war effort. Toward the end of hostilities in Europe, two of the series prototype YP-80As were delivered to the Italian theater to bolster troop morale and make an impression. The American jets did not come in contact with any of the advanced Axis designs; air-to-air jet combat was delayed until a future conflict. The P-80A *Shooting Star* had its moment of fame on November 8, 1950, when it became the first jet plane to shoot down another jet plane in combat after an American pilot scored a "kill" against a Soviet-built MiG-15 in the skies over Korea.[83]

The second American jet developmental program illustrates the growing importance of jet aircraft in military doctrine. The influence of speed over range in jet fighters was an indication of the technological considerations of the time. The Navy, impressed by the potential of the XP-59A more than the reality, turned to the nascent McDonnell aircraft company of St. Louis for design proposals for their first jet plane. The 1943 proposal evolved into the 1944 design of the McDonnell XFH-1, later called the *Phantom*.[84] The airframe layout was similar to the XP-80: the proposed jet was a straight-wing single-seat fighter. The twin-jet engine configuration was a departure from the Lockheed program; the engine intakes and exhausts were patterned after the original *Airacomet* design: the intakes for the engines were at the wing roots, and the individual exhausts exited directly behind the wings along the fuselage sides. The tail was distinct; the elevators slanted upward to avoid jet wash. The Navy design incorporated a stronger undercarriage for carrier landings and packed four .50 caliber machine guns in the nose. The sturdy but heavy plane was intended to be a frontline Navy jet fighter, and it is important to remember that it was the first specifically designed jet aircraft for the Navy, and the first jet airframe proposal from McDonnell. The importance was that the military was considering various manufacturers for jet plane designs.

The power plants also came from another source. GE was not consulted; the Navy turned to Westinghouse Electric Corporation, a large steam turbine manufacturer. Westinghouse had been involved in the original NACA

Special Committee on Jet Propulsion, where they had proposed an axial-flow turbojet engine. The original Navy contract was awarded on December 8, 1941, and the engine ran for the first time on March 19, 1943.[85]

The Westinghouse 19A axial-flow turbojet engine was designed with a 19-inch intake diameter, six-stage axial compressor, annular combustion chamber, and a single-stage turbine. The 19A was originally designed as a booster engine only; it produced mere 1,200 lbs thrust.[86] The 19XB—the 19A specifically for use in jet aircraft—was given the designation J30. The J30 boosted the flying speed of a Chance Vought F4U *Corsair* fighter in January 1944. Pratt & Whitney, a large piston-engine manufacturer was brought into the fold with a contract to produce license-built Westinghouse J30s. The engine came off the lines rated at 1,600 lbs thrust, and became the basis for the Navy's jet program.

The McDonnell XFH-1 prototype flew on January 25, 1945, powered by the Westinghouse J30 axial-flow turbojet engine. On the first flight, only one engine was available; the plane flew on half of its intended power, a tribute to its sound design.[87] This is one more apt example of the function of the airframe as well as the lack of available engines. But the point remains: America was getting serious about its jet engine and aircraft programs.

Westinghouse went on to develop some of the best Navy-sponsored turbojet designs. Into the postwar period, they were responsible for the J34 (3,500 lbs thrust) as well as the J40 projected to produce 7,500 lbs thrust—10,500 lbs with afterburner.

The American jet engine program was off to the races by mid-1945. GE and Allison were building centrifugal-flow J33s in quantity, and the combination of Westinghouse/Pratt & Whitney began production of the J30 axial-flow turbojet. Allis-Chalmers, another original member of the NACA Special Committee had proposed and was working on a ducted fan engine, unfortunately it never developed into a working product. But with the experience, Allis-Chalmers was shuttled into other turbojet manufacturing, including license-built de Havilland *Goblin* production. Thus, although the turbojet engine had come to America via Britain, by the end of the war it was the Americans who were in the lead with turbojet engine development.

Furthermore, the Americans were also in a position to take the lead in airframe design. Bell Aircraft Corporation had its third jet airframe on the drawing boards, and had already designed the first successful American jet airframe. The XP-59A *Airacomet* was America's first jet. And although it had been disappointing in many aspects, it was a technological breakthrough. One of the main problems facing Bell in the development of the *Airacomet* was the fact that wartime exigencies dictated extreme secrecy. The design was hampered from both novelty and lack of testing facilities. By limiting test data and facilities, and prohibiting academic and engineering interaction outside the "Secret Six," the *Airacomet* was a conservative design based on hypothetical assumptions and partial information. The Bell plane was overengineered for safety and stability, not for high-speed potential. Bell hoped for the best, but the first American jet did not live up to expectations. Bell turned to other jet projects and theoretical designs.[88] Jet aircraft development found its home outside of Buffalo.

America expanded jet development by the end of the war to include Lockheed, the new leader in American jet aviation. Lockheed went on to entrench the Skunk Works in the military-industrial complex with designs such as continued improvement on the P-80 design, the U-2 spyplane, the F-94 *Starfire*, the F-104 *Starfighter*, and the ultimate high-speed turbojet aircraft, the SR-71 *Blackbird*. In the closing stages of the war, North American[89] and Republic[90] submitted other Army Air Forces jet fighter proposals. The circle of jet airframe manufacturers expanded to include the premier wartime airframe designers. Not to be outdone, and also in need of jet aircraft, the Navy incubated other nascent jet airframe programs. Ryan was the first to develop the hybrid—both piston- and jet-engine-powered—FR-1 *Fireball*, the plane was a bridge between the old and the new and enjoyed a brief, but important, life as a Navy aircraft. The *Fireball* became legend in November 1945 when in a carrier landing the piston engine failed and it became the first jet plane to land on a carrier.[91] In summation, McDonnell was responsible for the Navy's FH-1 *Phantom*, the F2H *Banshee*, and the F3H *Demon* jet airframes,[92] while other Navy projects were developed at North American,[93] Vought,[94] Douglas,[95] and Grumman.[96]

Development and implementation of turbojet technology was not limited to fighter designs. Speed was seen as a benefit for bombers, and advanced designs were soon in progress. The North American B-45 was the first four-engine jet bomber accepted by the Army Air Forces and was followed quickly by Convair and Boeing airframes.[97] By the end of the war the U.S. military had definitely become converts, the jet era began in earnest in America.

But the story of the American jet program during World War II must be labeled "reactionary." The Americans did not have a comprehensive turbojet developmental program before the war as those seen in Britain and Germany. The Americans did have substantial advantages when jets became viable, but America lacked an indigenous turbojet program.

The United States, led by its National Advisory Committee for Aeronautics (NACA), was more concerned with the improvement of existing aircraft technologies. As is amply illustrated by prewar research, NACA was involved with the evolution of piston-engine airframes and power plants. Research and Development in the United States concentrated on improving existing technology for national interests. American aircraft designers, on the whole, were interested in profitable aviation pursuits above all. That meant high-payload, long-range, low-overhead aircraft designed for transport. The emphasis was on commercial success over speed and experimental aircraft. In the last days of peace in 1939, American aircraft had developed into long-range, low-overhead, efficient piston-engine airframes with the emphasis on maintainability and cargo capacity. The Americans by default had great transport aircraft—military and civilian—and bombers but lacked R&D into theoretical and experimental designs.

There were Americans who had explored the fringes of turbojet technology, but by the start of the war, even with the American entry, there was no concentrated American effort into turbojet technology. Sanford Moss at GE had come the closest, his turbosupercharger designs were two-thirds of a working turbojet, but the Americans did not even attempt the radical new power plant technology in earnest.

The impetus for American turbojet technology came from General "Hap" Arnold and his interest in technology. He brought the British turbojet to the United States where it was copied directly. GE got the contract to build the revolutionary engine. GE copied the British Whittle engine, and made it work in the United States. But the technology came from outside American industry and academy. The Americans simply did not consider the turbojet engine as a viable propulsion system.

In the same vein, jet airframe development was also hampered early in the American jet program. Bell was hamstrung by secrecy and isolation; his team's design was too conservative. The XP-59A was built to fly, but not built to excel. Without wind-tunnel testing facilities the design was fundamentally flawed and overengineered. Without complete data the airframe was built for safety, not for combat. The *Airacomet* was a failure because it was a conservative airframe based on incomplete information and potentialities.

But America was the best place in the world for the development of jet airplanes. The North American continent controlled or had access to all of the materials that were necessary for the development of turbojet engines. Nickel and molybdenum were (in 1939) exclusive to Canada and the United States, respectively, and bauxite, vanadium, and zinc were in ample supply.[98] In addition, the United States outstripped the world in production of steel, oil, and aluminum every year after 1940; and Germany was only marginally ahead in aluminum for two years.[99]

America was also ideally situated for security reasons. First, it was difficult to spy on the jet program. The secrecy that hampered the program also secured it from prying eyes. The jet remained unknown to all but a few until the official press release in January 1944. The Allies and Axis alike were unaware of American forays into turbojet technology—only the British had an inkling as to the extent of the growing American turbojet program. Further, except for Pearl Harbor and isolated balloon bombs in the Northwest, America was safe from Axis attack. This meant that the American jet program progressed uninterrupted once the Americans decided to ante up. The relative quiet in the United States was an interesting undertone in "Tex" Johnson's book, where he unwittingly talks about the lack of concern about the war, even though he was testing potential combat aircraft. It is interesting to note the ambiguity about the American war on two fronts from the test pilot's memoirs.[100]

America also had by far the greatest industrial base in the world. Combined with materials and security, the Americans were ideally suited for wartime production. It is amazing that the United States had so many aircraft manufacturing companies that Arnold was able to find one where the engineers were not busy building anything, and could be put to work on the first American jet airframe. The Bell Aircraft Company was selected for location and ingenuity, but at the end of the day the "Secret Six" were not busy.

By the end of the war, the United States had the most active jet program. Both airframe design and engine development had made the transition from back burner to priority in American R&D. By 1945 there were at least five companies working on turbojet engines for the postwar American jet program. The Americans were building more "borrowed" British centrifugal-flow turbojet designs than the British themselves. And the axial-flow design had finally come of age in the United States and by 1945 was in final testing phases. The Americans had come out of the dark and had initiated and instituted homegrown turbojet engine programs.

In addition, by 1945 there were at least nine airframe companies working on the next generation of American jet planes. Jet planes emerged and entered the mainstream in American society and military thinking. It took years for consistent doctrine to develop, but the Army (and later Air Force) and Navy in the aftermath of war sought out high-speed, high-altitude fighting jets. Contracts were solicited, proposed, and awarded to all comers; even abhorrent jet aircraft were built as prototypes in order to explore the potential of jet aircraft. The point is that by 1945, the Army Air Forces and Navy had converted—in theory, the reality was in development—to jet aircraft. For every operation from fighting to close air support to reconnaissance to bombing, turbojet aircraft became the preferred platform.

Furthermore, the American turbojet developmental program got a boost as the war was winding down in Europe. Army personnel directed by scientists and engineers began rounding up German technicians, data, and equipment for capture and analysis. As we will see, the German jet program had an enormous impact on the American jet program in the immediate postwar period.

America started the jet race late, but not last. The American jet program began with interest from on high in the persona of "Hap" Arnold, and had the British to thank for turbojet engine technology. The Americans would have eventually developed turbojets, but had not yet started. In accelerated evolution brought on by war, the United States quickly took center stage in the development of turbojet aircraft. The Americans were ideally situated to excel, and did. But the American approach was fundamentally different than the Germans and the British. In the United States the answer to the question of turbojet technology was the development of the technology first, then the application of scientific R&D to refine the existing designs. The British engine was virtually copied and put into use. The Bell designers had scientific background, but were restricted from testing.

7

Into the Cold

May 1945 brought an end to the "Thousand Year Reich" in only 12 years. As opposed to the ambiguous end of the war in 1918, the Allies decisively defeated Nazi Germany both militarily and politically. The end of the European war was the defining moment in the fall of the European powers and the rise of the Superpowers. Germany was divided and occupied; there would be no question as to the identity of the victors or the vanquished.

Even before the end of the war the Allies realized that the Germans had had an enormous impact on the evolution of military technology. In the final year of the war in Europe, the Germans led in nearly all fields of military technology, industrial capability, and theoretical knowledge. Some of the most impressive gains were in the fields of rocket technology (both manned and unmanned), turbojet aircraft, submarine technology, as well as the widespread misperception that the Germans had an advanced atomic program. By the end of the war each of the major Allies—the British, the Americans, and the Soviets—were poised to capture German technology for future considerations.

The European war had been decided by the courageous soldiers of the Red Army, the stoic British—with substantial Commonwealth support—and the determined Americans. These were not the only Allied combatants, but these were the three that were the most influential in the outcome of the war in Europe and the postwar world. All three powers had men in the field in Germany in the waning days of the Reich, and all three were in a position to exploit German hardware and knowledge for their benefit.

That being said, the first to benefit from German technology were her Axis partners in the Pacific. The Japanese bartered data and materiel from the Germans in the form of military hardware. Fortunately for the Americans in the Pacific, the designs were not much of use in the Japanese war effort. The Nakajima *Kikka*, based loosely on the Me 262 and powered by BMW 003 turbojet engines, was constructed in Japan but did not fly until the final days of the war.[1] The Japanese demonstrated the first example of incorporation of German jet technology into their military programs, but the Japanese jets did not become operational.

The Soviets had the most obvious presence in shattered Germany. The Soviets had surrounded and taken Berlin, and had advanced westward to link up with the Americans at Torgau. The Soviets controlled large portions of Germany and also stood in all of the former eastern European countries. The victorious Soviet Red Army began to "liberate" German equipment as reimbursement for the war.

The Soviets were interested in all aspects of German technology. Initially, there was a race among the victorious Allies for the supposed German atomic program. But all of the powers quickly learned that the Germans were in fact deficient in atomic weapons production; although their theoretical program was fairly impressive.[2] Each of the Allies turned their attention on other German technological development.

The second most coveted German technology was the marginally effective yet very impressive rocket program. And although the Soviets were on the ground at the rocket-testing facility in Peenemünde, the most influential German rocket scientists had traveled to southern Germany in order to surrender to the American forces. Thus, the Soviets got the hardware but the Americans got the theoretical data and personnel.[3] This of course incensed Stalin who is reported to have fumed, "We defeated Nazi armies; we occupy Berlin and Peenemünde; but the Americans get the rocket engineers... How and why was this allowed to happen?"[4]

Other German technology was gathered including material from the German jet program. The Soviets were the first to capture the fruits of the German jet program, and also the first to put it to use. Recently discovered Me 262s, Ar 234s, and He 162s were brought back to the Soviet Union for dissection by Soviet engineers. The Soviets quickly realized that the German jets were years beyond Soviet technology and ordered immediate reverse engineering and production of both Jumo 004 and BMW 003 engines.[5] Before the end of the war, in April 1945, the People's Commissar of Aircraft Industry ordered the construction of the new Soviet Red Air Force jet fighter based on German turbojet engine technology.

Although the Soviets decided against copying the Me 262 airframe outright, there was intrinsic interest in making use of the German engines. The Soviets began applying German technology to their nascent turbojet aircraft development, aware of the fact that they were years behind not only the Germans but also their erstwhile allies, the British and the Americans.[6]

Interestingly, the Soviets looked to the West for postwar technology as well. In an interesting exchange, the British were willing to sell the Soviets turbojet technology in the first days of peace. British turbojet technology, in the form of the Rolls-Royce W.2B *Nene*, was brokered to the Soviets, and began its Russian life as the VK-1 engine.[7] This centrifugal-flow engine, and the basic evolution of the first Whittle designs, powered Soviet jet fighters well into the cold war.

The Soviets made use of the German technology they acquired; in the end the German jet program, in the form of copied engines, powered the Red Air Force's first jet fighters. But the Soviets lagged behind their Western counterparts. The Germans, the British, and the Americans all had jets in production by the end of the European war; the Soviets did not. The first Soviet jet plane, the Mikoyan I-300 (also known by the designation F-1, the basis for the MiG 9 airframe) was not flight-tested until April 1946. The twin-jet engine fighter was followed chronologically by the Yakovlev Yak-Jumo prototype (the subsequent Yak 15), which flew in August 1946, and the Lavochkin "aircraft 150" that made its unimpressive first flight in October 1946.[8] The Soviets used German technology almost exclusively in their first jets; the first indigenous Soviet jet program, which finally improved on the German designs, was based on the original Lyul'ka designs, preempted by the war. But the Lyul'ka TR-1 was still not ready for testing by the end of the war, and it would be another year, until mid-1946, before the Soviets could apply homegrown technology to the newest arms race.

The Soviets gathered up what they could, but the Western Allies as well as the Germans stymied Soviet attempts to gather German technological expertise. Both the British and the Americans carried out planned programs for the capture and use of German technology and equipment, both focusing on the scientists and engineers. Further, the Germans made it easier for the Western Allies through their own actions.[9]

The Americans set plans in motion as early as November 1944. The U.S. Army gathered their own technical advisors, and drew up a list of names of German scientists who were considered leaders in their fields and therefore valuable. The operation was entitled Alsos and was put under the direction of Lieutenant Colonel Boris Pash, the former security chief for the Manhattan Project.[10] Alsos initially targeted the German atomic program. But as the Americans advanced across Europe, they came to the realization that the German program was in fact substantially inferior to the American program underway in New Mexico.[11] The team widened their focus and changed their operational name.

Operation Overcast was put into effect in the first months of the new year 1945. Building on information gathered from the OSS in Paris, the teams went in search of other German technology.[12] High-priority programs and their scientists included rockets, submarines, and turbojet technology, to name a few. The Americans were intent on capturing German hardware and engineers and whisking them away to the United States. This accomplished two goals: it gave the Americans access to high technology and denied the same to the Soviets.

With the end of the war in May, Operation Overcast was once again renamed, this time as Operation Paperclip. Special scientific teams were set up under the command of Supreme Headquarters Allied Expeditionary Force (SHAEF)–T (for "target") Sub-Division. The teams were sent into occupied Germany to gather technology and scientists for the advancement of postwar weapons. The "holy grail" for the Paperclip team were the scientists and engineers from *Mittelwerk*, the German rocket plant at Nordhausen. There, the Americans found the Peenemünde rocket scientists, along with 14 tons of data and paperwork, who had relocated to avoid Soviet capture. The most impressive acquisition of the Paperclip operation was Werner von Braun, the eminent German rocket scientist.

Under the aegis of Paperclip was a less well-known operation intended to gather German aeronautical technology. Colonel Harold Watson, a former USAAF test pilot, led Operation Lusty (named for Luftwaffe Secret Technology). The Lusty team was sent to Europe from Wright Field, Dayton, Ohio, where they were tasked with the capture of German aircraft technology.[13] The documents chronicle the journey of Watson and his men to Germany and their efforts to capture German planes.

Lusty was a complete success. Watson's team quickly collected captured German aircraft as the Allies overran German airfields. They constantly struggled to collect flying airplanes as the Germans had a tendency to disable aircraft before capture. But, eventually Watson was able to assemble an impressive array of captured German aircraft. Among his new acquisitions were the latest German hardware, the Arado 234 jet bomber, several Me 262s, and even a few Me 163 rocket planes. The biggest coup came with the capture of nine flight-worthy Me 262s accompanied by willing jet technicians and pilots. Given the choice of POW camps or instructing the new American jet pilots, three German flight officers joined Watson's team. The team was given a crash course on flying the revolutionary plane, and the propeller-less "Watson's Whizzers" were born. The flyable planes were flown to the coast of France, the rest were brought on trains, and the lot was packed on a loaned British escort carrier, *HMS Reaper*, and shipped to the United States for further evaluation.

Between the testing at Wright Field and later at Freeman Field, Indiana, the Americans came to some interesting conclusions about the value of German aircraft technology. "Hap" Arnold initiated postwar Air Force planning based on future projections, not on catch-up. He was insistent that the United States does a better job of technical intelligence—estimating others' strengths—as well as well-funded R&D. On both these points he argued, "In an age of nuclear weapons and strategic air power, we cannot afford to be caught by surprise again, as we were in World War II by German research and development."[14] The Americans, from the commander of the Air Forces to the test pilots and engineers, were extremely impressed by German technology.

As well, the Americans were impressed by German theoretical knowledge. The Germans had committed three turbojet types to combat (Me 262, Ar 234, and He 162), two pure rocket types (Me 163 and Bachem Ba 349), and one unmanned pulse-jet aircraft, the Fiesler Fi 103, better known as the V-1. The Germans were on the cutting edge of technology with their existing aircraft types; the postwar German theoretical knowledge stunned the Americans. German designs were married with American manufacturing to produce the most advanced aircraft of the time. German theory built the American "X" series experimental planes.

Under investigation, there were recognized problems with the German jet engines. By far the most frequent comment attesting to the drawbacks of the German jets was the poor performance at low speeds. The German jets suffered from poor performance at takeoff and landing, a condition that was never rectified during the war.[15] But the Germans had been able to develop axial-low turbojet engines during the war, realizing their potential for better efficiency and power. The Allied British and Americans had not been able to duplicate this feat. The Americans reverse-engineered German axial-flow turbojet engines and that information, combined with American materials technology and availability, was able to improve on forthcoming American designs. Information gathered from German Jumo 004 turbojet engines led to substantial improvements in General Electric's J47 axial-flow turbojet engine.[16]

Furthermore, the Americans were impressed by the existing German aircraft technology. The Me 262 provided a quantum leap in airframe technology. From the new undercarriage to the swept-wing design, from the fabrication to the structural efficiency, the German jet was revolutionary. The Me 163 rocket fighter was even more amazing. The delta-wing tail-less design fueled American aerodynamic research and development. "Hap" Arnold was quoted saying that captured German technology advanced American R&D by 6 months; von Kármán—a lot closer to the scientific world—said 2 years![17] By 1945 the Americans were developing very advanced aircraft, but even these were improved by German technology.[18] The Americas were immediately able to use captured German technology in Arnold's vision for a new all-jet-powered air force.

German experimental design work was also brought Stateside and incorporated into American aircraft development. The Me 262, the first plane with swept-back wings, would be the model for future high-speed interceptor aircraft. Another Messerschmitt project, P. 1011, was brought unfinished to the United States for inspection. The P.1011 was the first aircraft to incorporate swing-wing technology that was designed to maximize performance of early turbojet aircraft. The P.1011 became the basis for the Bell X-5, which investigated this idea. The Horton and Lippisch "tail-less" aircraft designs were investigated in the United States by Northrop (the X-4) as well as Ryan (and the ill-fated X-13 *Vertijet*). As well, German rocket planes influenced the development of another Bell product, the XS-1 (for Experimental Supersonic number 1), affectionately named *Glamorous Glennis* for the wife of the daring young pilot, Chuck Yeager. On October 14, 1947, Yeager piloted the XS-1 to Mach 1.06, the first pilot to break the sound barrier. Further work was done at Wright Field with the help of Hans von Ohain and Alexander Lippisch who actually came to the United States in the postwar period and helped the USAAF develop cutting-edge aircraft technology. German aeronautical development continued in America even after the end of the war; there were a number of prominent scientists and engineers who offered their services to the Americans in the aftermath of the war in Europe.

Britain also carried out a capture of German equipment in the closing days of the war. But, for their own reasons, the British did not build on German technology. The British were disappointed by existing German technology, and by the end of the war thought they were ahead of the Germans. Still, under the "Fedden Mission," the British gathered German artifacts for postwar consideration.[19] The mission was designed to investigate aeronautics in Germany in general, with specific reference in Section 4:

> To investigate gas turbines and jet engines, and to endeavor to make a broad review of their relative development in Germany in comparison with this country, and to ascertain the cost of manufacture and general techniques of jet engines, as compared with piston engines in Germany.[20]

The report argues that although the German jet engines were more easily built and maintained, they were built with inferior materials. German turbojets, therefore, were good, but plagued with problems. German equipment collected by Fedden Mission was brought back to Britain for display rather than testing. The recovery team, led by Group Captain Alan Hards, the commanding officer of Experimental Flying, went to Germany in the final stages of the war to capture and test Me 262s.[21] His small team comprised not only jet pilots but also British jet scientists. The British team went to Leck airfield in Schleswig-Holstein to fly captured Me 262s back to England. After visiting all of the airfields in the British Zone, as well as others outside the "official" British Zone, they were able to gather nine Me 262s; three each of the fighter, *Jabo*, and two-seat night-fighter versions. The planes were flown to Farnborough where two of the Me 262 fighters were put through extensive testing.[22] In the end, the British were content to show their public captured German material and did not feel the necessity of incorporating German technology into future development. This stands to reason, as the British in the immediate postwar period had other more pressing concerns with the Commonwealth and their crumbling Empire.

The story of the French utilization of the German jet program is somewhat more shrouded. After the war in Europe, France acquired seven Me 262s from captured airfields, but only three were airworthy.[23] Of the three flyable machines, one crashed in 1947 or 1948, leaving only two operational. These last two flew for the *Armee de l'Air* until September 1948 as France worked to rebuild its air forces.[24] By that point, however, the French had developed an independent air industry, based around the excellent designs of Dassault; little of the German technology was incorporated into evolving French designs.

A most unlikely postwar country was the beneficiary of German aviation technology. The Czechs in the immediate postwar period possessed a substantial portion of the German wartime turbojet manufacturing. In an interesting twist to history, the Czechs in May 1945 had what can be argued as the finest jet air force in the world. The new Czech government gained control of a number of factories that produced Me 262 components, including the Jumo 004 engines, following the German surrender. The factories, particularly *Avia*, continued production of the Me 262 under the Czech designation S-92 in the months after the end of the war.[25] The S-92 eventually formed the basis for the new Czech air force. By reconditioning several wartime Me 262s and building several new S-92s the Czechs were able to form one complete jet squadron. However, the story was short-lived; the communist takeover of Czechoslovakia in 1948 ended the use of the Me 262/S-92 as the Czech factories were retooled to produce "proper" Soviet designs like the MiG 15. The remaining S-92s were relegated to training roles.[26]

The relevant factor was speed. Turbojets were devised, designed, and developed for their revolutionary potential. The Germans were the first—and in the end the best—in developing turbojet technology during the war for a number of reasons. Initially, turbojet development was a natural evolution of German academic predisposition. The advanced theoretical knowledge in the institutes of higher learning in Germany translated directly into conditions for developing nontraditional aircraft and power plants. The "shackles" of Versailles actually forced the Germans to start fresh without technological baggage. The young Doctor of Physics, Hans von Ohain, searching for "elegance" in flight, wanted to develop an alternative to the dirty, noisy, and rough propeller engine. Fortunately, for Germany, his ideas were accepted by an aviation industrialist who was searching for speed and efficiency. German aircraft designers were looking for revolutionary technology at the exact time it was becoming available. And that is not all;

Dr. Franz, responsible for the development of the German axial-flow designs, also found the right time and climate for acceptance. His theories were proven correct; the Germans were the first to develop working, efficient axial-flow turbojets. Further, the Germans were devoted to increasingly higher theoretical advancement. In all forms of military hardware, the Germans were dedicated to developing the highest quality weapons by pursuing the boundaries of theoretical knowledge. Although this actually detracted from production on more than one occasion, and influenced more than one weapons system, the Germans were committed to the highest technology in the face of Allied quantitative capacity. Finally, the Germans faced the necessity of developing high-technology weapons systems. By the time turbojet aircraft became operational—indeed, as they were in the final stages of prototype—the Germans found that the turbojet aircraft, in the form of the Me 262, was a dire need. The air war had turned against Germany, the Allies were on the offensive, and Germany needed an air superiority fighter to combat the Combined Bomber Offensive. The Germans needed turbojet aircraft to an extent that the Allies did not.

The key variable that strangled the entire German turbojet production was the lack of necessary raw materials. It was not the infamous "Hitler Order" to construct the Me 262 only as a bomber; it was not the lack of pilots or fuel. What held up the development of German turbojet aircraft was the lack of raw materials—chrome, nickel, and molybdenum—in Germany. Substitutes were found; the machines were built. In fact, with consideration for the developmental chronology, the evolution was accelerated because of the war. But German turbojet engines, the Jumo 004 and BMW 003, were plagued with short operational life spans. The engines were consciously produced with defects because they were the potential answer to the weight of the Allied air offensive. The Germans made do with what they had because they had to. There were no other alternatives. And still the Me 262—and later Ar 234 and He 162—were better than any Allied turbojet aircraft built during the same time period.

The longevity of the German turbojet program is evident in the impact on postwar military and civilian applications. The Americans virtually copied most German theoretical data and applied it directly to experimental programs. Further, German aeronautical engineers, designers, and technicians were brought to the United States to advance theoretical knowledge for their new bosses. The impact of German turbojet engineering was substantial.

During World War II, the Americans and British were content to continue testing and with the development of conservative designs. Neither of the Western Allies felt the pressing need for turbojet aircraft throughout the war. Although they both possessed the know-how and the technical ability, there were few concerted efforts into development of non–piston-engine aircraft until well into the war. This is evident in the fact that the Americans, even with funds, materials, and ability, did not produce designs until prompted by collected data and extravagant government contracts. The jet pioneers in Britain and the United States were still concerned with speed, but took an entirely different approach than the Germans. Both were more concerned about postwar implications, thus designed conservative aircraft and engines. Both the United States and British designers considered endurance as an important factor, and spent more time on the development of more reliable centrifugal-flow turbojet engines. And finally, both the Americans and British were convinced that the war would be completed in the Allies favor with existing technology and concurrently impressive industrial capacity. The Allies had lots of material that was good enough to fight the Germans.

The Allies did not need turbojet aircraft to beat the Germans; the Germans needed their turbojet aircraft to have any hope of combating the Allied bombers over Germany. The Germans did it first and did it right; and after the war, the Germans kept doing it for the powers that combined to defeat them in World War II.

Epilogue

It has been 67 years since the first jet flight. In the interim, turbojet technology has become commonplace. Jet aircraft of all types fill the skies and provide invaluable services. Uses vary from transport to travel, protection to policing. And yet, it all began in the exigencies of wartime. Turbojet technology developed from a perceived need for high-technology weapons system as the world went to war in 1939. Had it not been for World War II, the world would have waited for turbojet technology. In peacetime, the evolution would have been years, perhaps decades slower.

Currently, the aircraft that did the most to prove jet propulsion—and provided the impetus for this project—is once again flying. In an interesting interconnection of capitalism and history, the Messerschmitt Me 262 is making a comeback. The most famous World War II German jet plane has found favor in the United States.

In 1993 Classic Fighter Industries was founded in New Jersey. Steve Snyder from Philadelphia was interested in resurrecting the historical German jet. He began researching, and got funding from private investors for a proposal to rebuild German jets. Although accurate and detailed blueprints were virtually nonexistent, the Navy dedicated their static Me 262B-1 to the group for disassembly and study on the condition that it was returned to Silver Hill Maryland as a restored static model. The Me 262B-1 was taken apart and drawings were made for future Me 262 construction.

The project was relocated to the Texas Air Factory, where Herb Tischler began construction of initially three, later five, reproduction Me 262s. The intention was that the planes were to be built using the same materials and jigs as the originals, the only difference in the American models were the engines. More reliable General Electric GE J19s will replace the unreliable Jumo 004 engines for the modern reproductions. The Texas team began construction of the Me 262 planes backed by private investors eager to see the German jet fly again.

Trouble ensued between investors and the design team, and the whole project was relocated to Seattle, Washington, in 1997. With increasing support and technical advice from Boeing, the project forged ahead. At this writing, the Me 262s have now flown; their triumphant return was the highlight of the 2006 Berlin Air Show. It is interesting in that there are investors willing to resurrect the German jet program for personal satisfaction and public notoriety. At the same time, the resurrection of the German jet program is a testament to the lasting legacy of the early jets in that the German jets need considerable financial investment to fly, while around the world there are still flying examples of the American P-80 and the British Meteor. The defeated Germans, who provided the world's most advanced jet fighter design of the war, were eclipsed by the victorious Americans, who were able to out-produce the Germans in all aspects of wartime production.

Appendices

APPENDIX A: THE CHOICE BETWEEN PISTON AND TURBOJET ENGINES

In retrospect, the decision in favor of the turbojet engine over the piston engine is obvious. But in 1935, this was not the case. By the mid-1930s there had been substantial changes and improvements in existing piston-engine technology. But, a presumptive anomaly[1] was foreseen with regard to existing and future piston engine power plants. Gas turbine technology was not the only answer; there were many different proposals and experiments. In the end, however, the gas turbine in the form of the turbojet engine was the answer to all of the questions: a high-speed, high-altitude, high-endurance, and long-range prime mover for aircraft. This Appendix will outline not only the reasons for the replacement of piston-engine technology but also some of the other ideas and experiments.

Aircraft piston-engine technology had developed substantially since World War I. At the end of the Great War, the U.S. *Liberty* V-12 Engine, as an example, produced 400 horsepower for 790 pounds. The *Liberty* was later supercharged for added horsepower, especially at high altitude. Sanford Moss's Pike's Peak experiments with a supercharged *Liberty* engine in 1918 proved that piston-engine technology could be improved for high-altitude flight. Both main types of piston-engine technology continued development throughout the interwar period. Liquid-cooled and air-cooled engines were tested, improved, and redesigned for better performance. Of these two types, the British Rolls-Royce liquid-cooled *Merlin* and the American *Wasp* series air-cooled radial engines were the apex of piston engine technology. The *Merlin* III (1940), which powered the Supermarine *Spitfire*, was a 12-cylinder liquid-cooled V engine of 27 liters displacement (1,649 c.i.d.). It was rated at 1440 hp (supercharged at altitude) for a dry weight of 1,375 pounds (625 kg) and a specific weight of 1.047 hp/pound.[2] The American Pratt and Whitney R2800 *Double Wasp* (1941) was an air-cooled 18-cylinder radial engine configured in two rows of nine cylinders. The R2800 was a 2,804 c.i.d. air-cooled engine that was rated at 2,500 hp (at 2,800 rpm) for a dry weight of 2,360 pounds (1,072.7 kg) and a specific weight of 1.059 hp/pound.[3]

But piston-engine designers were reaching the limits of their technology. All of the improvements possible were explored and attempted with only slight advantages. Materials engineering had built lighter yet powerful engines, but the piston engine was still constrained by fundamentals. The engine was made up of the block and the individual pistons; further modifications to these parts were nearly impossible. Further, development continued in the peripheral technologies: fuels, wiring, support cradles, fairings, and finally propellers. Of all of the developmental and experimental organizations, none was more concerned with making the piston-engine-powered aircraft more viable than the American National Advisory Committee for Aeronautics (NACA). Formed in 1915, NACA was very prolific on engine research. But, that being said, NACA was more interested in piston engines for commercial viability than anything else. They focused on the evolution of piston engines for long-range transport aircraft at the expense of other technology. NACA did succeed in analyzing and perfecting excellent long-range aircraft engines that were fuel-efficient and long-lasting. But NACA also ignored other possibilities.[4] The Americans led in high-altitude, long-range engine technology which evolved directly into excellent transports and heavy bombers, but failed in other areas.

The British were more concerned with speed than long range. They experimented with and built some of the fastest piston engines of the interwar period. But the British were also conservative; there were few attempts to develop alternate aircraft power plant technology.

In the Treaty of Versailles, the Germans were restricted from building aircraft engines. But German theoretical analysis continued. The Germans were open to new ideas in efforts to compete with both the British and the Americans. By 1939 the Germans were competing with existing piston-engine technology when Fritz Wendel broke and held the record for the world's fastest piston-engine aircraft in a new Messerschmitt design powered by a Damlier Benz DB 601X.[5] Furthermore, the Germans were open to other ideas. In order to compete on a world stage, the Germans considered many high-technology options for powered flight. Among the ideas were rockets (both solid and liquid fuel), pulse jets, ram jets, and turbojets (gas turbines). The Germans went on to lead the field in experimental aircraft power plants.

The limitations of piston engines can be broken down into two areas: the weight of the engine and the propeller system. Engine designers quickly realized that as their engines became more powerful, the corresponding weight increased. By 1935, for a conventional piston engine to increase horsepower twice (2x) the weight of the engine would increase by four 2^2, an exponential increase in weight for a linear increase in power. In aircraft technology this was a disaster. With the delicate balance between speed, range, and payload, an increase in weight took away from the performance of the plane. For large bombers and transports this was an important factor, but for single-engine fighters, planes that relied on high-speed, the considerations were an imperative.

In addition, there was increasing concern about the propeller system. Since World War I, propeller technology had evolved from wooden propellers to metal variable-pitch propellers, designed to maximize piston-engine performance. But one problem remained. As propellers turned ever faster, the tips reached supersonic speeds. Propellers flirted with the recently recognized compressibility boundary of air, and lost efficiency at high speeds. Therefore, even as engines became more powerful, efficiency was falling off at high speeds and at high altitude.

The simple solution, for a number of reasons, was the gas turbine for aircraft. First and foremost, it was much lighter. For the output (specific weight), turbojet engines were more efficient. They were easier to construct, once actual production began, and required fewer parts. Further, whereas piston engines are reciprocating, turbojets are rotational. The reciprocating piston engine can literally tear itself apart with the back and forth motion of the pistons and the crankshaft. Turbojet engines rotate around a central shaft with virtually no vibration and no reciprocating forces. The rotational speeds were (and remain) high, around 16,000 to 18,000 revolutions per minute (rpm), but are more easily dealt with than reciprocating engines that turn at 3,500 to 4,300 rpm.

Further, turbojet engines avoid propeller problems by deleting it. Vanes inside the engine compress the air for propulsion thus avoiding the need for a propeller. Turboprops (turbojet-powered propeller engines) are an evolution of the turbojet engine, but were developed after the original turbojet concept.

Thus, the turbojet overcame piston engine problems simply and efficiently. The weight was reduced for more efficiency and the propeller was deleted. The turbojet engine was the answer to the presumptive anomaly of the piston engine for aircraft.

Other experiments that attempted to supersede the piston engine were carried out primarily in Germany. As early as 1939 Heinkel had built both a rocket-assisted plane[6] and a pure rocket plane.[7] Further tests were conducted with pure rocket power for aircraft with the Messerschmitt Me 163

Komet, the Bachem Ba 349 *Natter,* and various rocket-assisted takeoff (RATO) configurations on a multitude of planes. The V-2 rocket program at Peenemünde under Werner von Braun was of course the most famous rocket program of the war. German tests continued with pulse-jets, in the infamous V-1 (Fiesler Fi 103) flying bomb known as the "Buzz Bomb" to the British, and various ramjet experiments to test their viability. But, even though successful, it was the turbojet engine, developed first in Germany and then in Britain, that has had the greatest impact on the continued evolution of aircraft power plant technology to this day.

APPENDIX B: CENTRIFUGAL-FLOW VERSUS AXIAL-FLOW TURBOJETS

This appendix will outline some of the basic premises behind the differences between centrifugal-flow and axial-flow turbojets.

The early construction of turbojets in all three countries relied on the easiest and most direct design of aircraft turbojet, the centrifugal-flow type. Stemming directly from technology and principles set forth in steam and water turbines, the centrifugal-flow type was the most easily adapted as a prime mover for aircraft. The centrifugal-flow engines designed by both Whittle and Ohain were simple, relatively easy to construct, and adapted well to use in aircraft. The more complex, difficult, and costly axial-flow turbojets were not developed until after certain high-speed and high-temperature principles were worked out in the centrifugal-flow types.

Turbojet construction is less about individual parts and more about a coordinated system.[8] The three turbojet stages are the compressor, the combustion chamber, and the turbine. In the centrifugal-flow system, the air is drawn in the front and comes in contact with the compressor. The compressor turns, and forces the air outwards centrifugally; the air is compressed as it is forced outwards at 90° from its original path. Compressed air flows to the next stage in the system, the combustion chamber or chambers. The first prototype turbojet engines employed single-sided impellers; ambient air was drawn in from the front of the engine and compressed by a one-sided impeller. Interestingly, the earliest production centrifugal-flow engines used double-sided compressors, a second stage of vanes was added to the back side of the compressor, air was drawn in from intakes on either side, thus increasing compression and therefore efficiency, while keeping the engine radius the same.

The next stage is the combustion chamber (or the plural, combustion chambers). The compressed air flows into the combustion chamber where it mixes with fuel and ignites, combusting the mixture. This causes a heat reaction wherein the volume of air expands and is forced past the third stage of the system, the turbine. There were immediate problems with the combustion chamber stage, materials engineering met head-on with thermodynamics in high-temperature testing. Temperatures reached 800°C in the combustion chambers, and the designers had to develop chambers that were not only heat-resistant but still lightweight for use in aircraft. In reciprocating engines the temperature and pressure are often higher, but only cyclical. Four-stroke piston engines are only "hot" during one cycle (of the four-cycle intake–compression–combustion–exhaust), while turbojet combustion chambers experience constant high temperature and high pressure. The difficulty was in developing combustion chambers that could withstand these new requirements and still be light enough to preserve the concept of the turbojet for aircraft.

The problem both Whittle and Ohain faced was making the engine viable for use as an aircraft power plant in the face of immense heat, pressure, and weight restrictions. In the end, Whittle decided on, and designed, a configuration of 10 combustion chambers for his W.1 engine; distributing the pressure and heat to a number of different chambers in the same stage. The Ohain engine had 16 combustion chambers of similar design. Both engines were designed as experimental flying prototypes and nothing more. Ohain went on to design further Heinkel centrifugal-flow engines such as the HeS 8. The heated and expanded air escaped the combustion chambers and flowed across the next stage: the turbine.

In the centrifugal-flow turbojet engines designed by Whittle and Ohain, the turbine was a single-wheel with vanes that turned as the heated, expanded air flowed through the final stages of the engine. The turbine turned on a shaft that was connected to the compressor, thus driving the entire engine and drawing yet more air in. The system was self-repeating; more air brought in, heated, and forced across the turbine meant that more air was drawn into the engine. The heated, expanded air not only turned the engine, it also became the thrust to power the aircraft in flight. Initial results with the W.1X (Whittle) were: 860 lbs thrust at 16,500 rpm. The E.28/39 powered by the W.1X flew for the first time to speeds of 370 mph at 20,000 ft altitude.[9] The main competition, the HeS 3b (Ohain) produced 1,100 lbs thrust for its first flight, but was also heavier than the W.1X.[10] The engines were very efficient for their construction, design, and technological development, but both men realized that there was more potential for the centrifugal-flow turbojet engine as developmental changes were made.

Some of the changes in the centrifugal-flow type over the course of the war were larger compressors, better and more efficient combustion chambers, and multistage turbines. Both Whittle and Ohain continued the development of their respective engines. By the end of the war, Whittle was working on his W.2/700 centrifugal-flow turbojet engine, which became the basis for the Rolls-Royce *Derwent* engine. Ohain's designs were modified and developed into more efficient centrifugal-flow engines, but in the end, the Germans decided on axial-flow over centrifugal-flow turbojets. Today, the centrifugal-flow turbojet engine has become an efficient, powerful workhorse in the world of aviation technology and is still in use. From its humble beginnings, the centrifugal-flow turbojet is an intricate technological component to aviation technology and engineering.

But the centrifugal-flow turbojet had its drawbacks as well. The diameter of the engine was inherently large. Because the airflow had to be forced outwards centrifugally, the engine itself was shallow, but wide. In the early jet aircraft, this was not a problem. The German He 178, the British Gloster E.28/39, and the American Bell XP-59A all incorporated centrifugal-flow engines within their fuselage cavities. The planes were, in effect, built around the power plants; all of these models were realistically only test beds for the new engine technology. When the second-generation jet aircraft were designed, considerations were made for the placement and type of engine(s). For the Allies in Britain and the United States, the choice was made to improve the centrifugal-flow type for maximum thrust, and build aircraft around the engine technology—as in the American Lockheed (X)P-80 *Shooting Star*—or cover the engines in low-drag nacelles as the British attempted in the Gloster *Meteor*. The Germans took a different tack: they called for radically different engine design. Later German jet aircraft, such as the Messerschmitt Me 262, were based on engineered airframe design with incorporated jet technology. The engines were designed to complement the aircraft, not the other way around.

Furthermore, the novel technology was the "first cut" at turbojet design. Early construction was trial and error, with lots of trial and frequent error. The early designers had to deal with unforeseen difficulties with temperatures, materials, and rotational speeds of the early turbojet engines. There was even the question of fuels for the nascent technology. Whereas Ohain and the Germans employed liquid hydrogen for the first turbojet engine, the British used kerosene. Eventually more common fuels were used, the British kept with the kerosene/paraffin family of fuels, the Germans worked with low-grade diesel, a fuel they still possessed in quantity at the end of the war. The most temperamental stage of the engines continued to be modified; the combustion chambers were designed and redesigned throughout the development of centrifugal-flow turbojet engines.

Alternately, other designs offered more promise as aircraft power plants. Engine designers in all three countries developed, tested, and—in Germany at least—flew a potentially more efficient turbojet engine: the axial-flow turbojet. The premise was the same. The engine system was composed of the three above-mentioned stages; in the axial-flow engine the layout was different. The axial-flow compressor relied on stages of alternating impeller and stator vanes to compress incoming air. There were revolving compressor blades (impeller vanes) that compressed air against stationary blades (stator vanes) in stages. The beauty of the axial-flow turbojet was that stages could be added to increase compression hence efficiency. In the most famous wartime example, the Junkers Jumo 004, the compressor stage was made up of eight stages in the compressor. The compressed air did not, however, change direction as in the centrifugal-flow type, instead it was compressed axially.

The compressed air next entered the combustion chambers. The compressed air was mixed with fuel and fired, increasing both the temperature and volume of the gas. Interestingly, the axial-flow combustion chamber was also the most problematic stage of the system. There were difficulties with this stage throughout the war; materials and thermodynamics had to evolve with the development of technology. The Jumo 004 incorporated six combustion chambers in the second stage of the engine. The prototype Jumo 004 engine was built without consideration for materials restrictions, but German designer, Dr. Anselm Franz, quickly realized that future development and mass production would be restricted by materials shortages. The redesigned 004 B-1 used less of the scarce resources but engine longevity suffered. The Germans built Jumo 004s in 1944–1945 with the recognition that the engine was flawed, there were few other options. However, the German jet program can be hailed for two reasons: they were able to build thousands of Jumo 004 engines—no matter how flawed—and they also realized the shortcomings but were simply unable to rectify the problems with the exigency of war. The Germans got it right and were able to mass produce a viable jet engine for combat use. The combustion chambers continued to be the main concern. In the prototypes, they were made of high-temperature and high-stress steel alloy, with significant amounts of chrome, nickel, and molybdenum. In the production model the combustion chambers were formed from "mild" steel alloys with an aluminum coating to prevent oxidation. This translated into problems with longevity. The Jumo 004 engine was scheduled for complete overhaul after only 10 hours flight time.

The Jumo 004 turbine was an improvement, but not a significant change from earlier types. The turbine was in the exhaust stage where heated gas flowed over the turbine wheel turning the central shaft that drove the entire engine. In the Jumo 004 production engine (004B-1 and on), the added improvement was a variable position tail cone inside the exhaust chamber of the engine which could be manipulated to increase thrust.

The dilemma for the early turbojet aircraft designers was the question of which engine design to pursue. For the Allies it was straightforward; the centrifugal-flow turbojet engine was the chosen power plant for the entire war, receiving all consideration and effort. A few axial-flow projects were considered—and funded—but for the most part these engines were seen as postwar developmental programs for future advancement. The Germans put funding and effort into all designs from the start. Under the technical branch of the *Reichsluftfahrtministerium* (RLM), German jets received attention and funding throughout the war. There were programs in many facilities, the Jumo Company simply happened to produce the most lasting impression. For example, the RLM funded rocket, pulse-jet, ramjet, and several different turbojet programs. The Heinkel company—with Ohain at the fore—continued to develop centrifugal-flow turbojets throughout the war. Although these engines were overshadowed, there was significant advance in the evolution of German centrifugal-flow types. There were other axial-flow programs in addition to Jumo. BMW was actually the first to produce axial-flow turbojets for the Me 262 program, but the engines failed on the ill-fated March 25, 1942, flight. But, by the end of the war the BMW company had developed a viable turbojet engine, the BMW 003. The BMW was the power source for the Heinkel He 162 as well as testing in a number of different experimental planes and configurations.

The choice for centrifugal-flow versus axial-flow turbojet was not exclusionary; it was based on several considerations.[11] The benefits of the centrifugal-flow type, after successful tests by both Whittle and Ohain, were straightforward. Whittle argued, successfully, that the centrifugal-flow type was easier and cheaper to make, that the potential had not been met and could be improved upon, and ultimately that the engine was already working and would not require extensive modification for production and use. Further, Whittle stated that the centrifugal-flow turbojet engine could match the compressor and turbine stages more closely (and more easily) thus reducing surging in the engine. To Whittle, the centrifugal-flow design was proven and robust, and was the obvious choice for further development.

By comparison, Whittle considered the axial-flow turbojet more expensive, more fragile, and more troublesome. Although the axial-flow type predicted higher efficiency and power, as well as a smaller frontal area, Whittle derided the type because it did not offer the same benefits that the centrifugal-flow engine promised. For Whittle, the axial-flow engine was more costly in materials, construction time, and developmental funding. The axial-flow engine was also considered more fragile and temperamental. Whittle also argued that the axial-flow engine required closer tolerances: it was a more precise system. And Whittle was right. The axial-flow engine was more troublesome for all of these reasons, and Whittle was not optimistic about the potential of the axial-flow over the centrifugal- flow types.

But the Germans were. The German tradition of machinists and engineers translated directly into excellent designs and relative ease of manufacture. Furthermore, German turbojet theory promised substantial improvement over the centrifugal-flow engine with the axial-flow type. The Germans (literally and figuratively) invested in the axial-flow turbojet for their jet program. Dr. Anselm Franz believed that his Jumo 004 axial-flow turbojet design would live up to not only theory but also be, in practice, a revolutionary aircraft power plant. The Germans invested in the axial-flow

turbojet engine, but it must be remembered that there was concurrent research and development of many types of turbojet engines; the Jumo 004
was simply the success story of the German jet program.

Furthermore, the fundamental conception of turbojet engine technology
was different between the Germans and the Allies. The Germans considered
the engines peripheral within the entire aircraft system. The engines were
the prime movers but the aircraft itself was the focus. This is evidenced
by the importance of the aircraft designers themselves—Messerschmitt and
Heinkel, as well as others—who were given the contracts for jet aircraft and
later shopped for engines. Ample funding was given to Junkers Motorenbau
(Jumo) and BMW for development, but the airframes were the focus, the
engines were secondary. Thus, the RLM records reflect the ongoing debate in
Germany over the airframes and development at Heinkel and Messerschmitt
rather than more than a cursory mention of the concurrent engine programs.
In Germany, the engines were less important than the airframes; the axial-
flow engine was developed because it promised the best performance. The
Germans were interested in developing the most capable aircraft possible
under the constraints of war and time.

The Allies on the other hand focused on the engines. The British, led by
Whittle's developments, and the Americans, building directly on the British
turbojet program, continued development of the centrifugal-flow type. The
Allies made the engine the center of attention, and developed airframes
around the power plant. Developmental funding and effort went into improvements in the engine; airframes were an afterthought. In all three Allied
wartime turbojet programs, Gloster's *Meteor* as well as Bell and Lockheed,
the airframe designers were given engine specifications and told to develop
airframes around the power plants. Centrifugal-flow engines were improved
during the war, but the Americans and British considered the turbojet aircraft superfluous to the war effort. Both of the Allies wanted continued
development of turbojet aircraft for postwar considerations, neither saw the
jet as decisive—from either side—for the concurrent conflict. The Allies were
content to develop centrifugal-flow turbojet technology along evolutionary
(albeit accelerated) timelines, while postponing serious axial-flow R&D into
the future. Both the Americans and British ended the war with good, but
still unimpressive, turbojet aircraft designs in production. Neither had committed to producing overwhelmingly superior turbojet aircraft by the end of
hostilities.

Both the Allies and the Germans avoided making the choice between
centrifugal-flow and axial-flow turbojet engines during the war. The Allies knew that the axial-flow turbojet promised higher potential, but given
the inherent constraints of turbojet engines were content to push axial-flow
R&D into the future. The Germans avoided the decision by funding both
programs; either privately or through government sponsorship the Germans

continued development of both centrifugal-flow and axial-flow turbojet engines throughout the war.

APPENDIX C: CALL SIGNS AND OFFICIAL DESIGNATION OF THE EARLY JET AIRCRAFT

The first turbojet-powered aircraft to fly was the Heinkel He 178. As an experimental prototype this plane carried neither civilian nor military markings. In fact, the plane was unpainted, maintaining its natural metal finish. Two He 178 aircraft (V1 and V2) were built for experimental testing only.

The first Allied turbojet aircraft to fly was the Gloster Meteor E.28/39. Two were built for experimental testing, and designed around Whittle's engine. The unofficial name given to the plane by the men who designed and tested it (from both Gloster and Power Jets) was the *Squirt*. The eventual "official" Air Ministry moniker was *Pioneer*. The Gloster manufacture number for the first E.28/39 was 4041 and fell under the contract from the Air Ministry SB/3229/c 23A. The fuselage designation was initially bare metal, later painted camouflage with RAF roundels applied followed by ⓅW4041/G (the last "G" designated that the plane must be under armed guard whenever it was away from its home airfield). The Air Ministry numbers for the two *Pioneers* were W4041 and W4046, respectively.

Heinkel's next jet project, his first He 280 prototype was given the fuselage designation DL and carried that letter grouping in front of the German cross "+" followed by the plane letter grouping AS. Thus, the call sign of the first He 280 prototype (also reported as V1, for "first prototype") reads: DL+AS. The second prototype was designated GJ+CA, the third was GJ+CB. V4 through V6 had no designations; V7 was assigned NU+EB (and is also seen in photos with the civilian registration D-IEXM). The final constructed prototype V8 was designated NU+EC. Eight prototypes were built, exclusively for testing purposes. Another four were planned but never constructed. The He 280 program was cancelled by the RLM before official numbers could be assigned to the airframes, and the plane was never given a name.

Meserschmitt's Me 262 jets were designated with the letter grouping PC, and the prototypes began with the letter grouping UA. Thus the first prototype was PC+UA, the third prototype (the first to fly on pure jet power) was designated PC+UC. Ten prototypes were built and tested. A further 10 were "Series 0" aircraft, preproduction airframes for weapons and stability testing. Production began with the Me 262a-1 *Schwalbe*, and continued with other versions including a two-seat night fighter, reconnaissance version, and various experimental weapons platform configurations. The official German records, supported by cross-referenced American and British documents, state that 1,294 Me 262s of all types were constructed and accepted by the Luftwaffe. A significant number of these were damaged or destroyed in noncombat accidents, another portion were destroyed on the ground by Allied air power. Only an estimated one-third reached operational squadrons for use in air combat. As an illustration, on the most active day of German jet operations, only 55 Me 262s were able to intercept over 2,000 Allied aircraft (April 10, 1945). The Me 262 carried RLM numbers for official registration, and each squadron had its own numbering system for its aircraft. For example, the National Air and Space Museum Me 262a-1a is RLM number 500491, and is painted with the call sign "Yellow 7" (a yellow number 7 on the fuselage directly in front of the German cross), and decorated with the squadron chevron from (*Jagdgeschwader*) *JG* 7. The U.S. Air Force Museum's Me 262a-1a awaits a proper paint scheme and designation.

The American Bell prototypes were designated Model 27 by the Bell Aircraft Company. The first U.S. turbojet aircraft was identified as the XP-59A to obscure its origins. The Bell Aircraft Company had been working on, but had dismissed, another piston plane called the XP-59, and the number was resurrected to maintain the secrecy of the new design. The XP-59A was named the *Airacomet* by the company after its line of "Aira-" aircraft, including the *Airacobra* and *Airacuda*. USAAF registration numbers began with the first prototype, 42-108784, and continued for three prototypes (784/785/786). Thirteen service trials aircraft were ordered and designated YP-59A (serial numbers 42-108771 through 783), and later 50 were ordered as trainers (P-59A 44-22609 through 628 and P-59B 44-22629 through 658). The first prototype carried no other markings besides the USAAF contract number on the tail and the USAAF chevron on the fuselage and wings. Later aircraft carried contract numbers, "stars-and-bars", squadron markings and call signs. The U.S. Air Force Museum (Dayton, Ohio) P-59B carries only USAAF contract number 44-22650 and the U.S. aircraft star in a field of blue. The first prototype, preserved at National Air and Space Museum (42-108784) is marked just as it was on its first flight on October 1, 1942.

The Gloster *Meteor* design was solicited from the Air Ministry under contract number SB21179/C.23(a) for the first 12 prototypes. These were given the Air Ministry batch number DG202 through 213. The First prototype was designated DG202 by the Air Ministry and carried this number on the fuselage and added the "/G" after the number described above (See E.28/39). The first *Meteor*, company designation F.9/40, was camouflaged with no other markings save the British national roundel. The first series production *Meteor* Mk I was designated EE210/G. With the first production model Gloster change the factory designation to Gloster *Meteor* F.1. EE210/G was later sent to the United States where it carried U.S. markings but retained the call sign "EE210/G" on the tail boom. A total of 3,875 Gloster *Meteor*s (up to and including Mk 20) were produced and flown all over the world, each with their own numbers and national designations.

Lockheed's *Shooting Star* began with the official Army Air Forces Designation XP-80. The plane had USAAF serial number 44-83020 and on the first flight was decorated with only a Lockheed company logo on the nose and a U.S. "stars-and-bars" on the tail and wings. The first flight was on January 8, 1944, with a borrowed British Halford H.1 engine; the plane was nicknamed "Lulu Belle" by the test pilot Milo Bercham. The first flights with American engines did not occur until June 1944, by which time the General Electric powered *Shooting Star* had been redesignated XP-80A. Two production prototype XP-80A were ordered (44-83021, 44-83022) as testing continued. Thirteen YP-80A were ordered in March 1944 (44-83023 through 35), and service trials began in September of that year. The production version P-80A was ordered as early as April 1944 in two batches of 500 each, but this order was reduced after V-J Day. The first P-80A was delivered to the USAAF in February 1945, and the aircraft did not arrive in numbers before the end of the war. One famous *Shooting Star*, the XP-80R (now on display at the U.S. Air Force Museum, Dayton, Ohio), was the first plane to record a flight over 1,000 kmph on June 19, 1947. Another infamous P-80A was responsible for the death of Medal of Honor winner, and highest-scoring American ace Richard Bong, when he crashed and burned in August 1945. In all 1,732 *Shooting Star*s of all types were built by Lockheed, and the aircraft enjoyed a 30-year life span in different forms and around the world.

APPENDIX D: BIOGRAPHIES

Henry Harley "Hap" Arnold (1886–1950)

Born in 1886, Arnold was a graduate of the U.S. Military Academy (West Point) class of 1907. He rose through the ranks of the Army to become the commander of the Army Air Forces during World War II. Always interested in aviation technology, he promoted USAAF technological R&D and procurement of high-technology weapons systems and components. He was the driving force behind America's development of turbojet aircraft during World War II. Arnold retired from the USAAF in 1945, but was named general of the Air Force when the service was separated from the Army in 1947, thus making Arnold the only five-star Air Force general. Arnold retired to his family farm in Sonoma, California, where he died in his sleep in January 1950.

Lawrence A. "Larry" Bell (1895–1956)

Born in Mentone, Indiana, in 1895, Larry Bell's family relocated to California when he was only 13. Bell was fascinated with aircraft from a very young age, although he did not like to fly. He began his career in aircraft construction with the Glenn Martin Company in 1913. He continued within the industry until 1935 when he began his own aircraft construction company, Bell Aircraft in Buffalo, New York. Known for his unusual but successful designs, and without serious wartime contracts, General Arnold, as the head of the U.S. Army Air Forces, approached Bell about building America's first turbojet aircraft in 1941. Bell Aircraft built the first American jet, the Bell XP-59A *Airacomet*. After building the first jet, Bell focused his company's attention on experimental planes (a few inspired by captured German data) and the blossoming market for helicopters. To this day Bell Aircraft is synonymous with excellent helicopter design. Larry Bell retired in September 1956, and died in October of the same year from heart failure.

Anselm Franz (1900–1994)

Born in Austria in 1900, Anselm Franz became one of the world's leading turbojet designers. He completed his doctorate in mechanical engineering at the University of Berlin. He joined Junkers (aircraft manufacturing company) in 1936 where he rose to the position of chief engineer. With his knowledge of turbosuperchargers he was put in charge of, and led the field in, the development of the axial-flow Jumo 004 turbojet engine. His work produced the main German jet engine of the war, despite severe wartime materials restrictions, of which over 6,000 units were actually produced. After the war, Franz went to the United States, where he was employed by the U.S. Air Force. He relocated to Avco-Lycoming (1951) and was responsible for the development of a number of aeronautical as well as nonaero turbine-engine programs, including the AGT-1500, the power source for the U.S. Army's M1 Abrams main battle tank. He retired in 1968 as a decorated engineer. He was a recognized leader in the field and held commendations from the Associated Society of Mechanical Engineers (The Tom Sawyer Award), the U.S. Army (The Outstanding Civilian Service Medal), and the government of Austria (The Grand Decoration of Honor). Franz died in 1994.

Adolf Galland (1912–1996)

Adolf Galland was born in Westphalia in 1912. He grew up in interwar Germany with a passion for flight and was adept at soaring. He was admitted to the airline pilot training school at Brunswick in 1932, a covert training center for future Luftwaffe pilots. He volunteered for, and served with the Kondor Legion during the Spanish Civil War (1936–1939) where he was credited with 12 victories. Galland went on to become a squadron leader (*JG* 26) during the Battle of Britain, and achieved distinction on the Western Front of the European Theatre. He was one of the first Luftwaffe pilots to fly the Me 262 and argued strongly in its favor. In 1944 Galland turned against Göring in an unofficial "mutiny" and was relieved of his command as general of Fighters. In a last-ditch effort, Hitler allowed Galland to form *Jagdverband* (*JV*) 44, an all Me 262 jet fighter squadron. Galland was shot down for the last time on 26 April 1945, and ended the war as a prisoner. After the war Galland was tried and served time as prisoner of war and was released in 1948. Galland worked as a consultant to the Argentina Air Force from 1948–1952. Galland returned to Germany in 1953. He worked as an independent aerospace consultant until his death in 1996.

Ernst Heinkel (1888–1958)

Heinkel was born in Grunbach, Germany in 1888. During World War I, he worked for the Albatross Company designing aircraft for the German *Luftstreitskräfte*. After the war, Heinkel moved to the Hansa-Brandenburg Aircraft Company where he designed several seaplanes. In 1922 he opened his own aircraft firm, *Heinkel Flugzeugwerke*, and began designing his own aircraft. With extensive rearmament contracts, Heinkel experimented with rocket- and turbojet-powered aircraft before and during World War II. Heinkel became famous in the last week of August 1939 when in successive days his aircraft became the first rocket-powered plane (He 176) and the first turbojet-powered plane (He 178). Heinkel's designs were important in Luftwaffe operations, but his experimental aircraft were often overlooked (and overshadowed). Although Heinkel designed, tested, and produced the rival for the Messerschmitt Me 262 turbojet, his jet plane was not accepted for series production. His anti-Nazi sentiments and open criticism of the Hitler government led to seizure of his holdings in 1942, but also led to his acquittal after the war. Following Germany's surrender, the Heinkel Company was restricted to manufacturing small engines, scooters, and minicars until 1955 when Heinkel once again began aircraft construction. Ernst Heinkel died in Germany in 1958.

Clarence L. Kelly Johnson (1910–1990)

Clarence L. "Kelly" Johnson was born in 1910 in Michigan. He received his master's in Aeronautical Engineering in 1933 from the University of Michigan. He was able to work his way through college by experimenting and consulting on aircraft, train, and race car design based on wind-tunnel testing at the University of Michigan. He was hired by Lockheed in 1933 as a tool designer. His groundbreaking work on the Lockheed P-38 *Lightning* assured his place in the annals of aviation history. But Johnson did not rest on his laurels; he went on to design the XP-80 *Shooting Star*, America's first operational combat turbojet aircraft. He was put in charge of the "Skunk Works" and rose within the ranks of the Lockheed corporation. He was the brainchild of many of the U.S. Air Force's most famous planes, including the F-104 *Starfighter* as well as the SR-71 *Blackbird*. For his work, Johnson received the Collier Trophy twice in addition to the Medal of Freedom, the highest American civilian award. Johnson retired from Lockheed in 1975 and died in California in 1990.

Theodore von Kármán (1881–1963)

Theodore von Kármán was born in Budapest, Hungary, in 1881. An intuitive genius in the field of mathematics and physics, Kármán excelled at his schooling. He received his doctorate from University of Göttingen. Kármán became interested in the designs of Henri Farman, the French aviator, and embarked on a career of aeronautics. His early work focused on his now famous theory of Kármán's Vortex Street and fluid mechanics.

Kármán became a professor of Aerodynamics and Mechanics as well as director of the Aerodynamics Institute at Aachen, Germany in 1912. During World War I, Kármán was recalled to Austria-Hungary, where he was appointed head of aviation research for the Austro-Hungarian Army Aviation Corps. After the war Kármán returned to Aachen and resumed his post until 1930. He first visited the United States as a lecturer at California Institute of Technology in 1926, where he returned in 1930 as the director of the school. His research and graduate students were the basis for the Jet Propulsion Laboratory (designated in 1944) as well as his role in the birth of the U.S. Air Force Scientific Advisory Board. Kármán eventually returned to Aachen, where he died in November 1963.

Willi Messerschmitt (1898–1978)

Willi Messerschmitt was born in Germany in 1898. Throughout his childhood, Messerschmitt was enthralled by aircraft and the promise of flight. After serving his country in battle during World War I, Messerschmitt went to technical college in Munich, where he graduated as an engineer in 1923. Messerschmitt opened *Beyerische Flugzeugmotor Werke* (BFW) in 1923 with funds from the Bavarian government. Armed with contracts, BFW began to rebuild the German Luftwaffe in 1934. His design, the Messerschmitt Bf 109 became the backbone of the Luftwaffe's fighter force with eventually 35,000 built. But Messerschmitt was also interested in speed and R&D. He submitted plans for a twin-engine turbojet fighter before the war, and was intent on building progressively better aircraft for the Luftwaffe. Although some of his aircraft were complete failures, his Messerschmitt Me 262 will go down in history as the first operational combat turbojet aircraft. After the war Messerschmitt was tried and imprisoned for war crimes; his factories had made extensive use of slave labor. He spent two years in prison. After his release, the Messerschmitt Company could not build aircraft and was confined to manufacturing sewing machines, cars, and prefabricated housing. But by 1958 Messerschmitt began building aircraft once more, specifically the Lockheed F-104 *Starfighter*, under license. Messerschmitt combined with Bolkow-Blohm in 1969 for a new conglomerate, and he served as chairman of the aircraft giant until his death in 1978.

Sanford Moss (1872–1946)

Sanford Moss was born in the United States in 1872. He was a pioneer in American aviation circles, and a leader in the field. His doctoral dissertation (Cornell University, 1903) was on the use of turbosuperchargers for aviation. He was employed by General Electric in 1903 to design turbines for the company. Moss's work led him to the field of aviation. He theorized that a supercharged piston engine would run better at high altitude and set to work to prove his theory. In the 1918 Pike's Peak experiments he did just that. Using a supercharged Liberty piston engine, he set new horsepower records at high altitudes. His retirement in 1938 was short-lived. Called back to work due to the war, Moss was influential in the development of high-speed high-altitude flight and the supercharged Boeing B-17 *Flying Fortress*. For his work he received the Collier Trophy in 1941. His work in turbosuperchargers translated directly to the development of gas turbine (turbojet) engines when GE was awarded the contract to build American jet engines in 1941. His influence allowed GE to build and even improve the British turbojet design. Dr. Sanford Moss died in 1946

Hans Joachim Pabst von Ohain (1911–1998)

Hans von Ohain was born in Germany in December 1911. While completing his doctorate at the University of Göttingen, he formulated his idea for a three-cycle turbojet engine. Based on his idea that flight should be elegant and smooth, Ohain set out to build a turbojet engine. Assisted by his auto mechanic, Max Hahn, and encouraged by his advisor, Dr. Robert Pohl, Ohain was able to present the idea to Ernst Heinkel as early as 1936. His engine was the prime mover for the first turbojet aircraft in history, the Heinkel He 178. Powered by Ohain's HeS 3b engine, the He 178 took to the skies on August 27, 1939. He continued to work for Heinkel throughout the war, building and improving further turbojet designs. He was invited to the United States immediately after the war where he went to work for the U.S. Air Force at Wright-Patterson Air Force Base and the Aero Propulsion Laboratory at Dayton, Ohio. He retired in 1975 but maintained his contacts as a consultant through the University of Dayton Research Institute. Ohain died in 1998 at his home in Florida.

Ludwig Prandtl (1875–1953)

Ludwig Prandtl was born in Germany in 1875. He became known as the "Father of Modern Fluid Mechanics" through his discovery of the principles of boundary layer phenomenon. He was a master of mathematics and was an excellent professor beginning at the University of Hanover (1901) and culminating with his appointment to the University of Göttingen. He was concurrently named the director of the Kaiser Wilhelm Institute for Fluid Mechanics. Prandtl was an important influence on Hans von Ohain at Göttingen as one of Ohain's advisors. Prandtl died in the city of Göttingen in 1953.

P.E.G. "Gerry" Sayer (1905–1942)

Gerry Sayer was born in England in 1905. He was a test pilot for the Royal Air Force (RAF) before joining Hawker in 1930. When Hawker and Gloster joined in 1934 he was named chief test pilot. Sayer's claim to fame was that he was the first Allied pilot to fly a turbojet-powered aircraft. On May 15, 1941, Sayer took to the skies in the Whittle-powered Gloster E.28/39 *Pioneer*. His flight was historic in that it was the first Allied jet flight. Unfortunately for Gloster, Sayer was killed in 1942 when the Hawker *Typhoon* he was flying crashed.

Robert Stanley (1912–1977)

Robert Stanley was born in Oklahoma in 1912. He graduated from California Institute of Technology with a degree in Aeronautical Engineering in 1935. While in school, Stanley took a job at Douglas Aircraft Corporation to help pay his school bills. His aptitude for aircraft was evident in his involvement in the development of the Douglas DC-1 and DC-2 as well as his early patents on the mechanical reversible pitch propeller. Stanley earned his flight wings with the Navy in 1936, and later became an instructor pilot. In 1940 Stanley took the position of chief test pilot with the Bell Aircraft Corporation in Buffalo, New York. On October 1, 1942, Stanley became the first American to pilot a turbojet aircraft, the Bell XP-59A *Airacomet*. Stanley was promoted within the ranks at Bell Aircraft after the war rising to the position of Engineering Vice President and was intimately involved in both the Bell "X" planes and subsequent helicopter design and production. He formed Stanley Aviation Corporation in 1948 and was responsible for the design and implementation of the encapsulated ejection seat escape system as well as the rocket-assisted Yankee ejection system. He remained president of Stanley Aviation until his death in 1977.

Fritz Wendel (1915–1975)

Fritz Wendel was born in Germany in 1915. He joined the Luftwaffe on its inception and later was a Luftwaffe flight instructor. In 1936, Wendel joined the Messerschmitt team as a factory test pilot. In April 1939, while flying a prototype Messerschmitt Me 209 V1 (*Versuchs*—experimental, sometimes reported as a Bf 109 R), Wendel set the world speed record for piston-engine aircraft that stood for 30 years (755.136 kmph/469.22 mph). Wendel was later the chief test pilot for the Me 262, and flew for the factory throughout the development of the German jet program. He died in Germany in 1975.

Frank Whittle (1907–1996)

Frank Whittle was born in England in 1907. He was the son of a machinist, and quickly learned that he was a good mechanic. He was interested in aircraft from an early age, and set out to not only build airplanes but also to improve them. After some difficulty he entered the RAF, and became a test pilot. Because of his mechanical aptitude, he was sent to school to become a better mechanic. His first school was RAF machinist school, which was eventually followed by mechanical engineering at Cambridge. He passed at the top of his class, and went to work for the Air Ministry in Special Services. While at school, Whittle came up with the idea for a turbojet engine. He was intent on building one, and set his mind and his determination toward that end. Even in the face of adversity he overcame financial, material, and health issues to finally build his revolutionary engine. He was finally rewarded by the Air Ministry with the developmental oversight of the production of his turbojet engine which was to take place at Rolls-Royce. Although not pleased with the outcome, Whittle was finally recognized for his invention. His company, Power Jets Ltd., was nationalized in 1943, and Whittle was out of a job. He was promoted within the RAF ranks, but did not receive any monetary compensation for his discovery. He retired from the RAF in 1948, but was given an award of £100,000 by the Royal Commission on Awards to Inventors, and was knighted by King George VI. Whittle immigrated to the United States in 1976, where he became a faculty member at the U.S. Naval Academy at Annapolis. Whittle died in 1996 in Baltimore, Maryland.

APPENDIX E: TURBOJET AIRCRAFT SPECIFICATIONS REQUESTED BY THE *REICHSLUFTFAHRTMINISTERIUM*

On April 9, 1939, the RLM solicited proposals for high-speed, high-altitude turbojet fighter aircraft for consideration by Germany's aviation industries. Two companies, Messerschmitt and Heinkel, immediately offered ideas on the future of military aviation. This contract led to the development of the Heinkel He 280 and the Messerschmitt Me 262. The following is a translation of the original solicitation and requirements for turbojet fighter aircraft proposals.

Purpose: High-speed fighter for use against aerial targets

Number and type of engine: Two jet engines—installation of various types of engine must be possible without major structural changes

Crew: One

Armament: Four MG 17 each with 800 rounds, two MG 131 each with 400 rounds

Gunsight: Revi C12C, installation of weapons in fuselage nose

Signals and equipment: One FuG 18, identification 1 flare pistol with six rounds

Fuel tank requirements: Forward removable protected tank, rear removable metal or sealed riveted tank

Electronic equipment: Aircraft must be capable of being operated at night.

Performance: Maximum speed as high as possible

Landing speed not to exceed 140 kmph

Takeoff run not more than 600 meters to an altitude of 20 meters

Endurance of approximately 1 hour at 85 percent power at an altitude of 6,500 meters (fuel quantity 2,000 liters)

Time to climb to 6,000 meters not to exceed 8.5 minutes

Flight characteristics: Flight characteristics must satisfy E-Stelle Reichlin guidelines for the assessment of flight characteristics for the required role

Stress limit: H5

Airframe: The aircraft is to be of all-metal construction. Simple and cheap design is required

Table 1. First-Generation Turbojet Aircraft by Nationality

	Germany Heinkel He 178	Britain Gloster E. 28/39	United States Bell XP-59A
Length	24' 6" (7.47 m)	25" 33/4" (7.72 m)	38' 1.5" (11.63 m)
Height	6' 10.5" (2.1 m)	9' 3" (2.7 m)	12' (3.66 m)
Wingspan	23' 9" (7.2 m)	29' (8.84 m)	45' 6" (13.87 m)
Wing area	84.98 sq. ft (7.9 sq. m)	146.5 sq. ft (13.5 sq. m)	385.8 sq. ft (35.8 sq. m)
Weight (max)	4,290 lbs (1950 kg)	3,700 lbs (1,678 kg)	10,822 lbs (4,915 kg)
Weight (tare)	3,454 lbs (1570 kg)	2,890 lbs (1,311 kg)	7,950 lbs (3,610 kg)
Wing loading (pounds per square foot)	50.48 lbs/ft²	25.25 lbs/ft²	28.05 lbs/ft²
Configuration	Single-seat, single-engine, shoulder-wing monoplane experimental turbojet aircraft	Single-seat, single-engine, low-wing monoplane experimental turbojet aircraft	Single-seat, twin-engine monoplane experimental turbojet aircraft
Engine(s)	(One) Heinkel He S3b centrifugal-flow turbojet	(One) Whittle (Power Jets) W.1 centrifugal-flow turbojet	(Two) General Electric I-A centrifugal-flow turbojets, direct copies of the Whittle W.1X
Thrust rating	1,100 lbs thrust (500 kg) @13,000 rpm at a dry weight of 795 lbs (361.3 kg)	860 lbs thrust (390.9 kg) @ 16,500 rpm at a dry weight of 623 lbs (283.1 kg)	1,250 lbs thrust each (568 kg) @ 16,500 rpm at a dry weight of 780 lbs (354.5 kg)
Specific weight (pounds dry per pound thrust)	0.722	0.724	0.624
Specific fuel consumption (pounds of fuel per pound of thrust per hour)	1.6	1.4	1.1
Speed (max)	400 mph (640 kmph)[a]	338 mph (541 kmph)	389 mph (622 kmph) (XP version)
Speed (cruise)	312.5 mph (500 kmph)	300 mph (480 kmph)	280 mph (448 kmph)
Ceiling	Experimental only, figures unavailable	32,000 ft (9,753 m)	40,000 ft (12,192 m)
Rate of climb	Experimental only, figures unavailable	1,366 ft (414 m) per minute	1,200 ft (366 m) per minute
Range	125 miles (200 km)	187.5 miles (300 km)	520 miles (832 km)
First flight	August 27, 1939	May 15,1941	October 1, 1942
Number built	2	2	66

Table 2. Second-Generation Turbojet Aircraft by Nationality

	Germany				Britain		United States
	Heinkel He 280	Messerschmitt Me 262	Arado Ar 234	Heinkel He 162 Volksjäger	Meteor Mk I	De Havilland DH100 Vampire F.1	Lockheed P-80 Shooting Star (figures for XP-80A)
Length	34' 4" (10.4 m)	34' 9.75" (10.59 m)	41' 5.5" (12.64 m)	29' 8.5" (9 m)	41' 3" (12.5 m)	30' 9" (9.37 m)	34' 6" (10.45 m)
Height	10' (3.06 m)	12' 7" (3.83 m)	14' 1.25" (4.3 m)	8' 6.5" (2.6 m)	13' (3.9 m)	8' 10" (2.68 m)	11' 4" (3.43 m)
Wingspan	39' 6" (12 m)	40' 11.5" (12.49 m)	46' 3.5" (14.11 m)	23' 7" (7.2 m)	43' (13.1 m)	40' (12.19 m)	39' 11" (12.1 m)
Wing area	231.3 sq. ft (21.5 sq. m)	234 sq. ft (21.73 sq. m)	284.17 sq. ft (26.41 sq. m)	120.56 sq. ft (11.21 sq. m)	374 sq. ft (34.7 sq. m)	261 sq. ft (24.24 sq. m)	238 sq. ft (22.11 sq. m)
Weight (max)	9,460 lbs (4,300 kg)	14,101 lbs (6,395 kg)	21,715 lbs (9,850 kg) with RATO; 18,541 lbs (8,428 kg) without	5,940 lbs (2,694 kg)	11,775 lbs (5,351 kg)	10,480 lbs (4,752.6 kg)	13,780 lbs (6,263.6 kg)
Weight (tare)	7,073 lbs (3,215 kg)	9,741 lbs (4,417.5 kg)	11,464 lbs (5,200 kg) without RATO[a]	4,800 lbs (2,176 kg)	9,654 lbs (4,378 kg)	6,372 lb (2,889.7 kg)	7,225 lbs (3,284 kg)
Wing loading (pounds per square foot)	40.89 lbs/ft²	60.26 lbs/ft²	65.25 lbs/ft² without RATO[a]	49.27 lbs/ft²	31.48 lbs/ft²	40.15 lbs/ft²	57.89 lbs/ft²

(continued)

Table 2. (*continued*)

	Germany				Britain		United States
	Heinkel He 280	Messerschmitt Me 262	Arado Ar 234	Heinkel He 162 Volksjager	Meteor Mk I	De Havilland DH100 Vampire F.1	Lockheed P-80 Shooting Star (figures for XP-80A)
Configuration	Twin-engine turbojet fighter (prototypes only)	Twin-engine turbojet fighter/bomber	Twin-engine turbojet reconnaisance/bomber	Single-engine turbojet fighter	Twin-engine turbojet fighter	Single-engine twin tail-boom turbojet fighter	Single-engine turbojet fighter
Engine(s)	Heinkel He S8A centrifugal-flow turbojet	Jumo 004B axial-flow turbojet	Jumo 004B axial-flow turbojet	BMW 003 A-1 axial-flow turbojet	Rolls-Royce W2B/23C Welland centrifugal-flow turbojet	De Havilland H-1 Goblin II centrifugal-flow turbojet	General Electric I-40 (later J33) centrifugal-flow turbojet
Thrust rating	1,584 lbs (720 kg)	1,980 lbs (900 kg)	1,980 lbs (900 kg)	1,760 lbs (800 kg)	1,600 lbs (725 kg)	3,000 lbs (1,364 kg)[c]	4,000 lbs (1,818 kg)
Engine dry weight	836 lb (380 kg) engine	1,639 lb (745 kg) engine	1,639 lb (745 kg) engine	1,309 lb (595 kg) engine	1,510 lb (686.4 kg) engine	1,500 lb (681.8 kg) engine	1,820 lb (827 kg) engine
Specific Weight (pounds dry per pound thrust)	0.52 lb/lb thrust	0.83 lb/lb thrust	0.83 lb/lb thrust	0.74 lb/lb thrust	0.94 lb/lb thrust	0.5 lb/lb thrust	0.455 lb/lb thrust
Specific fuel consumption (pounds of fuel per pound of thrust per	1.6	1.44	1.4	1.4	1.12	1.14	1.185

Speed (max)	477.4 mph (770 kmph)	521 mph (835 kmph)	461 mph (742 kmph)	522 mph (835 kmph)	415 mph (674 kmph)	540 mph (869 kmph)	502 mph (803 kmph)
Speed (cruise)	450 mph (720 kmph)	515.6 mph (825 kmph)	437.5 mph (700 kmph)	496.8 mph (795 kmph)	395 mph (632 kmph)	515 mph (824 kmph)	475 mph (760 kmph)
Ceiling	37,950 ft (11,500 m)	45,210 ft (13,700 m)	39,600 ft (12,000 m)	39,400 ft (12,009 m)	40,000 ft (12,192 m)	40,000 ft (12,192 m)	45,000 ft (13,715 m)
Rate of climb	3,780 ft (1,146 m) per minute	3,963 ft (1,201 m) per minute	1,650 ft (500 m) per minute	4,200 ft (1,280 m) per minute	1,765 ft (534.5 m) per minute	4,224 ft (1,280 m) per minute	3,960 ft (1,200 m) per minute
Range	231.25 miles (370 km) at altitude	768.75 miles (1,230 km) at altitude	1,015 miles (1,630 km) at altitude	410 miles (659 km) at altitude	312.5 miles (500 km) at altitude	1,220 miles (1,963 km) with drop tanks	1,165 miles (1,865 km) with drop tanks
Armament	3x MG 151/20 20 mm machine guns	4 × 30 mm Mk 108 cannon	2 × rear firing 20 mm guns and up to 1,500 kg bombs	2 × 30 mm Mk 108 or 2 × 20 mm MG 151/20	4 × 20 mm cannon	4 × 20 mm cannon	6 × .50 in. machine guns
First flight	March 30, 1941	July 18, 1942	June 15, 1943	December 6, 1944	March 5, 1943[b]	September 20, 1943	January 9, 1944[d]

[a] A bomber of course usually drops a significant portion of its max weight on mission.
[b] First flight flown with de Havilland H.1 engines, later converted to Metrovick F.2s and then R-R engines.
[c] The de Havilland Goblin II was not ready for production until July 1945.
[d] First flight with the de Havilland H.1 engine; the first flight with a GE I-40 (J33) was on June 10, 1944.

Notes

INTRODUCTION: THE STATE OF AERONAUTICAL ENGINEERING AND AIRCRAFT TECHNOLOGY IN THE WORLD, 1919–1939

1. The French began the era of "strategic" bombing with the Alsace-Lorraine bombing campaign in 1915, arguably for strategic reasons. By 1917, both the Germans—first with Zeppelins and later with heavier-than-air bomber planes—and the British began attacking enemy population centers as strategic targets.

2. The Treaty of Versailles (June 28, 1919), Part V, Section III, "Air Clauses," Articles 198–202. See specifically Article 201, which forbids Germany from "manufacture or importation" of aircraft or parts and Article 202 that the Germans had to deliver all aircraft and parts to the "Governments of the Principal Allied and Associated Powers." However, it is important to note that there is no mention of German aeronautical research or theoretical development.

3. By specifically allowing the Germans to once again build low-power (in HP) aero engines. The French were not, however, willing to let the Germans completely rebuild to their industrial potential.

4. Barton Whaley, *Covert Rearmament in Germany, 1919–1939* (Frederick, MD: 1984), pp. 10–11.

5. Kees Gispin, *New Profession, Old Order* (Cambridge: 1989), p. 166.

6. Helmuth Trischler, *Luft- und Raum-fahrtforschung in Deutschland 1900–1970* (Frankfurt: 1992). In his book, Trischler gives an important account of aerospace research in Germany for the entire period in question.

7. Joseph Ermenc, *Interviews with German Contributors to Aviation History* (London: 1990), pp. 10–11; interview with Hans von Ohain where he refers to his classes with Prandtl.

8. Karl-Heinz Ludwig, *Technik und Ingenieure im Dritten Reich* (Düsseldorf: 1974), pp. 218–219.

9. Trischler, *Luft- und Raum-fahrtforschung in Deutschland 1900–1970*, pp. 208–228.

10. Anthony Kay, *German Jet Engine and Gas Turbine Development 1930–1945* (Shrewsbury, England: 2002), p. 11. See also Edward Homze, *Arming the Luftwaffe* (Lincoln, NE: 1976), pp. 57–62, Trischler, *Luft- und Raum-fahrtforschung in Deutschland 1900–1970*, pp. 213–228.

11. Homze, "German Aircraft Production 1918–1939," in Horst Boog (ed.), *The Conduct of the Air War in the Second World War* (New York: 1992), pp. 115–130.

12. Edward Homze, *Arming the Luftwaffe* (Lincoln, NE: 1976), pp. 28–29.

13. One example of this was a prewar competition for a rocket propelled fighter/interceptor aircraft. Three companies submitted proposals: Messerschmitt, Heinkel, and Bachem. Even if the basic concept of a rocket-propelled combat-operational fighter had been valid—which is debatable—the three competing programs diverted scarce technical and engineering resources that were wasted.

14. Edward Constant, *The Origins of the Turbojet Revolution* (Baltimore: 1980), *passim*. Constant's idea of presumptive anomaly was that the piston-engine combination was reaching its peak, and a specific few engineers realized this and began looking for alternatives. I would add that the industrialists Heinkel and Messerschmitt were also looking for revolutionary power plants for their aircraft in the spirit of industrial competition.

15. Of course, many German "civilian" aircraft projects were thinly disguised military aircraft. The Heinkel He 111 medium bomber was initially designed as a commercial airliner.

16. The He 178 turbojet airplane and the He 176 rocket-powered plane, both flew before the war started in Europe (August 1939). Both of these are dealt with in length; the discussion of the Gunther twins continues below.

17. William Green and Gordon Swanborough, *The Complete Book of Fighters* (London: 1994), pp. 108–110, and the discussion of the Italian fighter planes from 1937 (F.4 and F.5) to the 1941 F.6. The in-line engine Italian fighters were powered by license-built German Daimler-Benz DB 601 and later DB 605 engines, but were in fact faster than the CC.2 prototype.

18. Brian Sullivan, "The Impatient Cat: Assessments of Military Power in Fascist Italy, 1936–1940," in Allan Millett and Williamson Murray (eds.), *Calculations: Net Assessment and the Coming of World War II* (New York: 1992), pp. 97–135.

19. Yefim Gordon and Keith Dexter, *Polikarpov's I-16 Fighter* (Hinckley, UK: 2002), *passim*.

20. James Corum, *The Luftwaffe, Creating the Operational Air War 1918–1940* (Lawrence, KS: 1997), pp. 182–223. See also Werner Beumelburg, *Kampf um Spanien* (Berlin: 1939), *passim*.

21. Bill Gunston, *World Encyclopedia of Aero Engines*, p. 96.

22. Including the sentiments of Hugh Trenchard and Arthur "Bomber" Harris. See specifically Scot Robertson, *The Development of RAF Strategic Bombing Doctrine 1919–1939* (Westport, CT: 1995), *passim*, as well as Malcolm Smith, *British Air Strategy Between the Wars* (Oxford: 1984).

23. John Ferris, "Fighter Defense before Fighter Command: The Rise of Strategic Air Defense in Great Britain, 1917–1934," *The Journal of Military History*, 63(4) (October 1999), 845–884.

24. According to the bias of Graham White, *Allied Aircraft Piston Engines of World War II* (Shrewsbury, England: 1995) and L.J.K. Setright, *The Power to Fly: the Development of the Piston Engine in Aviation* (London: 1971), in which both men say that the *Merlin* series engines were the best in the world. But it must be remembered that by 1939 the Germans were mass-producing the Daimler-Benz DB 601, another excellent aircraft piston engine. Furthermore, the Americans were producing their *Wasp* series engines, massive radial engines for long-range transport and later bombers. But, for short-range, high-speed interceptors, one-on-one the Rolls Royce was comparable.

25. NACA study #159, "Jet Propulsion for Airplanes," written 1923, published 1924 by Government Printing Office, Washington, DC. In the 1923 study, "jets" were defined widely and included liquid and solid fuel rockets as well as rudimentary turbines.

26. NACA studies in 1944, 1945, and finally in 1946, on the viability of turbojet engines—which were already in use—in American aircraft development.

27. Robert Schlaifer and E.P. Heron, *The Development of Aircraft Engines and Fuels* (Chicago: 1950), pp. 628–630 (propellers), and Part II of the book as a whole that discusses the *Development of Aviation Fuels*. This book still contains the fundamental analysis of developing aviation engine and fuel technology, with special reference to the interconnectedness of industry–military–and R&D.

28. Beginning with the Martin B-10, the first all-metal bomber aircraft. The American built B-10 was powered by two Wright R-1820 *Cyclone* engines. The B-10 was the cutting edge of bomber design in the 1930s and initiated the trend of impressive American transport and heavy bomber designs that would later lead to the Douglas DC-2 and DC-3, the Boeing B-17 and later B-29, as well as the Consolidated B-24.

29. Once again, an idea that needs to be put on paper. The Mitsubishi A6M *Zero* was the finest carrier-borne fighter at the start of the war and was only later eclipsed by American designs (specifically the Chance Vought F4U *Corsair*). For specifics on the Mitsubishi A6M *Zero* see *Jane's*.

30. Bill Gunston, *The World Encyclopedia of Aero Engines* (Wellingborough, England: 1986), pp. 81–82.

31. Geoffrey Dorman, *Fifty Years Fly Past* (London: 1951), p. 160.

32. Ibid., pp. 161–162.

33. Ibid., p. 148. Seaplanes were chosen for the simple reason that they had unlimited runway space on water. Thus, fine pitch propellers could be used (for high top speeds) even though this meant longer takeoff runs. Land-based planes would have been constrained by short runway length.

34. See specifically Dorman's chapter XXVII on the F.A.I., pp. 195–199.

35. The plane was a Supermarine S.6B seaplane powered by a Rolls-Royce "R" engine.

36. The plane is frequently mislabeled a Bf 109R; according to Messerschmitt the plane was actually one of the prototype Me 209 second-generation fighters.

37. Dorman, see also David Wragg, *Speed in the Air* (New York: 1974), p. 93.

38. See specifically Ernst Heinkel, *Stürmisches Leben* (Stuttgart: 1953), translated as *Stormy Life* (Stuttgart: 1991), p. 255 (Messerschmitt flight), 244–252 (Heinkel He 100 record-breaking flight).

39. Lockheed test pilot Darryl Greenamayer piloted a Grumman F8F-2 *Bearcat* to 771 kmph (478.8 mph) on August 16, 1969, finally breaking Wendel's 1939 record.

40. See specifically Richard Smith, "The International Airliner and the Essence of Aircraft Performance," in *Technology and Culture*, 24(3) (July 1983), 428–449.

41. See specifically *Luchtvaart en Luchtpost Encyclopedie* (Tschroots-Beor: 1991), under the citation for the mentioned race and the specific plane (translated for me by my colleague Dr. John Stapleton). The Dutch DC-2, named *Uiver* (Stork) gave the British team concern because it was so close behind. The DC-2 was forced to delay the night before the finish because of bad weather and was stranded 40 miles from Melbourne the night before the finish. Instead of accepting the second-place trophy, the Dutch team opted for a first place finish in the "handicapped" division because of the size of the plane.

42. *Convegno di Scienze Fisiche, Matematiche e Naturali* (published by the Reale Accademia D'Italia, 1936), p.29. The conference theme that year was high-speed aviation (*Tema: Le Alte Velocita in Aviazione*) and was held on September 30 through October 6, 1935. Hereafter cited as the Volta Conference.

43. The Volta Conference was—and is—held regularly; in 1935 the theme happened to be High-Speed Flight. The themes change yearly.

44. Participants included 36 Italian intellectuals as well as 22 invited international guests. The roll call was a "who's who" of aviation technology and theoretical work. In attendance were the some of the most important aeronautical theoreticians of the interwar period, including Theodore von Kármán and Eastman Jacobs representing the United States; D.R. Pye (later the director of Scientific Research), George Stainforth, Geoffrey Taylor, and Harry Wimperis from England; Henri Bénard, René Dévillérs, and Albert Toussaint from France (the latter from St. Cyr); and the German representatives Ludwig Prandtl, Adolf Busemann, among others. There were also individual Polish, Soviet, and Dutch representatives.

45. Volta Conference, *passim*. It is interesting to see that the Americans—with the exception of Kármán—and the British were skeptical of high-speed flight. One commentator asked how they would be able to interest passengers to fly that fast.

46. Volta Conference, Wimperis presentation "The British Technical Preparation for the Schneider Trophy Contest, 1931," pp. 23–29; in which he outlines not only the 1931 Schneider Race but also his personal speculation on future research.

47. Volta Conference, Wimperis comments following N.A. Rinnin's (Leningrad) presentation on rocket propulsion (*"Propulsione a Reazione Senza Utilizzazione Dell'arei Esterna"*), p. 650.

48. Ibid., *passim*. Throughout the conference, the Göttingen representatives were constantly offering suggestions and comments to the other presenters. Prandtl was the chair on the second day of the conference focusing on Aerodynamics (*Aerodinamica*), and also gave a paper on "German Research on Fluid Dynamics and Flow" (*Allgemeine Überlegungen über die Strömung Zusammendrückbarer Flüssigkeiten*), pp. 169–196 and figures. Also, in the appendices of the conference text, comments for each panel are reported by name and pages: Prandtl offered frequent comments during the proceedings.

49. Margaret Connor, *Elegance in Flight* (Reston, VA: 2001), *passim*. See specifically the introduction.

50. World War II aircraft capable of top speeds of 450 mph included the British Hawker *Typhoon* and *Tempest* and Supermarine *Spitfire* Mk XV; the German Focke Wulf FW 190H-1/Ta 152, the Messerschmitt Bf 109K, and the Dornier Do 335; the American North American P-51 D *Mustang*, the Lockheed P-38 J *Lightning*; and the Soviet Mikoyan Guerevitch MiG-3.

51. Thanks to turbosupercharged piston engines, these planes included most of the American heavy bombers such as Boeing B-17 *Flying Fortress*, the Consolidated B-24 *Liberator*, and the Boeing B-29 *Superfortress*; British aircraft were also high-altitude, but because of mechanical superchargers, and included the de Havilland *Mosquito*.

52. See specifically the Boeing B-29 *Superfortress* with a range of 4,100 miles with a payload of 20,000 pounds.

CHAPTER 1: THE BIRTH OF THE GERMAN JET PROGRAM

1. Including, but not limited to, the outstanding Heinkel He 64 *Roter Teufel* (Red Devil), the He 70 *Blitz* (Lightning), and the closest competitor to the Messerschmitt Bf 109 (Germany's most important fighter aircraft of WWII), the He 112.

2. Among the reasons were insufficient range and more often inferior firepower. In an effort to maximize speed, Heinkel often planned for fewer or smaller caliber guns. Fighter aircraft are designed to very close tolerances, and replacing guns with more or larger models is generally infeasible, effectively requiring complete redesign.

3. Vincent Orange, "Fortunate Fascist Failures: The Case of the Heinkel Fighters," in *Historical News* (Number 47, December 1983), pp. 7–13.

4. David Wragg, from *Speed in the Air* (New York: 1974), outlines Heinkel's (and others') air speed records. In May 1939, Heinkel's He 112 set the absolute world speed record which was eclipsed by Messerschmitt's plane's record in August 1939. This is only one indication of the continuing competition between the German aircraft manufacturers.

5. Ernst Heinkel, *Stürmisches Leben* (Stuttgart: 1953), translated as *Stormy Life*, by Cindy Opitz (Stuttgart: 1991), pp. 197–204. See also Barton Whaley, *Covert German Rearmament, 1919–1939* (Frederick, Maryland: 1984), pp. 3–39, where he outlines the development of the Heinkel He 111 first as a commercial airliner for *Lufthansa*, easily converted to a bomber for the Luftwaffe. The He 111 first flew in 1935, and by 1937 was the Luftwaffe's staple reconnaissance/bomber aircraft; the RLM offered funding for production of 100 units per month.

6. From "Interviews with Hans von Ohain," in *Interviews with German Contributors to Aviation History*, Joseph Ermenc (ed.) (Westport, CT: 1990), p. 10.

7. Ibid.

8. Ibid., p. 12.

9. The conversion rates for interwar currency are tenuous at best. All countries' currencies were in constant flux, but according to a pair of historical currency calculators online (including The Inflation Calculator http://www.westegg.com/inflation/ and Online Conversion http://www.onlineconversion.com/) the 1935 figure DM 3,500 roughly equaled $1,411 or £282.

10. From Ermenc, *Interviews with German Contributors*, pp. 13–14.

11. Ibid., p. 16.

12. Ibid., pp. 21–25.

13. Ibid., p. 24.

14. Again, using rough calculation, DM 500 would have been equal to about £40 at the time.

15. Ermenc, *Interviews with German Contributors*, p. 17.

16. Ibid.

17. Margaret Connor, *Hans von Ohain: Elegance in Flight* (Reston, VA: 2001), pp. 41–42.

18. Ermenc, *Interviews with German Contributors*, p. 18.

19. It is important to note that the temperatures involved were not significantly higher than in piston engines. But, whereas the piston engine experiences intermittent high heat (once in a four-stage—intake, compression, combustion, exhaust—cycle, the turbine engine had to deal with constant high-temperature in the combustion stage. The high heat and pressure requirements of the combustion stage of the turbojet engine would be the Achilles' heel of the program throughout its developmental evolution.

20. It is important to note that the first British turbojet, the Whittle W.U. was not run until April 1937. And, although the W.U. ran on kerosene, a liquid fuel, the British team found they had similar difficulties in controlling the combustion in the three-stage cycle. Combustion problems were the constant source of aggravation in the development of the turbojet engine for applicable use throughout wartime development. And, as will be addressed in Chapter 7 "Into the Cold," the continuing debate on the importance of the early engine designs will be answered. Frank Whittle was attempting to build a working turbojet engine in Britain whereas Ohain was trying to prove the viability of the experiment, while his employer, Heinkel, was very hopeful of a successful outcome.

21. J. Richard Smith and Eddie Creek, *ME 262* (London: 1998), Volume 1, pp. 38–40.

22. Ermenc, *Interviews with German Contributors*, p. 27. See also Edward Constant, *The Origins of the Turbojet Revolution* (Baltimore: 1980), p. 179.

23. Ermenc, *Interviews with German Contributors*, p. 27.

24. Ibid., p. 28.

25. Ibid., p. 39.

26. The Heinkel He 176 rocket plane was a single-seat experimental rocket plane under testing at the same time at the Heinkel factory. Powered by an early Walter rocket engine, the He 176 was the first rocket plane to be tested.

27. Ohain says June 1939 (Ermenc, p. 42), Michael Neufeld says July 3, 1939 in "Rocket Aircraft and the 'Turbojet Revolution'" in Roger Launius, *Innovation and the Development of Flight* (College Station, TX: 1999), pp. 206–234.

28. Meaning two main wheels and a tailwheel.

29. Geoffrey Dorman, *Fifty Years Fly Past* (London: 1951), p. 212. The Messerschmitt Bf 109 would officially retain the "Bf" prefix throughout its operational career as it had been designed while Messerschmitt was still the *Beyerische Flugzeugwerke*. All models built after the 1938 name change to Messerschmitt AG would carry the prefix "Me." However, the designations Bf 109 and Me 109 are frequently interchanged.

30. See Chapter 1 above. Wendel's 1939 fastest piston-engine aircraft world speed record was not broken until 1969 when Darryl Greenamayer (United States) beat the 1939 record.

31. David Masters, *German Jet Genesis* (London: 1982), pp. 76–77.

32. Connor, *Hans von Ohain*, p. 93.

33. Ibid., pp. 95–96. See also Heinkel, *Stürmisches Leben*, pp. 311–313.

34. Connor, *Hans von Ohain*, p. 96.

35. Volta High Speed Conference, Rome, Italy, September 30 to October 6, 1935.

36. Constant, *The Origins of the Turbojet Revolution*, p. 143.

37. Ibid., p. 155. Von Kármán is an interesting case, and is not dealt with in detail. Although he was connected to the German brain trust, he had relocated to the United States in 1930 and was the head of the Fluid Dynamics research lab at Cal Tech.

38. As outlined in the RLM's "Preliminary Technical Guidelines for Jet-Powered High-Speed Fighters," dated April 9, 1939, and reproduced in Ebert, Kaiser, and Peters, *Willi Messerschmitt—Pionier der Luftfahrt und des Leichtbaues – Eine Biographie* (Bonn: 1992) (translated as *The History of German Aviation, Willy Messerschmitt: Pioneer of Aviation Design*, Volume 2, in The History of German Aviation series from Schiffer Military History (Atglen, PA: 1999) by Theriault and Cox, the English translation will be used for citations), pp. 236–237. Also reprinted in Manfred Boehme, *JG7, The World's First Jet Fighter Unit 1944/1945* (Atglen, PA: 1992), David Johnston (translator), pp. 15–16.

39. Wolfgang Wagner, *The History of German Aviation: The First Jet Aircraft* (Atglen, PA: 1998), translated by Don Cox, Volume 1 in the History of German Aviation Series, pp. 228–234, 237–242. See also Nicholson, Chapter 3, "The Axial-Flow Compressor Realizes its Potential," pp. 93–135.

40. Antony Kay, *German Jet Engine and Gas Turbine Development 1930–1945* (Shrewsbury, UK: 2002), pp. 15–17.

41. Hans von Ohain, "The Evolution and Future of Aeropropulsion Systems." As reported in Walter Boyne (ed.), *The Jet Age: Forty Years of Jet Aviation* (Washington, DC: 1979), pp. 25–46. The Jumo 004 B-1 produced 1,980 lbs thrust (900 kg), the BMW 003 A-1 gave 1,760 lbs (800 kg)—both of these were developed and used operationally by the end of the war—the British Power Jets W.2/500 produced 1,600 lbs (725 kg) thrust, and the American General Electric I-16 gave 1,600 lbs (725 kg) as well.

42. Michael Koziol, *Rustung, Krieg and Sklaveri* (Sigmaringen: 1986), pp. 43–45, 62–64.

43. Especially after Albert Speer created the Fighter Staff (*Jägerstab*) as mentioned in Edward Zilbert, *Albert Speer and the Nazi Ministry of Arms* (London: 1981), pp. 239–240. See also Ebert et al., *Willi Messerschmitt*, p. 244.

44. Richard Suchenwirth, *Historical Turning Points in the German Air Force War Effort*, USAF Historical Studies Number 189 (New York: 1968), pp. 50–51.

45. Harold Faber (ed.), *Luftwaffe, A History* (New York: 1977), p. 116.

46. Suchenwirth, *Historical Turning Points*, pp. 51–52.

47. Boehme, *JG7*, pp. 22–23. See also Smith and Creek, *Me 262* (West Sussex, England: 1997), Volume I, pp. 96–97.

48. See Robert Schlaiffer, *The Development of Aircraft Engines and Fuels* (Chicago: 1950).

49. J.R. Smith, Anthony Kay, and Eddie Creek, *German Aircraft of the Second World War* (London: 1972), pp. 293–295.

50. As is evidenced by the fact that the He 280 V2 was powered by axial-flow turbojets by April 1943 (Smith et al., *German Aircraft*, pp. 295–296), and Ohain's work was sidelined.

51. Smith et al., *German Aircraft*, pp. 295–296. The decision is dated Autumn 1942, when the HeS 30 could have been a suitable powerplant for either jet program (He 280 or Me 262).

52. Joachim Dressel, Manfried Griehl, and Jochen Menke (eds.), *Heinkel He 280, The World's First Jet Aircraft* (West Chester, PA: 1991), p. 13.

53. Smith et al., *German Aircraft*, pp. 294–295.

54. Wing loading refers to the weight of the aircraft as compared to the area of the wing (mtow/wing area= wing loading). The higher the weight/wing area, the higher the max speeds, but also the higher the landing speeds. The Me 262 at 60.26 lbs/ft incorporated high wing loading, meaning high tolerances in the fighter aircraft. For reference and comparison, see below Appendix IV: Second-Generation Fighter Jets of WWII, page 243.

55. Boehme, *JG7*, p. 23. The Messerschmitt documents come from Boehme's personal collection.

56. Ibid., p. 40. See also Horst Boog, *Die Deutsche Luftwaffenführung 1935–1945* (Stuttgart: 1982), pp. 124–130. And, this order is evident in the development of all the Luftwaffe fighter types. The Bf (Me) 109 E-4b was the first example of the single-engine fighter-bomber, and later models including the Me 109F and the (Focke Wulf) FW 190 A-3/U1 and U7, A-5, A-10, and D-9. All of the above are mentioned in Smith et al., *German Aircraft*, pp. 173–196 (FW 190), pp. 467–492 (Me 109).

57. As mentioned in James Corum, "The Luftwaffe's Army Support Doctrine, 1918–1941," in *The Journal of Military History*, 59(1) (January 1995), 53–76.

58. Ibid., pp. 76–77.

59. Heinz Nowarra, *Messerschmitt Bf 109* (Somerset, England: 1989), pp. 94–112, in the chapter titled "The Battle of Britain" where he discusses the development of the Bf 109 E-4B (bomber version) and its use as a fighter/bomber in the Battle. See also Ebert et al., *Willi Messerschmitt*, pp. 241–242.

60. Nowarra, *Messerschmitt Bf 109*, p. 118. See also John Turner, *British Aircraft of World War II* (Edinburgh: 1975), pp. 47–47.

61. See specifically Walter Vincenti, *What Engineers Know and How They Know It* (Baltimore: 1990), *passim*, for his discussion of "presumptive anomaly."

62. See P.J. McMahon, *Aircraft Propulsion* (London: 1971). Specifically the chapters "Propulsion Cycles," pp. 75–117, and "The Piston Aero-Engine," pp. 308–329.

63. In the words of Edward Constant, *The Origins of the Turbojet Revolution*.

64. Smith and Creek, *ME 262*, p. 45. See also Hans von Ohain, "The Evolution of Future Aeropropulsion Systems."

65. Boyne, *Messerschmitt . . .* , p. 28.

66. Smith and Creek, *ME 262*, p. 86.

67. Ibid.

68. Hugh Morgan, *Me 262 Stormbird Rising* (London: 1994), pp. 20–21.

69. Smith and Creek, *ME 262*, p. 47.

70. Ibid.

71. Bill Gunston, *Jet and Turbine Aero Engines* (Somerset, England: 1995), pp. 84–85, Anthony Kay, *German Jet Engine and Gas Turbine Development 1930–1945* (Shrewsbury, England: 2002), pp. 57–89.

72. Smith and Creek, *ME 262*, p. 49.

73. Smith et al., *German Aircraft*, pp. 536–537.

74. T.A. Heppenheimer, "Jet Plane" in *Invention and Technology* (Fall 1993), pp. 45–57. See also Jeffrey Ethell and Alfred Price, *World War II Fighting Jets* (Annapolis, MD: 1994), pp. 19–20.

75. For a complete discussion of the production Junkers Jumo 004 engines see John Foster, Jr., "Design Analysis of the Me 262 Jet Fighter, Part II—The Power Plant" in *Aviation*, 44 (November 1945), 115–130. In it he gives complete technical analysis of the Jumo 004 engine that the Germans used in the Me 262.

76. Morgan, *Me 262 Stormbird Rising*, pp. 22–25.

77. Albert Speer, *Inside the Third Reich* (New York: 1970), pp. 194–197.

78. Burton Klein, *Germany's Economic Preparations for War* (Cambridge: 1959), pp. 220–224.

79. R.J. Overy, *The Air War 1939–1945* (Chelsea, MI: 1980), pp. 158–159.

80. Zilbert, *Albert Speer and the Nazi Ministry of Arms*, pp. 239–240. See also Ebert et al., *Willi Messerschmitt*, p. 244.

81. Ebert et al., *Willi Messerschmitt*, p. 232.

82. RLM documents collected from the Imperial War Museum (IWM), hereafter "IWM Milch Documents," Volume 36, dated March 22, 1943, "Decision of the Me 262 over the He 280."

83. The Bf 109 began its career as a product of the *Bayerische Flugzeugwerke*. The plane was initially labeled Bf 109 with respect to its parent company. But, the Bf 109 later became—and is more commonly known as—the Me 109, after Messerschmitt changed the name of the company to reflect his influence.

84. IWM Milch Documents, Volume 20, May 25, 1943.

85. IWM Milch Documents, Volume 21, June 22, 1943.

86. Ibid., with two production centers producing Me 262s exclusively. The numbers projected were (for the months following November 1944) 40, 90, 140, 180, and increasing to a total of 400 by September 1945.

87. Heinz Nawarra, *Messerschmitt Bf 109* (Somerset, England: 1989), p. 297, figures taken for 1943, a total of 6,247 Me 109s produced.

88. IWM Milch Documents, Volume 21, June 22, 1943. See also Mano Ziegler, *Turbinenjäger Me 262* (Stuttgart: 1978), pp. 70–73.

89. Tony Wood and Bill Gunston, *Hitler's Luftwaffe* (London: 1977), pp. 164–168.

90. IWM Milch Documents, Volume 24, August 13, 1943.

91. Ibid.

92. Ibid.

93. Boehme, *JG7*, p. 35.

94. Ibid., p. 88. See also Boehme, *JG7*, pp. 20–21.

95. Boehme, *JG7*, p. 29.
96. Boyne, p. 30.
97. Smith and Creek, *ME 262*, p. 89.
98. For a complete transcript of the Galland report see Smith and Creek, *ME 262*, p. 108. For the conference minutes see IWM Milch Documents, Volume 20, May 25, 1943.
99. Smith and Creek, *ME 262*, p. 113.
100. IWM Milch Documents, Volume 20, May 25, 1943.
101. Adolf Galland, *The First and the Last* (New York: 1954), p. 274.

CHAPTER 2: FRANK WHITTLE AND THE "Squirt"

1. Frank Whittle, *Jet: The Story of Pioneer* (New York: 1954). p. 14.
2. Ibid., p. 15.
3. John Golley, *Whittle— The True Story* (Washington, DC: 1987), pp. 6–7.
4. Whittle, *Jet*, p. 17.
5. Whittle, *Jet*, pp. 20–21. See also (Flight Cadet) Frank Whittle, "Speculation" in *RAF Cadet College Magazine* (Fall 1928, pp. 106–110), where he attempts to answer the question of the future of aero engines with the response of "the air turbine."
6. Ibid. See also Golley, *Whittle*, p. 24, and Edward Constant, *The Origins of the Turbojet Revolution* (Baltimore: 1980), p. 182.
7. Whittle, *Jet*, pp. 22, 27. See also Golley, *Whittle*, pp. 19, 21, 25–30.
8. Golley, *Whittle*, p. 27.
9. Ironically after the Germans had already flown a "pure" turbojet aircraft on August 27, 1939, see Chapter 2 above.
10. Bill Gunston, *World Encyclopedia of Aero Engines* (Wellingborough, England: 1986), p. 38. Gunston refers to the CC.2 according to the civilian designation "N.1." See also, *Jane's Encyclopedia of Aviation* (New York: 1996 edition), p. 237; Constant, *The Origins of the Turbojet Revolution*, p. 227.
11. Whittle, *Jet*, p. 24.
12. Ibid., p. 26.
13. Ibid.
14. According to Whittle, "the invention was published throughout the world." p. 26, the two most often cited references to this breach of security are in the German magazine *Flugsport* and the American newspaper *The New York Times*, both in 1939.
15. According to Whittle, *Jet*, p. 27, probably a turn-and-bank indicator being put into use in RAF aircraft.
16. Ibid., 27–28, Golley, *Whittle*, p. 45.
17. Whittle, *Jet*, p. 31.
18. Ibid., p. 38.
19. Ibid., p. 39.
20. Ibid., pp. 39, 40. See also Gunston's descriptions, Rolls-Royce Type R, p. 134, and Whittle WU, pp. 107–108.
21. Whittle, *Jet*, p. 41.
22. Reprinted in Whittle, *Jet*, p. 42.

23. Whittle, *Jet*, p. 44.

24. Example Hawker Hurricane, developed in 1934, operational in the RAF by 1937. The 1934 Hurricane prototype was powered by a Rolls-Royce "C" to a top speed of 260 mph at sea-level and 315 mph at 15,000 ft. Although there was extensive use of aluminum in the construction, in the 1934 prototypes the wings and rear fuselage were still fabric-covered surfaces. From *Combat Aircraft of World War Two* (1977), *Great Aircraft of the World* (1992), and *Jane's Encyclopedia of Aviation* (1996 edition) among others. The most advanced American fighter of the time was the Boeing P-26 "Peashooter," prototypes developed in 1932 with a top speed of 234 mph. By 1934, due to the Treaty of Versailles, the Germans were still using biplane and parasol monoplanes that could not compete with British or American types. The infamous Bf 109 was not developed until late 1934, and the first was not delivered (Bf 109A) until September 1935—with a British Rolls-Royce Kestrel VI engine!

25. Whittle, *Jet*, p. 44.

26. Ibid., p. 45.

27. General Electric Aircraft Engine Archives (hereafter GEAE), housed at Wright State University, Dayton, Ohio, as the "Whittle Papers," MS-241, Box 1, File 1, no date given, "The Theories and Inventions forming the basis of Developments undertaken by Power Jets Ltd," Flight Lieutenant Frank Whittle. The document was assuredly written by Whittle as the funding proposal for the nascent Power Jets. This is the "scientific" proposal that would have accompanied Bramson's financial proposal. In the document it is obvious that Whittle is excited about his project, but that he has yet to confront some of the major obstacles in his research. This, in addition to the signature, Flight Lieutenant, and the title incorporating Power Jets, as well as its contents, places the document in time as the engineering portion of the financial proposal.

28. Whittle, *Jet*, p. 50.

29. Whittle, *Jet*, p. 52, and Constant, *The Origins of the Turbojet Revolution*, p. 188.

30. Whittle, *Jet*, pp. 52–53.

31. Ibid., p. 53.

32. Constant, *The Origins of the Turbojet Revolution*; p. 189, Golley, *Whittle*, p. 73.

33. See Constant, *The Origins of the Turbojet Revolution*, pp. 188–189. See also G. Smith, *Gas Turbines and Jet Propulsion*, 5th edition (London: 1950), pp. 43–45.

34. Whittle, *Jet*, p. 56.

35. Ibid.

36. Whittle, *Jet*, pp. 58–60. See also Gunston, *World Encyclopedia*, pp. 98–99.

37. Whittle, *Jet*, p. 62.

38. Ibid.

39. Letter reprinted in Whittle, *Jet*, p. 66.

40. Whittle (pp. 65–68) mentions Air Ministry support without specifying the details, James St. Peter in *The History of Aircraft Gas Turbine Development in the United States: A Tradition of Excellence* (Atlanta, GA: 1999), p.9, makes this distinction clear. When the Air Ministry reduced its financial support to £5,000 *total*, it was because it did not purchase the W.U.

41. Whittle, *Jet*, pp. 68–69.

42. Ibid., pp. 71–75.

43. Constant, *The Origins of the Turbojet Revolution*, p. 191.

44. Whittle, *Jet*, p. 77.

45. Ibid.

46. Ibid.

47. Ibid., p. 78.

48. Frank Whittle, *Gas Turbine Thermodynamics* (Oxford: 1981), pp. 166–167.

49. Whittle, *Jet*, pp. 79–82.

50. Ibid., p. 82.

51. Ibid., p. 85.

52. GEAE, Box 3, File 4, "The Advent of the Aircraft Gas Turbine" by Air Commodore Frank Whittle, p. 7, no date given (but sometime after 1948 when he retired with that rank). Whittle, *Jet*, p. 86. See also St. Peter, *The History of Aircraft Gas Turbine Development in the United States*, p. 13.

53. Dr. D.R. Pye had been at the Volta High-Speed Conference in Italy in 1935. We can assume from his attendance and participation at the conference that he had a good idea about what was going on in the rest of Europe with regard to high-speed flight and aeronautical technology. See specifically the Introduction (pp. 17–19) for a discussion of the different national perspectives presented at the conference. Suffice it to say that Pye and the British were overshadowed by their German counterparts.

54. Whittle, *Jet*, p. 88.

55. Ibid., p. 89.

56. Ibid., p. 90.

57. Ibid., p. 97. See also St. Peter, *The History of Aircraft Gas Turbine Development in the United States*, p. 15, and Golley, *Whittle*, p. 124.

58. Whittle, *Jet*, p. 93.

59. GEAE, Box 3, File 8. From the Power Jets Engineering Department, "A Note on Production, Design, and Research, with Special Reference to Aircraft Gas Turbine Power Plants," Whittle, no date given, but the document corresponds to Whittle's record of the discussion (Whittle, *Jet*, p. 95.), and the contents of the file which outlines machinery and proposed production at Power Jets.

60. Whittle, *Jet*, p. 96.

61. Ibid.

62. Ibid., p. 97.

63. Ibid., pp. 98–100; St. Peter, *The History of Aircraft Gas Turbine Development in the United States*, p. 16.

64. Whittle, *Jet*, pp. 100–101; Golley, *Whittle*, pp. 135–136; St. Peter, *The History of Aircraft Gas Turbine Development in the United States*, p. 16.

65. Whittle, *Jet*, p. 107; Golley, *Whittle*, p. 138; St. Peter, *The History of Aircraft Gas Turbine Development in the United States*, p. 17.

66. Whittle, *Jet*, p. 104, Golley, *Whittle*, p. 139.

67. Whittle, *Jet*, p. 104.

68. Ibid., *fn.*

69. Whittle, *Jet*, p. 104, italics in original.

70. Ibid., p. 105.

71. I.C.B. Dear, *The Oxford Companion to World War II* (Oxford: 1995), pp. 117, 1150.
72. Whittle, *Jet*, p. 112.
73. Ibid., p. 114.
74. Ibid., p. 116.
75. Ibid.
76. Ibid., p. 122.
77. Ibid., italics in original.
78. Ibid., pp. 123–124.
79. Ibid., pp. 124–125; St. Peter, *The History of Aircraft Gas Turbine Development in the United States*, pp. 19–20.
80. Whittle, Jet, pp. 129–130; St. Peter, *The History of Aircraft Gas Turbine Development in the United States*, p. 20.
81. Whittle, *Jet*, p. 130.
82. Ibid., p. 132.
83. GEAE, Box 3, File 11, "Memorandum No. 2 on Power Jets Defence," by Frank Whittle, 2 pages, dated July 4, 1940.
84. Whittle, *Jet*, p. 134.
85. Ibid., p. 134–135.
86. Ibid., p. 144–145.
87. Ibid., p. 147.
88. Ibid., p. 148.
89. Ibid.
90. 1 Whittle gives a great description of the first flight on pages 151–152, while the actual flight report is purely technical. GEAE, Box 3, File 9, "Gloster E28/39—Aircraft W.4041—Contractors Preliminary Flight Tests at Cranwell," filed May 17, 1941. In the flight report, Sayer records that he reached 240 mph air speed at an altitude of 4,000 feet and 15,000 rpm. He reports that overall the aircraft was easy and enjoyable to fly.

CHAPTER 3: THE JET COMES TO AMERICA

1. Dik Daso, *Hap Arnold and the Evolution of American Airpower* (Washington, DC: 2000), p. 39.
2. Arnold's statement comes from an unpublished article from "before World War I" entitled "Pioneers of the Aerial Trails" cited in Daso, *Hap Arnold and the Evolution of American Airpower*, p. 39.
3. H.H. Arnold, *Global Mission* (New York: 1949), pp. 13–14.
4. Daso, *Hap Arnold and the Evolution of American Airpower*, p. 36.
5. Ibid.
6. Arnold talks about his awaited transfer optimistically in *Arnold, Global Mission*, p. 15, but Daso reports that Arnold actually failed his exams and would not therefore have been transferred in any case, Daso, *Hap Arnold and the Evolution of American Airpower*, p. 42.
7. Arnold, *Global Mission*, p. 15; Daso, *Hap Arnold and the Evolution of American Airpower*, p. 43; Thomas Coffey, *Hap, Military Aviator* (New York: 1982), p. 41.

8. Arnold, *Global Mission*, p. 21.

9. Ibid., p. 34.

10. Ibid.

11. John Morrow, Jr., *Building German Airpower, 1909–1914* (Knoxville, TN: 1976), pp. 45, 86–87.

12. National Archives and Records Administration (hereafter NARA), 233.5 Records of the Armed Services Committee and its Predecessors, Committee on Military Affairs, H.R. 5304, 1911, and repeated in Arnold, *Global Mission*, pp. 42–43.

13. Arnold, *Global Mission*, p. 43.

14. Ibid., p. 42.

15. Ibid., p. 43.

16. Ibid., p. 45.

17. Ibid., p. 46.

18. Ibid., p. 50.

19. Ibid., pp. 53–54.

20. Ibid., p. 62.

21. Ibid., p. 91.

22. Ibid., p. 93.

23. Ibid., p. 99.

24. Ibid., pp. 102–106.

25. See, for example, Giulio Douhet, *The Command of the Air* (New York: 1942). Translated by Dino Ferrari. Originally published as *Il Dominio Dell'Aria.* (1921).

26. From James Lowe, *A Philosophy of Airpower* (New York: 1984), p. 95.

27. *World Cruisers* reference in Arnold, *Global Mission*, pp. 111–112, and Jane's, p. 333; the Barling bomber (NBL-1), developed in 1923, a triplane bomber powered by six Liberty engines, and although a complete failure as a bomber it was an important lesson to aircraft manufacturers in aeronautical engineering; Arnold, *Global Mission*, p. 113, detail his orders to the AIC.

28. Arnold, *Global Mission*, p. 113.

29. Reported in Arnold, *Global Mission*, p. 118.

30. Ibid., p. 123.

31. Ibid., p. 131.

32. Ibid., p. 133.

33. Ibid., p. 137.

34. Ibid., p. 138.

35. Also known as the Boeing Model 299. The YB-17 was to become the famous B-17 Flying Fortress.

36. Daso, *Hap Arnold and the Evolution of American Airpower*, pp. 141–142. See also Dik Daso, *Architects of American Air Supremacy, General Hap Arnold and Theodore von Kármán* (Maxwell, AL: 1997), pp. 115–120.

37. Daso, *Hap Arnold and the Evolution of American Airpower*, p. 146, and Michael Sherry, *The Rise of American Airpower* (New Haven, CT: 1987), pp. 200–201.

38. Hap Arnold and Ira Eaker, *This Flying Game*, p.

39. Daso, *Hap Arnold and the Evolution of American Airpower*, p. 151.

40. Ibid., p. 153.

41. Ibid., p. 159.

42. Hap Arnold and Ira Eaker, *Winged Warfare* (New York: 1941), pp. 238–239.

43. Arnold, *Global Mission*, p. 193.

44. Craven and Cate, *Army Air Forces in WWII*, Vol. 6 (Chicago: 1948–1958), pp. 26–32.

45. Quoted in Daso, *Hap Arnold and the Evolution of American Airpower*, p. 162.

46. Arnold, *Global Mission*, pp. 195–196.

47. Daso, *Hap Arnold and the Evolution of American Airpower*, pp. 163–164.

48. It must be noted that initially there was no distinction between air-breathing combustion engines (turbojets) and fuel-burning, nonair, reaction engines (rockets). To the early scientists and technicians at the NAS and NACA the technology was similar and concurrently investigated.

49. David Carpenter, *Flame Powered, the Bell XP-59A Airacomet and the General Electric I-A Engine* (New York: 1992), p. 9.

50. NACA reports TN 239 (1926) "Steam Turbines in Aircraft," TN 431 (1932) "Tests on Thrust Augmentors for Jet Propulsion," and TN 442 (1933) "Jet Propulsion with Special Reference to Thrust Augmenters," which all disqualified jet, turbine, and turbojet research for use as aircraft power plants as underpowered and too heavy.

51. NACA reports 263 (1928), 283 (1929), 384 (1932), and so on up to 1938 which go into the impressive development of both mechanical and turbosuperchargers in the United States.

52. NACA "Committee on ..." and Carpenter, *Flame Powered*, p. 9.

53. Arnold, *Global Mission*, p. 216.

54. *Headlines* (published for the Aircraft Engine Group (GE) at Lynn and Everett, September 28, 1977), "Jet Technology Crosses Atlantic," a reprinted letter from H.H. Arnold to the Jet Pioneers of America.

55. Carpenter, *Flame Powered*, p. 11.

56. Ibid.

57. Reprinted in Carpenter, *Flame Powered*, p. 12.

58. Ibid. See also James O. Young, "Riding England's Coattails," in Roger Launius (ed.), *Innovation and the Development of Flight* (College Station, TX: 1999), pp. 277–279, as well as Edward Constant, *The Origins of the Turbojet Revolution* (Baltimore, MD: 1980), p. 218.

59. Max altitude, 35,000 ft. Combat performance was usually 25,000 feet at 295 mph (according to Jane's), and with a maximum speed of 320 mph due to the turbosupercharged engines, Wright R-1820-51 Cyclones.

60. Constant, *The Origins of the Turbojet Revolution*, pp. 218–222, and Young (in Launius), "Riding England's Coattails," pp. 271–277.

61. Reprinted in Carpenter, *Flame Powered*, pp. 12–13.

62. Ibid.

63. Ibid. See also Donald Norton, *Larry, a Biography: a Biography of Lawrence D. Bell* (Chicago: 1981), pp. 117–122.

64. Norton, *Larry, a Biography*, pp. 2–3. Norton compiled a complete biography of the aircraft designer based on his research at the Larry Bell museum (Mentone, IN) as well as oral interviews from former Bell acquaintances.

65. Ibid., p. 3.

66. Ibid., p. 17.
67. Ibid., pp. 18–19.
68. Ibid., pp. 20–21.
69. Ibid., pp. 21, 26–27.
70. Ibid., p. 34.
71. Ibid.
72. Ibid., pp. 43–45.
73. Ibid., p. 57.
74. Ibid., pp. 69–70.
75. Ibid., pp. 70–71.
76. Ibid., p. 72.
77. Ibid.
78. Ibid., p. 73.
79. Reprinted in Norton, *Larry, a Biography*, p. 74.
80. Norton, *Larry, a Biography*, p. 75.
81. Ibid., p. 96.
82. Ibid., pp. 96–97. Bell Aircraft Company was eventually able to produce 20 P-39s a day.
83. See *An Aviation Story*, published by the Bell Aircraft Corporation for the Tenth Anniversary, July 1945, specifically chapter XIV "Jet Propulsion" pp. 142–143. See also Norton, *Larry, a Biography*, pp. 117–118, Carpenter, *Flame Powered*, pp. 12–13, Alain Pelletier, *Bell Aircraft since 1935* (London: 1992), p. 50.
84. Norton, *Larry, a Biography*, p. 118.
85. Ibid.; Carpenter, *Flame Powered*, p. 19; Pelletier, *Bell Aircraft since 1935*, p. 50.
86. The "Secret Six" included Edgar Rhodes, Project engineer, H. Poyer, R. Wolf, J. Limage, H. Bowers, and B. Sparks. The XP-59A was Bell Aircraft Company's "Model 27" all Company serial numbers for this aircraft started with "27-." For example, the first prototype was 27-1.
87. Carpenter, *Flame Powered*, p. 14. See also United States Air Force Museum (hereafter USAFM), (X)P-59A/his Documents, Box 483, "Cost of Bell XP-59A Airplanes," dated September 30, 1941. The cost was estimated at $1,551,350.00 for the planes with a "Fixed-Fee" for Bell Aircraft Company of $93,081.00. Bell was to be paid $750,000 for the first prototype, $500,000 for the second, and $300,000 for the third. According to the contract, he would only receive $450 for the wind tunnel test model and $900 for the "final Engineering Data"!
88. Carpenter, *Flame Powered*, p. 14,
89. Sanford Moss, "The Gas Turbine, and 'Internal Combustion' Prime-Mover" (Doctoral Dissertation, Unpublished, Cornell University, 1903). In his dissertation, Moss discussed the potential of an extremely primitive steam/gas turbine as a prime mover. Although he was on the right track, his "engine" was only 4 percent efficient, and was not powerful enough to maintain the compression–combustion—exhaust cycle.
90. Robert Garvin, *Starting Something Big, the Commercial Emergence of GE Aircraft Engines* (Reston, VA: 1998), pp. 3–4. See also The General Electric Company, *Seven Decades of Progress* (Fallbrook, CA: 1979), pp. 12–13.
91. Garvin, *Starting Something Big*, p. 5. See also *Seven Decades*, pp. 27–27.

92. Constant, *The Origins of the Turbojet Revolution*, p. 220.

93. As is aptly discussed in Constant, *The Origins of the Turbojet Revolution*, pp. 218–222.

94. Carpenter, *Flame Powered*, pp. 12–13. See also Young, "Riding England's Coattails," pp. 263–298.

95. Nor did others. There were discussions of the turbojet as a prime mover in the United States, but studies had theorized that the Turbojet was not in and of itself efficient enough to power an airplane. Contemporary research showed that the turbojet powering a propeller (turboprop) was the most likely combination for a viable aircraft powerplant. See specifically National Advisor Report for Aeronautics (NACA) Report number 159, "Jet Propulsion for Airplanes," dated 1923, as well as NACA Wartime Reports E-78, "The Reaction Jet as a Means of Propulsion at High Speeds," dated June 1941.

96. See Sanford Moss, *Superchargers for Aviation* (New York: 1944) and Army Air Forces Technical Report Number 5234, "Final Report on the Development of the XP-59A and YP-59A Model Airplanes," courtesy of the United States Air Force Museum (hereafter USAFM) collection, P-59A, Box A1/his, Dated June 28, 1945. The engine is incorrectly reported as the General Electric "Turbosupercharger Model I-16." See also Major Rudolpf Schulte (Project Officer Turbojet and Gas Turbine Developments, HQ AAF), "Design Analysis of the General Electric Type I-16 Jet Engine," in *Aviation* (January, 1946), 43–50.

97. Note the official GE designation "I" ("eye"—not "one")—A. Although it is mislabeled in many articles, former GE designers and the citation in *Seven Decades of Progress*, pp. 46–47, are very insistent that the engine be labeled correctly.

98. Ibid., p. 47. See also Young, "Riding England's Coattails," p. 280. In addition consultation of the original blueprints of the W.1 and GE I-A engines: Wright State University Special Collections, Dunbar Archives (hereafter Wright State), Whittle Collection, engine blueprints in Box 1, File 13, and USAFM AAF Technical Report 5234, in File A1, P-59A/his.

99. *Seven Decades*, p. 47, and any and all of the info for this trip. See also *Headlines* (published for the Aircraft Engine Group (GE) at Lynn and Everett, September 28, 1977), "Secrecy Surrounds Birth of the First U.S. Jet."

100. *Seven Decades*, p. 47.

101. Ibid.

102. Frank Whittle, *Jet, the Story of a Pioneer* (New York: 1954), p. 218.

103. *Seven Decades*, p. 48, including a reprinted original test log page, underline in original.

104. *Seven Decades*, p. 49 records the name as "Whitley," Whittle, *Jet*, p. 219, says he used the name "Whiteley." But Whittle himself says that he did not remember from day to day the spelling of his new assumed name and often reverted to "Whittle."

105. Whittle, *Jet*, pp. 223–225.

106. Carpenter, *Flame Powered*, p. 19. See also Pelletier, *Bell Aircraft Since 1935*, pp. 50–54.

107. Carpenter, *Flame Powered*, p. 19.

108. Quoted in Norton, *Larry, a Biography*, p. 118.

109. Norton, *Larry, a Biography*, p. 118; Carpenter, *Flame Powered*, pp. 18–20.

110. Carpenter, *Flame Powered*, pp. 19–20.

111. Shoults and Keirn reprinted in Carpenter, *Flame Powered*, pp. 20–21.See also Norton, *Larry, a Biography*, p. 120.

112. Carpenter, *Flame Powered*, pp. 20–21; Norton, *Larry, a Biography*, pp. 120–121. See also Pelletier, *Bell Aircraft since 1935*, pp. 50–54, Young, "Riding England's Coattails," pp. 279–280.

113. NACA Wartime Reports L-485, "Wind Tunnel Tests of a Submerged-Engine Fuselage Design," dated October 1940, dealt with radial engines embedded in the aircraft fuselage—different concept, but relevant.

114. Relating to different air intakes on different aircraft, but most often researched was the North American P-51 *Mustang*, see specifically: NACA Wartime Reports L-331, "Effect of External Shape Upon the Drag of a Scoop" (July 1941), L-486, "High-Speed Tests of a Ducted body with Various Air-Outlet Openings" (May 1942), and L-438, "Wind Tunnel Investigation of Rear Underslung Fuselage Ducts" (September 1943), to name a few. While relevant to the Bell problem, and under consideration by the NACA, only the tests completed by the time the Bell team was working on the XP-59A were available for consultation. NACA could not be consulted, and the Bell team could not request specific test data.

115. *An Aviation Story*, pp. 142–145.

116. Carpenter, *Flame Powered*, pp. 27–28, Steve Pace, *X-Planes at Edwards* (Osceola, WI: 1995), pp. 9–10, Constant, *The Origins of the Turbojet Revolution*, pp. 281–282

117. Carpenter, *Flame Powered*, p. 28. And it is inherently interesting that an antiquated steam train was delivering the United States's most highly developed technology across the country.

118. Norton, *Larry, a Biography*, p. 122.

119. *An Aviation Story*, p. 146.

120. Carpenter, *Flame Powered*, p. 27.

121. Ibid., p. 25; Norton, *Larry, a Biography*, p. 123; Pelletier, *Bell Aircraft since 1935*, p. 50; *An Aviation Story*, p. 147.

122. Young, "Riding England's Coattails," pp. 282–283; Pace, *X-Planes at Edwards*, p. 15; *Seven Decades*, p. 51.

123. *An Aviation Story*, p. 147.

124. The Soviets "borrowed" captured German ME-262s for trials; and the Japanese built the Nakajima *Kikka* powered by BMW 003 engines, but the prototype was not flown until August 7, 1945, far to late for potential impact.

125. Edward Constant's "presumptive anomaly" in *The Origins of the Turbojet Revolution* (Baltimore, MD: 1980).

126. In Launius.

CHAPTER 4: JETS AT WAR

1. Adolf Galland, *The First and the Last* (London: 1954), p. 275, as well as pilot reports in J. Richard Smith and Eddie Creek, *Me262* (London: 1998) Vol. 1, *passim*, Hugh Morgan, *Stormbird Rising* (London: 1996), pp. 32, 34–36.

2. Galland diary entry reported in *The First and the Last*, pp. 280–281.

3. Based on reports from the records of the *Reichsluftfahrt Ministerium* (RLM). These documents are housed in three specific places: London, England, at the Imperial War Museum (IWM) and the Public Record Office (PRO), in Germany at the *Bundesarchiv-Militärarchiv* (BA-MA) in Freiburg, and in the United States at the National Archives and Records Administration (NARA). This author consulted the RLM records at all of these locations. The documents in this chapter are labeled according to the files at the IWM and hereafter cited as IWM Milch Documents, Vol. 20, May 25, 1943, "Conference on the Me 209 vs. the Me 262" as well as reported in Galland's diary, Drop Me 209, put the Me 262 in its place," and in Smith and Creek, *Me262*, p. 113.

4. The RLM decided in favor of the Me 262 over the He 280 in March, but was still cautious in the May meetings about halting all Me 109 production in favor of the nascent jet. See specifically IWM Documents Milch collection Vol. 36, March 22, 1943, "Decision of the Me 262 over the He 280."

5. IWM Milch Documents, Vol. 21, June 22, 1943.

6. Ibid., the numbers projected for the months following November 1944 were (by month): 40, 90, 140, 180, and up to 400 by September 1945.

7. Smith and Creek, *Me262*, Vol. 1, p. 120.

8. Ibid., p. 146.

9. Ibid., pp. 120–121.

10. Ibid., pp. 143, 146.

11. IWM Milch Documents, Vol. 24, August 13, 1943.

12. Walter Boyne, *The Jet Age: Forty Years of Jet Aviation* (Washington, DC: 1979), p. 158.

13. See specifically Morgan's Chapter 4, "Dispersal of Production Facilities," pp. 46–57.

14. Manfred Boehme, *JG7, the World's First Jet Fighter Unit 1944/1945* (Atglen, PA: 1992), translated by David Johnston, p. 40. See also Galland, *The First and the Last*, pp. 277–278.

15. The order was expressly ignored by Messerschmitt who did not even have a bombsight for the Me 262. This fact is clear from the operational units that flew the Me 262: there were 10 squadrons that flew the jet and only three were designated as bomber squadrons (and they were labeled Bomber/fighter squadrons). For an interesting design analysis of Me 262 technological specifications see John Foster, Jr., "Design Analysis of the Messerschmitt Me-262 Jet Fighter" Parts I and II (Airframe and Engines) in *Aviation*, Vol. 44, October and November 1945.

16. J.R. Smith, Anthony Kay, and Eddie Creek, *German Aircraft of the Second World War* (London: 1972), pp. 536–537.

17. Smith and Creek, *Me262*, Vol. 2, p. 234.

18. Boehme, *JG7*, p. 53. See also, John Foreman and S.E Harvey, *Messerschmitt Me 262 Combat Diary* (Surrey, England: 1995), p. 34.

19. Adolf Galland, *The Development of Jet and Rocket Airplanes in Germany 1938–1945*, extracted from *European Contributions to the History of World War II*, monograph Number 7, *Development and Planning in the German Air Force*, Part I of the von Rohden Monograph (Foreign Documents Section, Air University Library: Maxwell AFB, AL: 1951), p. 41. Galland states the production of Me 262s was one in March, none in April, and eight in May, 1944.

20. Ibid. Production figures were: May 1944: 8, June: 26, July: 55, August: 56, September: 81, October: 127, November: 86, December: 124, for a total of 564 in 1944.

21. Boehme, *JG7*, pp. 57–58.

22. Ibid., pp. 47–49.

23. Ibid., pp. 48–49. Boehme mentions a Messerschmitt document dated August 10, 1944.

24. For a complete discussion of the Jumo 004 engines and their models see John Foster, Jr., "Design Analysis of the Me-262 Jet Fighter Part I—the Powerplant," in *Aviation*, 4 (November 1945). In it he discusses the complete technical analysis of the Jumo 004 engine that the Germans used in the Me 262.

25. IWM Milch Documents, Vol. 58, May 28, 1944.

26. Smith and Creek, *Me262*, Vol. 1, p. 183.

27. Germany got supplies of chrome from Turkey, but in 1940 the world's supply of nickel came mainly (87%) from Canada, and molybdenum came from the United States (92.4%). See I.C.B. Dear, *The Oxford Companion to World War II* (Oxford: 1996 edition), p. 1063.

28. Göring's four-year plan for German aviation in 1936, see David Irving, *Göring, a Biography* (New York: 1989), pp. 162–169.

29. Albert Speer, *Inside the Third Reich* (New York: 1970), pp. 194–197.

30. Burton Klein, *Germany's Economic Preparations for War* (Cambridge: 1959), pp. 220–224.

31. R.J. Overy, *The Air War, 1939–1945* (Chelsea, MI: 1980), pp. 158–159.

32. Edward Zilbert, *Albert Speer and the Nazi Ministry of Arms* (London: 1981), pp. 239–240. See also Hans Ebert, Johann Kaiser, and Klaus Peters, *Willi Messerschmitt—Pionier der Luftfahrt und des Leichtbaues—Eine Biographie* (Bonn: 1992), p. 244.

33. IWM Milch Documents, Vol. 32, January 5, 1944. See also IWM Messerschmitt Papers, "Messerschmitt to *RLM*," March 30, 1944, "request for more manpower."

34. See for example Alfred Mierzejewski, *The Collapse of the German War Economy* (Chapel Hill, NC: 1988). See also David MacIssac, *Strategic Bombing in World War Two* (New York: 1976), pp. 76, 78. As well as Jesse Edgar (Lt. Col. (ret.)), *Bombs Away! Thirty was Enough, a Bombardier's Diary Account of Combat as a Member of a B-17 Crew with the Eight Air Force* (unpublished), pp. 61–62, 66–76; where he gives a first-hand account of bomb missions against German oil refineries and marshalling yards.

35. Smith and Creek, *Me262*, Vol. 2, p. 401.

36. *United States Strategic Bombing Survey* (USSBS),Vol. 1 (New York: 1976), pp. 8–9, 42–45. See in particular Chart 16, "German Production, Consumption, and Stocks: Aviation Gas, Motor Gasoline, Diesel Oil," p. 43. Whereas there was virtually no aviation gas left at the end of the war, there were still stockpiles of diesel available.

37. Harold Faber (ed.), *Luftwaffe, a History* (New York: 1977), pp. 269, 272.

38. Williamson Murray, *Strategy for Defeat, the Luftwaffe* (Maxwell, AL: 1983), pp. 310–1, 314.

39. Zilbert, *Albert Speer and the Nazi Ministry of Arms*, p. 262.

40. USSBS, II: chapter VI "Effects of bombing on Aircraft Production," pp. 76–93, Figure VI, "Comparison of United States and Germany Aircraft Production." See also *The Strategic Air War Against Germany 1939-1945, Reports of the British Bombing Survey Unit* (London: 1998), p. 72. British production of all types of aircraft in 1944 was 26,500 planes. See also Overy, *The Air War*, pp. 77, 120, and 150. Overy presents production figures for the United States and Britain for the year 1944, the average is over 9,000 fighters per month and 3,500 bombers per month. Production figures for 1945 can be calculated as 6,500 fighters and almost 4,000 bombers per month in the last five months of the war in Europe. See also Francis Dean, *America's Hundred-Thousand* (Atglen, PA: 1996), production figures per month for American fighter manufacture, the title of the book is the reference to the 100,000 fighters produced in the United States alone during the war.

41. Ibid., see USSBS figures for bomber production, as well as British survey Unit on the same topic.

42. Morgan, *Stormbird Rising*, pp. 46–47. See also USSBS, Vol. 2, pp. 30–31.

43. USSBS, Vol. 2, p. 27.

44. Ibid., p. 28.

45. Ibid., p. 32. See also Morgan, *Stormbird Rising*, pp. 47–49.

46. USSBS, Vol. 2, p. 32.

47. IWM Milch Documents, Vol. 21, June 22, 1943, "Messerschmitt to Milch: Production Schedule for the Me 262."

48. Ibid.

49. Adolf Galland, *The Development . . .* , p. 41.

50. Ibid.

51. IWM Milch Documents, Vol. 63, November 2, 1943, "Göring to Messerschmitt et al on the development of the Me 262."

52. Foreman and Harvey, *Messerschmitt Me 262*, pp. 38–39.

53. Ibid., p. 40.

54. Ibid.

55. The *Mosquito* had a maximum speed of 380 mph (cruising speed of 255 mph) and a service ceiling of 33,000 feet.

56. Boyne, *The Jet Age*, pp. 41–42, Boehme, *JG7*, p. 49, and Smith and Creek, *Me262*, Vol. 2, pp. 247–248.

57. Boehme, *JG7,*, pp. 42–44.

58. Foreman and Harvey, *Messerschmitt Me 262*, p. 53.

59. Boehme, *JG7*, p. 53. See also Smith and Creek, *Me262*, Vol. 2, p. 261.

60. Smith and Creek, *Me262*, Vol. 2, p. 263.

61. Foreman and Harvey, *Messerschmitt Me 262*, pp. 57–58.

62. *German Aircraft and Armament*, printed by the Office of the Assistant Chief of the Air Staff, Intelligence, Washington, DC: 1944 (Reprinted by Brassey's, Washington, DC: 2000), Report #112 (Me 262). The report suggests that the United States did not have any significant information on the Me 262 other than that it was a jet-propelled aircraft.

63. Smith and Creek, *Me262*, Vol. 2, p. 248.

64. Boehme, *JG7*, pp. 62–63. The American pilots of course reported that he was shot down whereas the observers on the ground deny any Allied planes in the vicinity.

65. Boyne, *The Jet Age*, p. 42.

66. Smith and Creek, *Me262*, Vol. 2, p. 363.

67. Foreman and Harvey, *Messerschmitt Me 262*, pp. 55–100. Their painstaking analysis of German and Allied records provides an accurate account of the day-to-day operational effectiveness of *Ekdo 262* and *Kommando Nowotny*.

68. Boehme, *JG7*, pp. 71–72.

69. Ibid., p. 73.

70. Ibid.

71. Morgan, *Stormbird Rising*, pp. 97–101.

72. Martin Windrow, *German Air Force Fighters of World War Two*, Vol. 1 (England: 1968), pp. 103–104. Morgan also gives a complete listing of operational and assigned Me 262 squadrons throughout the war.

73. Boehme, *JG 7*.

74. Morgan, *Stormbird Rising*, p. 103.

75. Galland, *The First and the Last*, p. 294. See also Boyne, *The Jet Age*, p. 48.

76. Galland, *The First and the Last*, pp. 299–301; Boyne, *The Jet Age*, p. 48.

77. Galland, *The First and the Last*, pp. 301–302.

78. Foreman and Harvey, *Messerschmitt Me 262*, pp. 236–244.

79. Galland, *The First and the Last*, pp. 297, 299.

80. Foreman and Harvey, *Messerschmitt Me 262*.

81. Foreman and Harvey, *Messerschmitt Me 262*, pp. 355–378. Appendices IV "USAAF Fighter Air Combat Claims Against Me 262 Aircraft," V "RAF Fighter Air Combat Claims against Me 262 Aircraft," and VI "Known Claims by Jet Pilots."

82. Galland, *The Development . . .* , p. 40.

83. Overy, *The Air War*, p. 150. The Allies (United States, Britain, and the USSR) combined to produce 167,654 aircraft of all types in 1944 and 84,806 in 1945. Some of these planes were obviously used in the Pacific theatre, and of those produced in 1945 some were built after the German surrender. But the figures are representative of the relative production capabilities of the Allies versus the Germans.

84. Foreman and Harvey, *Messerschmitt Me 262*, pp. 167–170.

85. Manfred Griehl and Joachim Dressel, *Luftwaffe Combat Aircraft* (Atglen, PA: 1994), p. 165–166.

86. Smith et al., *German Aircraft,*, p. 308.

87. Galland, *The Development . . .* , p. 41.

88. Ibid., p. 40.

89. Bryan Philpott, *German Military Aircraft* (London: 1981), p. 114.

90. Smith et al., *German Aircraft*, pp. 314–315.

91. John Gimbel, *Science, Technology, and Reparations* (Stanford: 1990), passim.

92. Foreman and Harvey, *Messerschmitt Me 262*, pp. 272–273.

93. Galland, *The First and the Last*, pp. 301–302.

94. Foreman and Harvey, *Messerschmitt Me 262*, pp. 274–275.

95. Ibid., p. 275.

96. Ibid.

97. See specifically Williamson Murray's argument in *Strategy for Defeat, the Decline of the Luftwaffe* (Maxwell, AL: 1983), passim.

CHAPTER 5: BRITAIN CATCHES UP

1. *Jane's Encyclopedia of Aviation* (London: 1996 edition), pp. 96, 105.
2. Ibid., pp. 848–850. See also Alfred Price, *Spitfire* (Leicester, England: 1993), *passim*, and *Jane's Fighting Aircraft of World War II* (London: 1989), pp. 139–142.
3. General Electric Aircraft Engine Archives (hereafter GEAE), housed at Wright State University, Dayton, Ohio as the "Whittle Papers," Gloster E28/39—Aircraft W.4041—Contractors Preliminary Flight Tests at Cranwell," Box 3, File 9, dated May 17, 1941. See also Henry Matthews, *Gloster-Whittle E. 28/39 Pioneer, a Flying Chronology* (Beirut, Lebanon: 2001), pp. 11–13, including a reprint of the first flight report, mentioned above, on p. 12. See also Derek James, *Gloster Aircraft since 1917* (London: 1971), pp. 237–245.
4. GEAE, "Gloster E28/39—Aircraft W.4041—Contractors Preliminary Flight Tests at Cranwell" (Second Flight, May 16), Box 3, File 9, dated May 17, 1941.
5. Frank Whittle, *Jet, the Story of a Pioneer* (New York: 1954), pp. 153–154.
6. Whittle, *Jet*, p. 154. By comparison, May 1941 production *Spitfires* had a top speed of 367 mph (see *Jane's*).
7. GEAE, "Gloster E28/39—Aircraft W.4041—Contractors Preliminary Flight Tests at Cranwell" (Second Flight, May 16), Box 3, File 9, dated May 17, 1941. See also Matthews, *Gloster-Whittle E. 28/39 Pioneer*, pp. 11–13.
8. See Matthews, *Gloster-Whittle E. 28/39 Pioneer*, p. 13.
9. James, *Gloster Aircraft since 1917*, pp. 245–306, specifically 245–246.
10. Ibid., p. 246.
11. Ibid., p. 247.
12. Bill Gunston, *World Encyclopedia of Aero Engines* (Wellingborough, England: 1986), pp. 51–53, 18–20, and 98–99, respectively.
13. *Headlines* (published for the Aircraft Engine Group (GE) at Lynn and Everett, September 28, 1977), "Jet Technology Crosses Atlantic," a reprinted letter from H.H. Arnold to the Jet Pioneers of America. See also H.H. Arnold, *Global Mission* (New York: 1949), pp. 242–243. See above Chapter 3, "The Jet Comes to America," pp. 104–106.
14. James, *Gloster Aircraft since 1917*, p. 247.
15. See above Chapter 2.
16. John Golley, *Whittle, the True Story* (Washington, DC: 1987), p. 174.
17. Golley, pp. 172–173.
18. Golley, p. 173.
19. Golley, pp. 176–177.
20. Bill Gunston, *Jet and Turbine Aero Engines* (Somerset, England: 1995), pp. 132–133.
21. See Gunston, *Jet and Turbine Aero Engines*, p. 133. Engine dry weight, for a specific weight of 2.31 lb thrust/lb
22. Gunston, *World Encyclopedia*, p. 51.
23. See Whittle, *Jet*, p. 195.
24. Ibid., pp. 194–195.
25. Ibid., pp. 198–215.
26. Ibid., pp. 220–221.
27. Ibid., p. 221.

28. Ibid., p. 224.

29. Ibid., pp. 224–225.

30. Ibid., p. 226.

31. Gunston, *Jet and Turbine Aero Engines*, p. 134.

32. Whittle, *Jet*, p. 226.

33. Gunston, *Jet and Turbine Aero Engines*, pp. 134–135, Gunston, *World Encyclopedia*, p. 108, Whittle, *Jet*, pp. 226–227.

34. Gunston, *Jet and Turbine Aero Engines*, p. 134. Also mentioned in Whittle, *Jet*, pp. 236–237.

35. Gunston, *Jet and Turbine Aero Engines*, pp. 134–135.

36. Whittle, *Jet*, p. 227.

37. Ibid., pp. 230–232; Gunston, *Jet and Turbine Aero Engines*, p. 134. Rover testing on the B.26—their design—was under 57 hours (Whittle), specific tests for 24 hours cited by Gunston. Whittle includes all testing of both of the B.26 engines at Rover (it is important to note that there were only two), as well as Rover's tests on the completed W.2Bs which were constructed according to strict Power Jets design. Whittle records that Rover counted 578 hours turbojet engine testing total during the year, but their records were vague and ambiguous, to say the least. Interaction with Power Jets and Rover was nonexistent, and neither knew of the other's problems that were cropping up with the engine, in either form. By Comparison, Power Jets, by the end of the year, had logged 57 hours on the W.2/500 prototype engine as well as 709 hours total testing of all engines available during the year (W.1, W.1A, and W.2B).

38. Whittle, *Jet*, p. 237.

39. Ibid., pp. 240–241.

40. Matthews, *Gloster-Whittle E. 28/39 Pioneer*, p. 16. The second E.28/39 prototype was numbered W4046.

41. Matthews, *Gloster-Whittle E. 28/39 Pioneer*, p. 16; Whittle, *Jet*, pp, 245–246. Note* Supermarine *Spitfire* Mk V max speed of 369 mph, Hawker *Typhoon* Mk I max speed of 412 mph, thus the *Pioneer* was approaching or even exceeding 400 mph.

42. Whittle, *Jet*, p. 246.

43. Matthews, *Gloster-Whittle E. 28/39 Pioneer*, p. 16.

44. Whittle, *Jet*, p. 243.

45. Ibid., pp. 243–245.

46. James, *Gloster Aircraft since 1917*, pp. 245+. It is interesting to note the similarities between the wing shapes of the Gloster *Meteor* (F.9/40), Supermarine *Spitfire*, and even the Heinkel He 111 bomber. The beautiful, stable design incorporated a rounded leading edge that met a rounded trailing edge at the tip of the wing. Unfortunately for the British, although aesthetically pleasing, the wing design actually hampered the Gloster jet's performance. By comparison, the German Me 262 employed a wing design that took into account interwar German research on fluid compressibility and theoretical physics. See Chapter 1 for a discussion of the German design and development of the Me 262.

47. James, *Gloster Aircraft since 1917*, p. 247.

48. Whittle, *Jet*, pp. 246–247.

49. See specifically Bill Gunston, *World Encyclopedia*, p. 51.

50. Gunston, *Jet and Turbine Aero Engines*, pp. 98–99.

51. Gunston, *Jet and Turbine Aero Engines*, p. 99; James, *Gloster Aircraft since 1917*, pp. 247, 249.

52. Gunston, *World Encyclopedia*, p. 140.

53. Whittle, *Jet*, pp. 247–251.

54. Ibid., pp. 250–251.

55. Ibid., p. 252.

56. James, *Gloster Aircraft since 1917*, pp. 250–251.

57. Public Record Office (hereafter PRO), pilot reports from No. 616 Squadron (Air 50/176).

58. PRO, pilot reports from No. 616 Squadron.

59. PRO, squadron records from No. 616 Squadron, dated 1945.

60. Jane's, pp. 305–316. See for example *Moth, Tiger Moth, Gypsy Moth, Moth Major, Hawk Moth*, etc.

61. Ibid., pp. 315–316.

62. Gunston, *World Encyclopedia*, pp. 51, 140. The *Goblin* was rated at 2,300 lbs thrust for the first *Vampire* flight, by October the Rolls-Royce W.2B/23 *Welland I* was rated at 1,600 lbs and by December only 1,700 lbs. The importance is of course that by December Rolls-Royce was in full production of their 100 unit contract while de Havilland had only four *Goblin* engines total (and only two were flight-ready).

63. See specifically Chapter 7 below.

64. David Watkins, *De Havilland Vampir* (Gloucestershire, England: 1998), pp.

65. James, *Gloster Aircraft since 1917*, pp. 251–252.

66. Gunston, *World Encyclopedia*, pp. 142–143.

67. Whittle, letter to MAP reprinted in *Whittle, the Story of a Pioneer*, pp. 262–263.

68. Whittle, *Jet*, pp. 262–264.

69. Ibid., pp. 266–269. He reports on page 268 that "the implication that Power Jets had willingly accepted the price was, of course, quite wrong. Having had the "pistol" of the threat of extinction pointed at them, they regarded is as something akin to "armed robbery."

70. Ibid., pp. 270–275.

71. Gunston, *World Encyclopedia*, pp. 141–142.

72. Whittle, *Jet*, p. 288.

CHAPTER 6: THE AMERICANS TAKE THE LEAD

1. First flight report reprinted in David Carpenter, *Flame Powered, The Bell XP59-A Airacomet and the General Electric I-A Engine* (New York: 1992), p. 33.

2. Carpenter, *Flame Powered*, pp. 34–35.

3. Ibid., p. 37; Donald Norton, *Larry, a Biography: a Biography of Lawrence D. Bell* (Chicago: 1981), p. 123.

4. "Preliminary Handbook of Service Instructions for the Model XP-59A Interceptor-Fighter Airplanes Manufactured by Bell Aircraft Corp." Dated October 31, 1942, published by Authority of the Commanding General, Army Air Forces

by the Air Service Command, Wright Field, Dayton, Ohio. Courtesy of U.S. Air Force Museum (hereafter USAFM), Box 484, (X)P-59A/mem.

5. "Service Manual" (con't), Column 33-Powerplant, maintenance requirements outlined on page 44.

6. Carpenter, *Flame Powered*, p. 38.

7. Norton, *Larry, a Biography*, p. 124.

8. Carpenter, *Flame Powered*, p. 39.

9. C.W. Smith, *Aircraft Gas Turbines* (John Wiley and Sons, New York: 1956).

10. Richard Leyes and William Fleming, *The History of North American Small Gas Turbine Aircraft Engines* (Washington, DC: 1999), pp. 237–238.

11. *Seven Decades of Progress* (Fallbrook, CA: 1979), p. 52.

12. Adrian Wyen, "They Flew the U.S. Navy's First Jets," in *Naval Aviation News* (March 1963), pp. 6–13.

13. Reprinted in Carpenter, *Flame Powered*, p. 42.

14. Wyen, "They Flew the U.S. Navy's First Jets," pp. 6–7.

15. Alain Pelletier, *Bell Aircraft since 1935* (Annapolis: 1992), pp. 50–51.

16. Francis Dean, *America's Hundred Thousand, The US Production Fighter Aircraft of World War II* (Atglen, PA: 1997), pp. 321–377. Dean outlines the production figures and capabilities of the Americans in WWII, which is a useful lesson in the amazing material ability of the United States in wartime. But, it must be noted that German fighter planes were also as good as the best American and British models, and the XP-59A would have been outclassed in the skies over Germany by its Axis counterparts as well.

17. USAFM, "412th Fighter Group [incorporation]", box 484, (X)P-59A/his.

18. Carpenter, *Flame Powered*, p. 43.

19. Arthur Irwin, "That Dummy Propeller," a letter to the editor of *Product Engineering* (March 1, 1965).

20. See Carpenter, *Flame Powered*, p. 42.

21. Ibid., pp. 45–46; Norton, *Larry, a Biography*, p. 128.

22. Carpenter, *Flame Powered*, p. 45; Norton, *Larry, a Biography*, p. 128.

23. Norton, *Larry, a Biography*, p. 128. Also reprinted in Carpenter, *Flame Powered*, p. 43.

24. Carpenter, *Flame Powered*, p. 43.

25. Ibid., p. 44.

26. Ibid.

27. See Appendix III and IV and their corresponding chart breakdowns of early turbojet aircraft.

28. Tex Johnston, *Jet-Age Test Pilot* (Washington, DC: 2000), pp. 1, 57–64. Although Johnston records his arrival at Muroc as "October, 1944" on page 1, he later (pages 57–58) correctly reports "October, 1943," which agrees with other sources including official Bell documents of his arrival, courtesy of The Bell Aircraft Museum (Hereafter Bell Museum), Mentone, Indiana; Tim Whetstone, Curator. See also Curtis Peebles, *Dark Eagles* (Presidio Novato: 1995), Chapter 1, "The First Black Airplane, The XP-59A *Airacomet*," pp. 3–17.

29. Peebles, *Dark Eagles*, p. 13.

30. NACA "Static Test Project Record," from USAFM, Box 484, (Y)P-59A/tes, YP-59A Airplane static test records.

31. Carpenter, *Flame Powered*, pp. 46–47.

32. Johnston, *Jet-Age Test Pilot*, pp. 2–3.

33. See for example the *New York Times*, *The Chicago Sun*, *The El Paso Times*, *The Bell Aircraft News*; all preserved at the Bell Museum. Also recorded in *An Aviation Story, The History of Bell Aircraft Corporation* (Tenth Anniversary Edition, Buffalo: 1945), pp. 150–151.

34. *El Paso Times*, Friday, January 7, 1944.

35. El Paso Times, New York Times, etc.

36. *Bell Aircraft News*, February 10, 1944.

37. Carpenter, *Flame Powered*, p. 47.

38. Ibid.

39. Ibid.

40. Johnston, *Jet-Age Test Pilot*, pp. 64–65; Carpenter, *Flame Powered*, pp. 47–48.

41. Carpenter, *Flame Powered*, p. 48.

42. Ann Carl, *A WASP among Eagles* (Washington, DC: 1999), pp. 98–102.

43. USAFM, Box 482, (Y)P-59A/his, "Summary of Case History," prepared by Historical Office, Wright Field [Dayton, Ohio], December 1947, a final compilation of the official records pertaining to the XP- YP- and P-59A and B aircraft. Also reprinted in Carl, p. 102.

44. Norton, *Larry, a Biography*, pp. 129–131.

45. Minor modifications in the wings to the P-59A resulted in the P-59B designation: the 50 production models included 20 P-59As and 30 P-59Bs.

46. Carpenter, *Flame Powered*, p. 51.

47. Norton, *Larry, a Biography*, p. 131.

48. Seven Decades of Progress, p. 53.

49. *Seven Decades*, pp. 54–56. See also Edward Constant, *The Origins of the Turbojet Revolution* (Baltimore: 1980), pp. 222–223. Constant discusses the development of the TG-100 (contract December 8, 1941) and the TG-180; both axial-flow turboprops (axial-flow turbojet engines powering propellers through shafts and gear boxes), neither of which were flight-tested before the end of the war. Axial-flow turbojet technology was brand new in the United States and development lagged perceptibly.

50. Bill Gunston, *World Encyclopedia of Aero Engines* (Wellingborough, England: 1986), pp. 60–61.

51. USAFM, "AAF Technical Report 5536: Final Report of Development, Procurement and Acceptance of the XP-83 Airplane," Box 284, (X)F-83/his. The Army Air Forces report states that the plane was designed for range and high-speed bomber escort. The production version would have six .60 caliber machine guns fixed in the nose (Type T17E3). The second prototype tested this weapons package.

52. USAFM, "XP-83 Pilot's Handbook of Flight Operating Instructions," Box 284, (X)P-83/ops.

53. USAFM, "AAF Technical Report 5536."

54. See Pelletier, *Bell Aircraft*, pp. 61–62.

55. Bell Aircraft Museum, "Venus Project" documents, unmarked box, dated March 10, 1945.

56. "Venus Project," p. 3.

57. Literally! I found this proposal in an unmarked box at the Bell Aircraft Museum, Mentone, Indiana; I thought it interesting that Bell was still proposing airframes without consideration of short ranges in low-altitude jet attack aircraft. The proposal was dated March 10, 1945, and an accompanying note stated that "Bell [Georgia Division] was advised unofficially by Wright Field that we had won the competition. Award was refused by L.D.B. (Larry Bell) at a meeting in Marietta!" The Army put $220,236.86 into the "Venus Project," but ultimately cancelled the contract on September 13, 1945. Only a wind-tunnel test model was constructed. But "Venus Project" still remains an interesting piece of aviation history that supplements the development of early jet airpower theory, doctrine, and implementation.

58. René Francillon, *Lockheed Aircraft since 1913* (Annapolis: 1987), pp. 235–254.

59. Ibid., pp. 13—14.

60. Constant, *The Origins of the Turbojet Revolution*, p. 224.

61. Ibid. Also Gunston, *World Encyclopedia*, p. 91, says 5,500 lbs.

62. Constant, *The Origins of the Turbojet Revolution*, pp. 223–224; Francillon, *Lockheed Aircraft since 1913*, pp. 22, 236, 484–485; Gunston, *World Encyclopedia*, p. 91; Young, pp. 276–277.

63. Constant, *The Origins of the Turbojet Revolution*, pp. 223–224.

64. See specifically *Of Men and Stars, a History of Lockheed Aircraft Corporation* (New York: 1980), reprinted by Arno Press from the official Lockheed History, see October 1957, Chapter VIII, "From War to Peace," pp. 6–10. See also Constant, *The Origins of the Turbojet Revolution*, p. 234, Francillon, *Lockheed Aircraft since 1913*, p. 22, and Young, p. 277. Some funding was thrown at the engine (L-1000) program in 1943, but the engine was still under development at the end of the war and the project was ultimately terminated.

65. Contract W535 ac-40680 was approved and signed on June 24, providing the proposed $515,018.40 to Lockheed for Project MX-409, the future XP-80 project. By October, the contract was extended to $1,044,335.36. Reprinted in Francillon, *Lockheed Aircraft since 1913*, p. 236.

66. Ben Rich and Leo Janos, *Skunk Works* (Boston: 1994), pp. 111–112. The name "Skonk Works" was later changed to "Skunk Works" when the comic's publisher objected to Lockheed's use of the term. p. 112, fn. See also Peebles, *Dark Eagles*, p. 17.

67. Kelly Johnson, "How We Engineered the Lockheed Shooting Star" in *Aviation*, 44(7) (July 1945), 149–151.

68. Ibid., p. 150.

69. Ibid., p. 151.

70. Ibid., p. 150. The design number is NACA 65213 from root to tip for the XP-80 airplane.

71. Ibid., p. 150.

72. Ibid., p. 151.

73. Francillon, *Lockheed Aircraft since 1913*, pp. 236–237.

74. Ibid., pp. 237–238. See also Roy Anderson, "A Look At Lockheed," a speech given to the Newcomen Society in North America, reprinted by the society (New York: 1983), pp. 30–31.

75. Francillon, *Lockheed Aircraft since 1913*, p. 238.

76. Johnston, p. 69. Also reprinted in Peebles, *Dark Eagles*, p. 16.

77. Gunston, *World Encyclopedia*, pp. 60–61.

78. Ibid. See also *Seven Decades of Progress*, pp. 53–54.

79. *Seven Decades of Progress*, p. 54. See also Gunston, *World Encyclopedia*, pp. 10–11, 61.

80. Francillon, *Lockheed Aircraft since 1913*, pp. 239–340.

81. Ibid., p. 240.

82. Ibid.

83. John Fredriksen, *Warbirds* (Santa Barbara, CA: 1999), p. 187.

84. Ibid., p. 224. See also R.J. Francillon, *McDonnell Douglas Aircraft Since 1920* (London: 1979), pp. 383–383; as well as Bill Yenne, *McDonnell Douglas, A Tale of Two Giants* (Greenwich, CT: 1985), pp. 64, 70–73.

85. Gunston, *World Encyclopedia*, pp. 169–170; also Constant, *The Origins of the Turbojet Revolution*, p. 223. See also Bill Gunston, *The Development of Jet and Turbine Aero Engines* (Somerset, England: 1995), p. 144.

86. See specifically Gunston, *World Encyclopedia*, p. 170, Constant, *The Origins of the Turbojet Revolution*, p. 223. As compared to the I-14 (1,400 lbs), I-16 (1,600 lbs), and the new I-40 (4,000 lbs thrust).

87. Gunston, *The Development* ... , p. 144; Fredriksen, *Warbirds*, p. 224.

88. Including specifically the entire range of Bell X planes, and by the end of the war helicopters.

89. North American F-86 *Sabre*.

90. Republic F-84 *Thunderjet*, designed to replace the unstoppable P-47 *Thunderbolt*.

91. Fredriksen, *Warbirds*, p. 277.

92. Ibid., pp. 221, 222, 224; Francillon, *McDonnell Aircraft*, pp. 380–383, 426–432, 480–487; Yenne, *McDonnell Douglas*, pp. 64, 70–74.

93. North American FJ-1 *Fury* Navy Fighter.

94. Vought F6U *Pirate*.

95. Douglas F3D *Skyknight*, two-seat Navy jet night-fighter.

96. Grumman F9F *Panther*.

97. North American B-45 *Tornado*, the AAF's first jet bomber, the Convair B-36 *Peacemaker*, originally designed as an intercontinental bomber to fly from the United States to bomb Germany and return, the B-36D incorporated both Pratt & Whitney R-4360 radials (six) in addition to four General Electric J47 turbojets. The Boeing B-47 *Stratojet* was a swept-wing, six-engine, jet bomber and a revolution in engineering design; in 1947 it flew for the first time.

98. ICB Dear, *The Oxford Companion to World War Two* (Oxford, England: 1996), pp. 1062–1063.

99. Ibid., p. 1062.

100. Johnson, "How We Engineered the Lockheed Shooting Star."

CHAPTER 7: INTO THE COLD

1. D.R. Maguire, "Enemy Jet History," in *The Journal of the Royal Aeronautical Society*, 52 (January 1948), 76–84. See also Walter Boyne, *The Jet Age: Forty*

Years of Jet Aviation (Washington, DC: 1979), p. 150; for a basic overview of the *Kikka* see Enzo Angelucci, *The Rand McNally Encyclopedia of Military Aircraft* (New York: 1980), pp. 296–297.

2. Alan Beyerchen, *Scientists under Hitler* (New Haven, CT: 1977), pp. 195–198.

3. Dieter Huzel, *Peenemünde to Canaveral* (Westport, CT: 1962), pp. 143–151. This is also outlined in Werner von Braun's own recollection in his book (written with Frederick Ordway), *History of Rocketry and Space Travel* (New York: 1969), and in Michael Neufeld, *The Rocket and the Reich* (Cambridge: 1995).

4. Eugene Emme (ed.), *The History of Rocket Technology: Essays on Research, Development, and Utility* (Detroit, MI: 1964), p. 279.

5. Yefim Gordon, *Early Soviet Fighters* (Hinckley, England: 2002), p. 4.

6. Ibid., pp. 4–7.

7. See Bill Gunston, *The World Encyclopedia of Aero Engines* (Wellingborough, UK: 1986), pp. 138–142.

8. Gordon, Early Soviet Fighters.

9. Clarence Lasby, *Project Paperclip: German Scientists and the Cold War* (New York: 1971), pp. 168–70.

10. See Earl Zeimke, The US Army in the Occupation of Germany, 1944–1946 (Washington, DC: 1975), passim, as well as Linda Hunt, Secret Agenda: The US Government, Nazi Scientists and Project Paperclip (New York: 1991); for a very critical look at the U.S. Government's policy regarding Nazi scientists.

11. Especially after the capture of Carl von Weizsäcker in Strasbourg in November 1944. See especially Beyerchen, *Scientists under Hitler*, pp. 195–198.

12. See the OSS reports from October through December, specifically Report No. GB-19971, in the collection at the USAFM archives, Box 683, on locations of aircraft engine construction (A/E Production). The document specifies where different types of aircraft engines are being produced and at what rates, including, "A visitor at the *Vereingte Deutsche Metallwerke* saw at the foundry a large number of engine components of a design unfamiliar to him. These he believed were parts for a completely new type of engine, possibly this same gas turbine unit [mentioned above]." Dated October 22, 1944.

13. The information for this section comes straight from documents collected from the USAF Museum in box 683–685 on the accounts of Operation Lusty. The German planes were brought straight to Wright Field, now Wright-Patterson AFB where they were tested, and where most are now on display at the Air Force Museum. See also Dik Daso, "Operation Lusty" in *Aerospace Power Journal*, 16(1) (Spring 2002), and Charles Christensen, *A History of the Development of Technical Intelligence in the Air Force 1917–1947* (New York: 2002), *passim*.

14. Reprinted in Christensen, *A History of the Development of Technical Intelligence ...* , p. 117.

15. USAFM, Files M and N, containing information on Colonel Harold Watson, Operation Lusty, and information on the German aircraft brought to Wright-Patterson AFB and later consigned to the U.S. Air Force Museum (USAFM).

16. Christensen, *A History of the Development of Technical Intelligence ...* , p. 137.

17. Ibid., p. 103.

18. General Hugh Knerr, [research and analysis of captured German equipment and data] "substantially furthered the XP-59 [sic] and XP-80 jet aircraft program[s]." Reprinted in Christensen, *A History of the Development of Technical Intelligence* ... , p. 136.

19. USAFM, box 683, "The Fedden Mission to Germany: Final Report" dated June 1945.

20. Ibid., p. 1.

21. Hugh Morgan, *Me 262 Stormbird Rising* (London: 1994), p. 146.

22. John Foreman and S.E. Harvey, *Messerschmitt Me 262 Combat Diary* (Surrey, England: 1995), p. 284.

23. Morgan, *Me 262 Stormbird Rising*, p. 190.

24. Ibid.

25. Morgan, *Me 262 Stormbird Rising*, pp. 158–159. See also Foreman and Harvey, *Messerschmitt Me 262*, p. 297.

26. Jon Guttman, "The Cold War Accelerated Jet Aircraft Development Without a Shot Being Fired in the 1940s," in *Aviation History* (January 1988), 1–13.

APPENDICES

1. This is the central theme of Edward Constant, *The Origins of the Turbojet Revolution* (Baltimore: 1980) which explains not only the advent of the turbojet engine but also the eclipse of the piston-engine power plant. See also Walter Vincenti's, *What Engineers Know and How They Know It*, an excellent book on the case studies of developing engineering technology in the interwar period. See also Frank Whittle's explanation in "The Advent of the Aircraft Gas Turbine," (box 3, file 4), General Aircraft Engine Archives held at Wright State University.

2. For German and British engine specifications see specifically L.J.K. Setright, *The Power to Fly, the Development of the Piston Engine in Aviation* (London: 1971), appendices. For confirmation as well as further information on the American figures see Graham White, *Allied Piston Engines of World War II* (London: 2000).

3. Graham White, R2800, *Pratt and Whitney's dependable masterpiece* (Warrendale, PA: 2002).

4. Specifically, "jet engines" (loosely defined) in 1924 with the report that dismissed "jet engines" for aircraft. NACA publications "Jet Engines for Aircraft" 1924.

5. When he flew the Messerschmitt ME 209 prototype (sometimes mistakenly referred to as a Bf 109R) powered by the DB 601X engine on a closed course at 469 mph (750.4 kmph). Hitler of course made the most of the achievement by suggesting that the Me 209 was the latest Luftwaffe fighter design and already in production. The Me 209 never made it past the experimental stage and was eventually scrapped in favor of the Me 262 turbojet fighter. But the record set in 1939 by Wendel for piston-engine aircraft stood until 1965 when an American finally outperformed the German. The DB 601X was a 12-cylinder inverted-"V" engine, rated at 1350 hp at 2700 rpm. The DB601X weighed 1,430 pounds (650 kg), giving it a specific weight (hp per pound weight) of .931; almost one hp per pound. See Setright, White.

6. A He 112 was tested with a liquid-fueled rocket motor in the tail, to increase speed at high altitude.

7. The He 176, a rocket plane that preceded the later Me 163 and Bachem Ba 349.

8. Hayne Constant, *Gas Turbines and their Problems* (London: 1948), pp. 11–15.

9. Frank Whittle, *Gas Turbine Aero-Thermodynamics* (Oxford: 1981), pp. 169–170. Whittle states that initial tests of the engine run up to 17,750 rpm produced 1,240 lbs static thrust, but for flight testing the engine was only run to 16,500 rpm.

10. Robert Schlaifer and S.D.Heron, *Development of Aircraft Engines and Fuels* (Chicago: 1950), p. 355 (fn). Schlaifer states that the Heinkel produced 1,100 lbs thrust for 795 lbs and the W.1 developed 850 lbs thrust for 623 lbs weight, thus the specific weights were "almost identical: 0.74 for the He S 3b and 0.73 for the W-1." Based on this author's research, the tolerances appear even closer: from the documents the specific weights (pounds thrust over pounds dry weight) were .722 for the HeS 3b and .724 for the W.1X. The point is that they were very equal in initial efficiency.

11. See specifically General Electric Aircraft Engine Archives at Wright State University, Dayton, Ohio, Box 2, File 20, Sir Frank Whittle, "Centrifugal v. Axial Flow Compressors for Aircraft Gas Turbines." These considerations were of course after successful tests of the early turbojet prototypes. See the above text for the difficulties that both Whittle and Ohain faced in getting initial funding for their engine ideas. But once the engines were tested and proven viable, choices were made in all three countries (Germany, Britain, and the United States) concerning the subsequent development of turbojet engines for aircraft.

Bibliography

PRIMARY SOURCES

Bell Aircraft Museum, Mentone, Indiana. Tim Whetstone, Curator.

The Bellringer, Bell Aircraft in-house newspaper. Citations for multiple dates.

Bell Aircraft News, February 10, 1944.

Bell Aircraft Museum, "Venus Project" documents, unmarked box, dated March 10, 1945.

General Electric Aircraft Engines Archives (GEAE) furnished to and held at Dunbar Special Collections, Wright State University, Dayton, Ohio. Also listed as "Whittle Papers" as the first GE turbojet engine was constructed based on the Whittle design.

Box 1, File 1, no date given, "The Theories and Inventions forming the basis of Developments undertaken by Power Jets Ltd.," Flight Lieutenant Frank Whittle.

Box 3, File 4, "The Advent of the Aircraft Gas Turbine" by Air Commodore Frank Whittle, p. 7, no date given (but sometime after 1948 when he retired with that rank).

Box 3, File 8, From the Power Jets Engineering Department, "A Note on Production, Design, and Research, with Special Reference to Aircraft Gas Turbine Power Plants," Whittle, no date given, but the document corresponds to Whittle's record of the discussion.

Box 3, File 11, "Memorandum No. 2 on Power Jets Defence," by Frank Whittle, 2 pages, dated July 4, 1940.

Box 3, File 9, "Gloster E28/39—Aircraft W.4041—Contractors Preliminary Flight Tests at Cranwell," filed May 17, 1941.

Box 3, File 9, "Gloster E28/39—Aircraft W.4041—Contractors Preliminary Flight Tests at Cranwell," (Second Flight, May 16), dated May 17, 1941.

In addition consultation of the original blueprints of the W.1X and GE I-A engines: Wright State University Special Collections, Dunbar Archives Whittle Collection, engine blueprints in Box 1, File 13.

The Imperial War Museum (IWM), London, England. Milch Documents Collection on the Official Records of the *Reichsluftfahrtministerium* captured after the war and copied by the Allies. Also at the IWM are selected Messerschmitt papers as relevant to the RLM record.

IWM Milch Documents, RLM's "Preliminary Technical Guidelines for Jet-Powered High-Speed Fighters," Volume 36, dated March 22, 1943, "Decision of the Me 262 over the He 280."

IWM Milch Documents, RLM minutes Volume 20, May 25, 1943, "Conference on the Me 209 vs. the Me 262."

IWM Milch Documents, Volume 21, June 22, 1943, "Messerschmitt to Milch: Production Schedule for the Me 262."

IWM Milch Documents, Volume 63, November 2, 1943, "Göring to Messerschmitt et al on the development of the Me 262."

IWM Milch Documents, Volume 24, August 13, 1943.

IWM Milch Documents, Volume 32, January 5, 1944.

IWM Messerschmitt Papers, "Messerschmitt to RLM," March 30, 1944, "request for more manpower."

IWM Milch Documents, Volume 58, May 28, 1944.

National Archives and Records Administration (NARA), Washington, DC.

233.5 Records of the Armed Services Committee and its Predecessors, Committee on Military Affairs, H.R. 5304, 1911

The Public Record Office (PRO), Kew, England.

PRO, squadron records from No. 616 Squadron, RAF, (Air 50/176).

The United States Air Force Museum (USAFM), Wright-Patterson Air Force Base, Dayton, Ohio. Dr. Jeffrey Underwood, Head Archivist.

(X)P-59A/his Documents, Box 483, "Cost of Bell XP-59A Airplanes," dated September 30, 1941.

USAFM AAF Technical Report 5234, in File A1, P-59A/his.

Box 484, (X)P-59A/mem, "Preliminary Handbook of Service Instructions for the Model XP-59A Interceptor-Fighter Airplanes Manufactured by Bell Aircraft Corp." dated October 31, 1942, published by Authority of the Commanding General, Army Air Forces by the Air Service Command, Wright Field, Dayton, Ohio.

USAFM, Box 482, (Y)P-59A/his, "Summary of Case History," prepared by Historical Office, Wright Field [Dayton, Ohio], December 1947, a final compilation of the official records pertaining to the XP- YP- and P-59A and B aircraft.

USAFM, Box 284, (X)F-83/his, "AAF Technical Report 5536: Final Report of Development, Procurement and Acceptance of the XP-83 Airplane."

USAFM, Box 284, (X)P-83/ops, "XP-83 Pilot's Handbook of Flight Operating Instructions."

USAFM, "AAF Technical Report 5536."

USAFM, Box 484, (X)P-59A/his, "412th Fighter Group [incorporation]."

USAFM, Box 484, (Y)P-59A/tes, YP-59A Airplane static test records, NACA "Static Test Project Record."
OSS reports from October through December, specifically Report No. GB-19971, in the collection at the USAFM archives, Box 683, on locations of aircraft engine construction (A/E Production). Dated October 22, 1944.
USAFM, Box 683, "The Fedden Mission to Germany: Final Report" dated June 1945.
USAF Museum boxes 683–685 on the accounts of Operation Lusty. The German planes were brought straight to Wright Field, now Wright-Patterson AFB where they were tested, and where most are now on display at the Air Force Museum.
Army Air Forces Technical Report Number 5234, "Final Report on the Development of the XP-59A and YP-59A Model Airplanes," P-59A, Box A1/his, dated June 28, 1945.
Miscellaneous unpublished primary documents:
Jesse Edgar (Lt. Col. (ret.)), "Bombs Away! Thirty was Enough, a Bombardier's Diary Account of Combat as a Member of a B-17 Crew with the Eight Air Force," (unpublished). Edgar gives a first-hand account of bombing missions against German oil refineries and marshalling yards.

PUBLISHED PRIMARY SOURCES

National Advisory Committee on Aeronautics (NACA) published Reports (all available on-line and through libraries around the United States):
NACA study #159, "Jet Propulsion for Airplanes," written 1923, published 1924 by Government Printing Office, Washington, DC.
NACA studies in 1944, 1945, 1946, (finally) on the viability of turbojet engines, which were already in use, in American aircraft development.
NACA reports TN 239 (1926) "Steam Turbines in Aircraft," TN 431 (1932) "Tests on Thrust Augmentors for Jet Propulsion."
NACA TN 442 (1933) "Jet Propulsion with Special Reference to Thrust Augmenters," which disqualified jet, turbine, and turbojet research for use as aircraft powerplants as underpowered and too heavy.
NACA reports 263 (1928), 283 (1929), 384 (1932), and so on up to 1938 which go into the impressive development of both mechanical and turbosuperchargers in the United States.
NACA Wartime Report L-485, "Wind Tunnel Tests of a Submerged-Engine Fuselage Design," (October 1940).
NACA Wartime Report L-331, "Effect of External Shape upon the Drag of a Scoop," (July 1941).
NACA Wartime Report L-486, "High-Speed Tests of a Ducted body with Various Air-Outlet Openings," (May 1942).
NACA Wartime Report L-438, "Wind Tunnel Investigation of Rear Underslung Fuselage Ducts," (September 1943).
An Aviation Story, published by the Bell Aircraft Corporation for the Tenth Anniversary, Buffalo, New York: July 1945.
Convegno di Scienze Fisiche, Matematiche e Naturali, (published by the Reale Accademia D'Italia, 1936), (Tema: Le Alte Velocita in Aviazione) and was

held on September 30 through October 6, 1935. Also known as the Volta Conference. Volta High Speed Conference, Rome, Italy, September 30 to October 6, 1935.

Douhet, Giulio, *The Command of the Air*, (New York: 1942). Translated by Dino Ferrari. Originally published as *Il Dominio Dell'Aria.* (1921).

Galland, Adolf, in *The Development of Jet and Rocket Airplanes in Germany 1938–1945*, extracted from European Contributions to the History of World War II, 1939–1945, Monograph number 7, Development and Planning in the German Air Force, Part I (The Von Rhoden Project), Maxwell AFB, AL: Foreign Documents Section, Air University Library, 1951.

Of Men and Stars, a History of Lockheed Aircraft Corporation, New York: 1980, reprinted by Arno Press from the official Lockheed History.

Seven Decades of Progress, published by the General Electric Company, Fallbrok, CA: 1979.

The Strategic Air War Against Germany 1939–1945, Reports of the British Bombing Survey Unit, London: 1998.

United States Strategic Bombing Survey (USSBS), New York: 1976, Volume I.

Flugsport, The New York Times, announcing Whittle's patent, both in March, 1939.

Headlines, published for the Aircraft Engine Group (GE) at Lynn and Everett, September 28, 1977.

El Paso Times, New York Times, and other American newspapers on the announcement of America's first jet plane Friday, January 7, 1944.

SECONDARY SOURCES

Anderson, Roy. "A Look at Lockheed," a speech given to the Newcomen Society in North America, reprinted by the society, New York: 1983.

Angelucci, Enzo. *The Rand McNally Encyclopedia of Military Aircraft.* New York: The Military Press, 1980.

Arnold, Henry (Hap). *Global Mission.* New York: Harper & Brothers, 1949.

Arnold, Henry (Hap) and Ira Eaker. *This Flying Game.* New York: Funk & Wagnalls, 1938.

———. *Winged Warfare.* New York: Harper & Brothers, 1941.

Beumelburg, Werner. *Kampf um Spanien, Die Geschichte der Legion Kondor.* Berlin: Gerhard Stalling Verlag, 1939.

Beyerchen, Alan. *Scientists under Hitler.* New Haven, CT: Yale University Press, 1977.

Boehme, Manfred. *JG7, The World's First Jet Fighter Unit 1944/1945*, translated by David Johnston. Atglen, PA: Schiffer Military History, 1992.

Boog, Horst. *Die Deutsche Luftwaffenführung 1935–1945.* Stuttgart: Deutsche Verlags-Anstalt, 1982.

———.(ed.). *The Conduct of the Air War in the Second World War.* New York: Berg Publishers, 1992.

Boyne, Walter (ed.). *The Jet Age: Forty Years of Jet Aviation.* Washington, DC: Smithsonian Institution Press, 1979.

Braun, Werner von and Frederick Ordway. *History of Rocketry and Space Travel.* New York: Thomas Y. Crowell Company, 1969.

Carl, Ann. *A WASP Among Eagles.* Washington, DC: Smithsonian Institution Press, 1999.

Carpenter, David. *Flame Powered, The Bell XP-59A Airacomet and the General Electric I-A Engine*. New York: Jet Pioneers of America, 1992.

Christensen, Charles. *A History of the Development of Technical Intelligence in the Air Force 1917–1947, Operation Lusty*. Lewiston, New York: Edwin Mellen Press, 2002.

Coffey, Thomas. *Hap: Military Aviator*. New York: The Viking Press, 1982.

Connor, Margaret. *Hans von Ohain: Elegance in Flight*. Reston, VA: American Institute of Aeronautics, 2001.

Constant, Edward. *The Origins of the Turbojet Revolution*. Baltimore: Johns Hopkins University Press, 1980.

Craven, Wesley and James Cate. *Army Air Forces in WWII*, Vols. 1–7. Chicago: University of Chicago Press, 1948–1958.

Daso, Dik. *Hap Arnold and the Evolution of American Airpower*. Washington, DC: Smithsonian Institution Press, 2000.

———. *Architects of American Air Supremacy, General Hap Arnold and Theodore von Kármán*. Maxwell, AL: Air University Press, 1997.

Dawson, Virginia. *Engines and Innovation*, NASA Historical Series. Washington, DC: NASA Historical Series, 1991.

Dean, Francis. *America's Hundred-Thousand*. Atglen, PA: Schiffer Military History, 1996.

Dear, I.C.B. *The Oxford Companion to World War II*. Oxford: Oxford University Press, 1995.

Dorman, Geoffrey. *Fifty Years Fly Past*. London: Forbes Robertson Publishers, 1951.

Dressel, Joachim, Manfried Griehl, and Jochen Menke (eds.). *Heinkel He 280, The World's First Jet Aircraft*. West Chester, PA: Schiffer Military History, 1991.

Eames, James. *Turbine- and Jet- Propelled Aircraft Powerplants*. New York: Chartwell House, 1954.

Ebert, Hans, Johann Kaiser, and Klaus Peters. *Willi Messerschmitt—Pionier der Luftfahrt und des Leichtbaues—Eine Biographie*, Bonn: Bernard and Graefe Verlag, 1992, translated by Theriault and Cox as *The History of German Aviation, Willy Messerschmitt: Pioneer of Aviation Design*, Volume 2 in The History of German Aviation series from Schiffer Military History, Atglen, PA: 1999.

Emme, Eugene (ed.). *The History of Rocket Technology: Essays on Research, Development, and Utility*. Detroit, MI: Wayne State University Press, 1964.

Ermenc, Joseph (ed.). *Interviews with German Contributors to Aviation History*. Westport, CT: Greenwood Press, 1990.

Ethell, Jeffrey and Alfred Price. *World War II Fighting Jets*. Annapolis, MD: Naval Institute Press, 1994.

Faber, Harold (ed.). *Luftwaffe, A History*. New York: Times Books, 1977.

Foreman, John and S.E. Harvey. *Messerschmitt Me 262 Combat Diary*. Surrey, England: Air Research Publications, 1995.

Francillon, René. *Lockheed Aircraft since 1913*. Annapolis, MD: Naval Institute Press, 1987.

———. *McDonnell Douglas Aircraft Since 1920*. London: Putnam Press, 1979.

Fredriksen, John. *Warbirds*. Santa Barbara, CA: ABC-Clio, 1999.

Galland, Adolf. *The First and the Last*. New York: Ballentine Books, 1954.

Garvin, Robert. *Starting Something Big, The Commercial Emergence of GE Aircraft Engines*. Reston, VA: American Institute of Aeronautics and Astronautics, 1998.

General Electric Company, *Seven Decades of Progress*. Fallbrook, CA: Aero Publishers, 1979.

Gispin, Kees. *New Profession, Old Order*. Cambridge: Cambridge University Press, 1989.

Golley, John. *Whittle—The True Story*. Washington, DC: Smithsonian Institution Press, 1987.

Gordon, Yefim. *Early Soviet Fighters*. Hinckley, England: Midland Publications, 2002.

Green, William and Gordon Swanborough. *The Complete Book of Fighters*. London: Smithmark Publishers, 1994.

Griehl, Manfred and Joachim Dressel. *Luftwaffe Combat Aircraft*, translated by Don Cox. Atglen, PA: Schiffer Military History, 1994.

Gunston, Bill. *The Development of Jet and Turbine Aero Engines*. Somerset, England: Patrick Stephens Limited, 1995.

———. *The World Encyclopedia of Aero Engines*. Wellingborough: Patrick Stephens Limited, 1986.

———. *Jane's Fighting Aircrat of World War II*. London: Studio Books, 1989.

Heinkel, Ernst. *Stürmisches Leben*. Stuttgart: Europäischer Buchklub, 1953, translated as *Stormy Life*, by Cindy Opitz, Stuttgart: Aviatic Verlag, 1991.

Homze, Edward. *Arming the Luftwaffe*. Lincoln, NE: University of Nebraska Press, 1976.

Hunt, Linda. *Secret Agenda: The US Government, Nazi Scientists and Project Paperclip*. New York: St. Martin's Press, 1991.

Huzel, Dieter. *Peenemünde to Canaveral*. Westport, CT: Greenwood Press, 1962.

Irving, David. *Göring, a Biography*. New York: Avon Books, 1989.

James, Derek. *Gloster Aircraft since 1917*. London: Putnam and Company, 1971.

Jane's Fighting Aircraft of World War II. London: 1989.

Johnston, Tex. *Jet-Age Test Pilot*. Washington, DC: Smithsonian Institution Press, 2000.

Kay, Anthony. *German Jet Engine and Gas Turbine Development 1930–1945*. Shrewsbury, England: Airlife Publishing, 2002.

Kerrebrock, Jack. *Aircraft Engines and Gas Turbines*. Cambridge, MA: McGraw-Hill, 1977.

Klein, Burton. *Germany's Economic Preparations for War*. Cambridge: Harvard University Press, 1959.

Koziol, Michael. *Rustung, Krieg and Sklaveri*. Sigmaringen, Germany: J. Thorbecke Verlag, 1989.

Lasby, Clarence. *Project Paperclip: German Scientists and the Cold War*. New York: Atheneum Press, 1971.

Launius, Roger. *Innovation and the Development of Flight*. College Station, TX: Texas A&M University Press, 1999.

Leyes, Richard and William Fleming. *The History of North American Small Gas Turbine Aircraft Engines*. Washington, DC: American Institute of Aeronautics and Astronautics, 1999.

Lowe, James. *A Philosophy of Airpower*. New York: University Press of America, 1984.

Ludwig, Karl-Heinz. *Technik und Ingenieure im Dritten Reich*. Düsseldorf: Droste Verlag, 1974.

MacIssac, David. *Strategic Bombing in World War Two*. New York: Garland Publishing Company, 1976.

Masters, David. *German Jet Genesis*. London: Jane's, 1982.

Matthews, Henry. *Gloster-Whittle E. 28/39 Pioneer, a Flying Chronology*. Beirut, Lebanon: HPM Publications, 2001.

McMahon, P.J. *Aircraft Propulsion*. London: Pitman, 1971.

Mierzejewski, Alfred. *The Collapse of the German War Economy*. Chapel Hill, NC: University of North Carolina Press, 1988.

Morgan, Hugh. *Me 262 Stormbird Rising*. London: Osprey Publishing, 1994.

Morrow, John, Jr. *Building German Airpower, 1909–1914*. Knoxville, TN: University of Tennessee Press, 1976.

Moss, Sanford. *Superchargers for Aviation*. New York: National Aeronautics Council, 1944.

———. "The Gas Turbine, and 'Internal Combustion' Prime-Mover," Doctoral Dissertation, Unpublished, Cornell University, 1903.

Murray, Williamson. *Strategy for Defeat, the Luftwaffe*. Maxwell, AL: Air University Press, 1983.

Neufeld, Michael. *The Rocket and the Reich*. Cambridge MA: Harvard University Press, 1995.

Norton, Donald. *Larry, a Biography: A Biography of Lawrence D. Bell*. Chicago: Nelson-Hall Company, 1981.

Nowarra, Heinz. *Messerschmitt Bf 109*. Somerset, England: Shiffer Publishing, 1989.

Overy, Richard. *The Air War 1939–1945*. London: Europa Press, 1980.

Pace, Steve. *X-Planes at Edwards*. Osceola, WI: Motorbooks International, 1995.

Peebles, Curtis. *Dark Eagles*. Presidio Novato, CA: Presidio Press, 1995.

Pelletier, Alain. *Bell Aircraft since 1935*. Annapolis, MD: Naval Institute Press, 1992.

Philpott, Bryan. *German Military Aircraft*. London: Crescent Books, 1981.

Price, Alfred. *Spitfire*. Leicester, England: PRC Press, 1993.

Rich, Ben and Leo Janos. *Skunk Works*. Boston: Little Brown and Company, 1994.

Saint-Peter, James. *The History of Aircraft Gas Turbine Development in the United States: A Tradition of Excellence*. Atlanta, GA: International Gas Turbine Institute of the American Society of Mechanical Engineers, 1999.

Setright, L.J.K. *The Power to Fly, The Development of the Piston Engine in Aviation*. London: George Allen and Unwin, 1971.

Sherry, Michael. *The Rise of American Airpower*. New Haven, CT: Yale University Press, 1987.

Smith, George. *Gas Turbines and Jet Propulsion*, 5th ed. London: Iliff & Sons, 1950.

Smith, J.R. and Eddie Creek. *ME 262*, Vols. 1–4. London: Classic Publications, 1998.

Smith, J.R., Anthony Kay, and Eddie Creek. *German Aircraft of the Second World War*. London: Putnam, 1972.

Speer, Albert. *Inside the Third Reich*. New York: Scribner, 1970.

Suchenwirth, Richard. *Historical Turning Points in the German Air Force War Effort*, USAF Historical Studies Number 189. New York: Arno Press, 1968.

Taylor, Michael (ed.). *Jane's Encyclopedia of Aviation*. New York: Crescent Books, 1996.

Trischler, Helmuth. *Luft- und Raum-fahrtforschung in Deutshcland 1900–1970.* Frankfurt: Campus Verlag, 1992.

Turner, John. *British Aircraft of World War II.* London: Sidgwick & Jackson, 1975.

Vincenti, Walter. *What Engineers Know and How They Know It.* Baltimore: Johns Hopkins University Press, 1990.

Wagner, Wolfgang. *The History of German Aviation: The First Jet Aircraft.* Atglen, PA: Schiffer Military History, 1998, Volume 1 in the History of German Aviation Series, translated by Don Cox.

Watkins, David. *De Havilland Vampire.* Gloucestershire, England: Budding Books, 1998.

Whaley, Barton. *Covert Rearmament in Germany, 1919–1939.* Frederick, MD: 1984.

Whittle, Frank. *Gas Turbine Thermodynamics.* Oxford, England: Pergamon, 1981.

———. *Jet: The Story of a Pioneer.* New York: Philosophical Library, 1954.

Windrow, Martin. *German Air Force Fighters of World War Two,* Vols. 1–2. London: Doubleday & Co, 1968.

Wood, Tony and Bill Gunston. *Hitler's Luftwaffe.* London: Salamander Books LTD., 1977.

Wragg, David. *Speed in the Air.* New York: Fell Publishers, 1974.

Yenne, Bill. *McDonnell Douglas, A Tale of Two Giants.* Greenwich, CT: Crescent Books, 1985.

Zeimke, Earl. *The US Army in the Occupation of Germany, 1944–1946.* Washington, DC: Government Printing Office, 1975.

Ziegler, Mano. *Turbinenjäger Me 262.* Stuttgart: Motorbuch Verlag, 1978.

Zilbert, Edward. *Albert Speer and the Nazi Ministry of Arms.* London: Fairleigh Dickenson University Press, 1981.

ARTICLES

Corum, James. "The Luftwaffe's Army Support Doctrine, 1918–1941." *The Journal of Military History,* 59(1) (January 1995), 53–76.

Daso, Dik. "Operation Lusty." *Aerospace Power Journal* XVI(1) (Spring 2002), 28–40.

Ferris, John. "Fighter Defense before Fighter Command: The Rise of Strategic Air Defense in Great Britain, 1917–1934." *The Journal of Military History,* 63(4) (October 1999), 845–884.

Foster, John, Jr. "Design Analysis of the Messerschmitt Me-262 Jet Fighter," Parts I and II (Airframe and Engines). *Aviation,* 44 (October and November 1945).

Guttman, Jon. "The Cold War Accelerated Jet Aircraft Development Without a Shot Being Fired in the 1940s." *Aviation History,* (January 1988), 1–13.

Heppenheimer, T.A. "Jet Plane." *Invention and Technology,* (Fall 1993), 45–57.

Irwin, Arthur. "That Dummy Propeller," a letter to the editor in *Product Engineering,* (March 1, 1965).

Johnson, Kelly. "How We Engineered the Lockheed Shooting Star." *Aviation,* 44(7) (July 1945), 149–151.

Maguire, D.R. "Enemy Jet History." *The Journal of the Royal Aeronautical Society,* 52 (January 1948), 76–84.

Orange, Vincent. "Fortunate Fascist Failures: The Case of the Heinkel Fighters." *Historical News*, (47) (December 1983), 7–13.

Schulte, Major Rudolpf (Project Officer Turbojet and Gas Turbine Developments, Hq., AAF). "Design Analysis of the General Electric Type I-16 Jet Engine." *Aviation*, (January 1946), 43–50.

Smith, Richard. "The International Airliner and the Essence of Aircraft Performance." *Technology and Culture*, 24(3), July 1983), 428–449.

————. "The Weight Envelope, An Airplane's Fourth Dimension—Aviation's Bottom Line" (unpublished, special handout to his History of Science and Technology students at the University of Maryland), dated 15 November 1985.

Whittle, Frank. "Speculation." *RAF Cadet College Magazine*, (Fall 1928), 106–110.

Wyen, Adrian. "They Flew the U.S. Navy's First Jets." *Naval Aviation News*, (March 1963), 6–3.

Index

About the Author

STERLING MICHAEL PAVELEC is the Program Chair for Diplomacy and Military Studies at Hawaii Pacific University.